WESTMAR COLLEGE

W9-APO-086

The President and the Public: Rhetoric and National Leadership

THE CREDIBILITY OF INSTITUTIONS, POLICIES AND LEADERSHIP
A Series funded by the Hewlett Foundation

Kenneth W. Thompson, *Series Editor*

The President and the Public: Rhetoric and National Leadership

The Credibility of Institutions, Policies and Leadership
Volume 7

Edited by
Craig Allen Smith
Department of Speech-Communication
The University of North Carolina
at Chapel Hill

and

Kathy B. Smith
Department of Politics
Wake Forest University

Series Editor
Kenneth W. Thompson

106937

University Press of America
Lanham • New York • London

Copyright © 1985 by

University Press of America® Inc.

4720 Boston Way
Lanham, MD 20706

3 Henrietta Street
London WC2E 8LU England

All rights reserved

Printed in the United States of America

Library of Congress Cataloging in Publication Data
Main entry under title:

The President and the public rhetoric and national
  leadership.

  (Credibility of institutions, policies and leadership ;
v. 7)
  Bibliography: p.
  Includes index.
  1. United States—Politics and government—Collected
works.   2. Presidents—United States—Messages—
Collected works.   3. Political oratory—United States—
Collected works.   I. Smith. Craig A. (Craig Allen),
1949-   . II. Smith, Kathy B.   III. Series.
J81.C86   1986   353.03′5   85-20299
ISBN 0-8191-4722-2 (alk. paper)
ISBN 0-8191-4723-0 (pbk. : alk. paper)

The views expressed by the author(s) of this publication do not necessarily represent
the opinions of the Miller Center. We hold to Jefferson's dictum that: "Truth is the
proper and sufficient antagonist to error, and has nothing to fear from the conflict,
unless, by human interposition, disarmed of her natural weapons, free argument
and debate."

Co-published by arrangement with
The White Burkett Miller Center of Public Affairs,
University of Virginia

Dedication

In memory of Sylvia Ruth Bahan, our earliest reader and supporter.

Acknowledgments

We would like to thank several people for their assistance in the development of this volume. Without the conscientious work of Bobbi Acord the actual process of compiling speeches would have been a much more arduous task. Kenneth Thompson has been most helpful in discussing our speech choices, although we take full responsibility for the final selections. The White Burkett Miller Center for Public Affairs at the University of Virginia provided invaluable assistance in the preparation of the final manuscript. Additionally, we greatly appreciate the support provided by the Wake Forest University Graduate Research Fund. Finally, and most importantly, we wish to thank our students at the University of North Carolina at Chapel Hill and Wake Forest University for their reactions to the speeches, their encouragement, and for the intellectual stimulation they constantly provide.

Table of Contents

UNIT III   Selected Presidential Responsibilities

Unit IV Looking Ahead

Introduction: Persuasion and the American Presidency

Presidents persuade. As candidates they persuade people to support them. Once in office they must persuade legislators, bureaucrats, and sub-national officials to enact and implement programs. They persuade the public, both directly and indirectly through the mass media, that they are fulfilling their obligations. And ultimately, they must persuade history. Clearly, presidential leadership entails influence through communication.

PRESIDENTIAL POWER AND PERSUASION

Richard Neustadt's argument that the power of the presidency *is* the power to persuade began to focus attention on the centrality of persuasion to presidential leadership (Neustadt, 1960). In *Presidential Power* Neustadt critiqued the presidential power to command and found that power wanting. In President Truman's dismissal of General Douglas MacArthur, Truman's steel seizure, and in President Eisenhower's use of troops in Little Rock the president was unable to make his "power" felt without a concomitant loss of that power.

Neustadt argued that our system of checks and balances is not one of "separated powers" but rather of "separated institutions sharing powers." The exercise of any power therefore requires the cooperation, or at least the acquiescence, of the other institutions. What matters most, he said, is the president's *prospects* for power, which prospective influence dims whenever the president alienates others through the use of command power. A president's prospects for power derive from three sources: his professional reputation among Washingtonians, his public prestige, and his choices. Put succinctly, every presidential choice influences his professional reputation and his public prestige. Neustadt advised presidents to make those choices with careful attention to these joint considerations.

"Persuasion," Neustadt noted, "deals in the coin of self-interest with [those] who have some freedom to reject what they find counterfeit" (p. 35). For this reason he further (and unnecessarily) defined a president's power to persuade as the power to bargain. Without detracting from the importance of presidential bargaining, it is important to distinguish between persuasion and bargaining as communication processes. Bargaining entails the efforts of two or more persons, each possessing some—but not all—of the resources necessary for task accomplishment, to overcome their mutual suspicions and to accomplish a task. Consequently, a bargain typically entails a *quid pro quo*. But as Neustadt's argument emphasizes, any *quid pro quo* or compromise involves a loss of power prospects *precisely because* each party must sacrifice some of its resources, whether present or future, to consummate the deal. When entering into a bargaining mode of communication, then, it is advisable for everyone to carefully guard their resources.

Persuasion, on the other hand, was aptly described by President Truman as getting people to do what they should have done in the first place without his having to tell them. It involves not a trading of resources but a restructuring of resources: a reconceptualization of one's resources and goals, a refocusing of purpose and ability such that the persuadee comes to voluntarily, perhaps even enthusiasticaly, adopt not only the persuader's recommendation but his or her general orientation as well. Thus, persuasion involves considerably less risk to the president than does bargaining, and it requires much less monitoring and enforcement.

Although persuasion is necessary for bargaining, bargaining is unnecessary for persuasion. A bargaining president, for example, must persuade his adversary that he possesses the resources in question, that he is willing and able to trade or use them, and that he will deliver his end of the bargain. But a president who induces congressmen, voters, or reporters to share his vision, or to "give it a chance," has neither taken their resources nor sacrificed any of his own. Thus persuasion is more nearly analogous to education than to warfare.

James MacGregor Burns distinguished between "Transactional" and "Transcendent" types of leadership (Burns, 1978). As he succinctly summarized the types:

> The relations of most leaders and followers are *transactional*—leaders approach followers with an eye to exchanging one thing for another: jobs for votes, or subsidies for campaign contributions. Such transactions comprise the bulk of the relationships among leaders and followers, especially in groups, legislatures, and parties. *Transforming* leadership, while more complex, is more potent. The transforming leader recognizes and exploits an existing need or demand of a potential follower. But, beyond that, the transforming leader looks for potential motives in followers, seeks to satisfy higher needs, and engages the full person of the follower (p. 4).

Burns's concept of transactional leadership rests upon a notion of political power as bargaining which echoes Neustadt's advice, while his preferred transforming leadership emphasizes persuasion.

The central argument here is this: Command, bargaining, and persuasion are three kinds of presidential influence, not two as described by Neustadt. There is a core area, primarily in the military, in which the president can issue commands and have them obeyed because he holds all the resources needed to accomplish his task. But as Neustadt's Truman-MacArthur illustration emphasizes, this is neither a large nor a clearly-defined area. Second, there is an area in which a president bargains because he has some of the necessary resources and the other resources are held by people beyond his control. Those people typically include the Soviet Union and other nations, the opposition party, the press, and other well-organized, politically sophisticated, and entrenched forces. Finally, there is an area in which a president persuades: either because his resources are meager and he must establish them (e.g., Johnson's "Gulf of Tonkin" maneuver and Nixon's construction of the "Great Silent Majority"), or because he thinks it either unnecessary or unwise to sacrifice any of his considerable resources through bargaining.

Yet whether one prefers to view the exercise of presidential power as command, bargaining, or persuasion, it is an unavoidably *communicative* process. That is the thrust of an important book by Colin Seymour-Ure: "What is at issue is not the appropriate way of naming different forms of A's capacity to control B, but rather the relation between these forms and the communication processes involved. *For the relational quality of power makes communication a pivotal factor*" (Seymour-Ure, 1982, p. 1, emphasis added).

ON STUDYING PRESIDENTIAL COMMUNICATION AS COMMUNICATION

Any consideration of power, presidential or otherwise, as communication necessarily emphasizes process over substance. Neustadt, Burns, and Seymour-Ure each in his own way focused less on power-wielders and policies than upon the process. Unfortunately, too few students of presidential power have taken the next small, yet significant step.

Having acknowledged that the process of communication is integrally related to the exercise of presidential power, students of presidential power have generally failed to consult the extant research literature in the discipline whose province this is: Speech-Communication. At a recent American Political Science Association meeting, for example, one panelist averred that presidential speech-making remains barely examined—this despite some 226 studies of president's and their communication published through 1979 in the Speech-Communication journals. Indeed, except for *Presidential Studies Quarterly*, it is almost impossible to find references to the discipline's journals in the historical and political journals. But when one is concerned with a communicative perspective on presidential power these 226 studies (and their more recent kin) merit wider attention and discussion.

But even more fundamental issues concern not conclusions about particular acts of presidential communication, but theory and method. If we acknowledge that presidential power can and should be studied communicatively, then logically we should adopt a theoretical framework and research methodologies appropriate for the study of communication. Once again, the literature in Speech-Communication has produced several such theoretical frameworks and research techniques that can be profitably extended to the study of presidential communication. The remainder of this chapter will briefly summarize one such appropriate theoretical framework.

A Theoretical Framework: The Coordinated Management of Meaning

W. Barnett Pearce, Vernon Cronen, Linda Harris and their colleagues at the University of Massachusetts have been primarily concerned with the study of interpersonal communication. They developed a theoretical perspective called, "Coordinated Management of Meaning" which emphasizes that *human beings create meaning, even where none exists* and that we create this meaning hierarchically (Pearce and Conklin, 1976; Pearce, Cronen, and Conklin, 1979; Harris and Cronen, 1979; Cronen, Pearce, and Harris, 1982;). Put simply, as symbol-using creatures, we interpret our environment and behave on the basis of our interpretations. Consistent with the works of Kenneth Burke, George Herbert Mead, Ernst Cassirer, and Murray Edelman, this approach emphasizes that persons mutually negotiate or create their own realities through the use of language.

The creation of understanding involves the coordination of meaning or, more precisely, meanings, since each individual creates or construes the meaning of something. But meaning is only partly idiosyncratic since each of us relies upon social and cultural guides or "Rules." It is these rules which permit us to coordinate or manage our meanings so that we move toward some kind of coordinated understanding.

But rules are not immutable laws of human conduct. Rather they are, themselves, a learned or developed product of communication. "Constitutive Rules" govern the kinds of behaviors considered meaningful in a particular case, while "Regulative Rules" govern the sequence or arrangement of behaviors. The kind of communication event is defined by its complex of rules in much the same way that a game of cards is governed by constitutive rules (e.g. the number, ranks, and suits of cards, the presence or absence of chips, and the number of players) and its regulative rules (e.g. the number of cards dealt, presence or absence of bidding, the playing and replenishing of cards, and the criteria for decision).

Now, just as a cardplayer can learn the rules, make the rules for a new game, or bend the rules as the game progresses, so too communicators learn the rules governing various kinds of communication activity, create new rules to clarify ambiguous or difficult tasks, and embellish the rules to enhance mutually acceptable understanding.

An important tenet of the CMM approach is that we create and employ our communicative rules *hierarchically*. The hierarchy consists of six levels of rules that govern, respectively, content, speech act, episode, relationship, individual life script, and culture.

Level 1: Content

Content rules affect the ways in which we render thoughts and ideas communicable. Foremost among these rules are those pertaining to culturally acceptable syntax, grammar, and vocabulary. The focus here is upon the semantic relationship between ideas and words. Linguistic choices like "recession" and "depression" are rule governed in so far as they refer to a set of predetermined economic criteria. Similarly, the terms "acceptable unemployment," "peace-keeping forces," "liberation," and "fairness" pervade American political discourse; and the careful citizen asks, "what does this person *mean* by 'acceptable'?" and "fair to *whom*, according to what *standards*?" These questions attempt to discover the regularities or patterns in the words and ideas of people, and to discover the implicit and explicit rules beneath them.

Level 2: Speech Act

These rules enable us to ascertain the type of *Speech Act* which these words constitute. Rising inflection at the end of a remark suggests a query, five-o'clock shadow and shifty eyes suggest deception, a smile suggests a compliment, and a scowl implies a threat. Indeed, presidents have been known to "punish" recalcitrant visitors by simply not smiling when the complimentary joint picture is taken. It is because of three distinct sets of speech act rules that reporters feel free to chaotically shout questions at the president as he walks along the street, but politely take turns at press conferences, and listen attentively to a presidential address. One can easily imagine the professional prospects of the reporter who waits to ask a question "on the run" until the others had finished, or who interrupts the State of the Union to ask a question. It is these and other rules which render speech acts comprehensible to those participating in them.

Level 3: Situation

Level three rules refer to communication *episodes* or situations. These rules help us to distinguish between political party conventions, church services, barroom political discussions, and protest marches. Episodic rules answer a communicant's question: what is going on here? The emphasis here is upon recurrent situational or scenic factors, consistent with Aristotle's definition of rhetoric as "The faculty of discovering *in a given situation* the available means of persuasion" (emphasis added).

Lloyd Bitzer has theorized that rhetorical discourse is a response to a "Rhetorical Situation" (Bitzer, 1968; 1980). A rhetorical situation consists of three elements. The first is an "Exigence" which Bitzer defines as "an imperfection marked by urgency." The exigence is the focal point of the situation, and rhetorical situations consist of those exigencies that can be positively modified through the introduction of human communication. The second element of a rhetorical situation is an "Audience" that is "capable of positively modifying the exigence." The third element is a set of "Constraints" upon communicative choices. These constraints are influences upon the rhetor's choices of audience and strategy—they can be resources as well as limitations.

Richard Vatz and others have criticized Bitzer's framework, arguing that the imperfection and its urgency, the existence of the audience and its ability to modify the exigence, and the presence, absence, and pertinence of constraints are all themselves products of rhetorical depiction (Vatz, 1972). Bitzer subsequently outlined a four stage developmental process through which the elements come into existence, peak, begin to disintegrate, and ultimately dissipate in response to communicative efforts. Central to Bitzer's framework is the "Fitting Response": the use of communication to bring about either terminal resolution of the primary exigence or the instrumental resolution of a subsidiary exigence such that the primary exigence becomes more amenable to resolution.

An important question facing presidents as persuaders, then, is: what episodic or situational rules apply to this communicative effort? Richard Nixon was roundly criticized for his failure to personally address Congress about the 1973 "State of the Union," even though nineteenth century presidents routinely sent the message via clerks.

But episodic rules are perhaps most notable in "Crisis" situations, as presidents describe the problem and its urgency and press for support. Of course, part of the presidents rhetorical task is definitional: does situation X constitute a crisis or does it not? Does it call for a UN response, or an American response? Are extraordinary, possibly extra-Constitutional powers, necessary? Crisis definition is no small question, in view of the dramatic increases in presidential support during "critical periods" (Mueller, 1970). Nevertheless, Presidents Nixon, Ford, and Carter were all unable to establish the urgency of the Energy Crisis and the consequent desirability of conservation.

Level 4: Relationships

Level 4 rules are *Relational*. These rules stem in part from culturally defined relationships (e.g., marital, parental, supervisory). But these cultural rules serve as grist for the interpersonal mill as individuals negotiate the terms of their own relationship. What one is *supposed to do* is modified in accordance with the likes, needs, and taboos of the actual communicators.

Even at the interpersonal or dyadic level, as Julia Wood has noted, relationships develop a culture: a climate of shared experiences, language, groundrules, expectations, and preferences. Whereas episodic rules focus on resolution of the exigence with the audience as transient factors, relational rules govern the rhetor-audience climate across varied exigencies.

As Neustadt argued, presidents want to maintain favorable working relationships with Congress, the public, and other important constituencies. Periodically, presidents damage a relationship for the sake of exigence resolution, and/or permit an exigence to fester for the sake of constituent relations. But relational rules are constantly in negotiation: while institutional rules (e.g. President-

Congress, President-Press) may remain stable, changes in personnel are bound to lead toward relational redefinition.

Level 5: Individual Life-Scripts

Level 5 rules concern *Life Scripts* of the participants. It is at this level that an individual considers the sayable and unsayable in light of his or her self-concept. As James David Barber, Erwin Hargrove, Neustadt, and common sense all argue, *who* is president makes a difference (Barber, 1977; Hargrove, 1966). Any communicator, certainly a president, makes choices on the basis of personal values, preferences, and norms. Harry Truman's concern for personal loyalty, Dwight Eisenhower's preference for order, Richard Nixon's focus on results, and Ronald Reagan's preference for simple explanations greatly influence their communication. Barber traces the importance of "Active-Positive" flexibility for the administrations of Franklin Roosevelt, Truman, and Kennedy; and of "Active-Negative" rigidification for the demise of the Wilson, Johnson, and Nixon presidencies. These idiosyncratic life scripts account for the discernible differences in the speeches of diverse presidents.

Level 6: Cultural Patterns

Level 6 rules concern *Cultural Patterns*. These rules broadly govern the communication activity of the society at large. They include normative inflections that differentiate British, Australian, and American versions of the English language. But they also include other normative patterns around which society communicates. Two studies by the authors illustrate this point.

The first study analyzed the audiences addressed by Presidents Johnson, Nixon, Ford, and Carter. Results revealed consistent patterns of audience selection with only minor partisan-geographic and temporal-functional variations. These and other cultural level rules provide a framework within which we can readily differentiate American political rhetoric from, say, British Parliamentary debates (Smith, 1983).

The second study was a content analysis of eighteen recurrent values in the 103 televised addresses of Presidents Johnson, Nixon, Ford, Carter, and Reagan. The results revealed no significant partisan variation, no significant temporal variation, and no significant idiosyncratic variation. Instead, a cultural pattern apparently constrained all five diverse presidents: a core set of American values (Puritan/Pioneer Morality, Peace, Patriotism, Effort/Optimism, and Change/Progress) dominated all 103 addresses to the nation, and there were clear-cut groups of Intermediate and Peripheral values as well (Smith and Smith, in press).

SUMMARY

The CMM approach suggests that (1) human beings inevitably create or construe meaning, (2) that we attempt to coordinate and manage our meanings with those of others for purposes of understanding, that (3) we accomplish this coordinated management through reference to rules, that (4) these rules are learned, adapted, created, and discovered through communication, and that (5) there is a hierarchy of rules encompassing content, speech act, episodic, relational, life script, and cultural pattern levels. *The key to understanding a particular sort of communication is therefore discovery of the rules in force; and discovery of the rules entails the systematic analysis of communication patterns.*

The first step toward a fuller and more meaningful understanding of presidential communication, then, is the discovery of patterns in presidential communication. But to do this, we must alter some of our familiar approaches to studying the presidency. Although we want to know about a president's personal qualities, about historical events, institutional relations, and changing sociocultural norms; we must resist the temptation to advocate any of these as univariate explanations of presidential leadership. Instead, we need to look for (1) recurrent episodic, relational, idiosyncratic, and cultural rules, (2) the interplay among these rules, (3) the influence of these rule systems on the exercise of presidential power, and (4) changes in the operative rule systems rather than changes in presidents.

OVERVIEW

Studies of presidential leadership continue to stress the centrality of communication to the process of presidential power. But if presidential power is communicative in nature, then our next task should be the communicative analysis of presidential leadership. This volume is designed to help us refocus our analyses of presidential communication. First, the presentation of a communication *theoretic* approach for the study of presidential power is a necessary step beyond extant calls for the examination of presidential power as communication. The Coordinated Management of Meaning framework offers two important advantages. First, it is a well-established theory of interpersonal communication which seems to offer new opportunities for explanations of presidential communication. And second, the CMM approach offers hierarchical levels which allow us to draw upon studies of presidents, speeches, American culture, and constituent relations.

Second, we have organized a collection of major presidential addresses which merit serious attention—whether that attention be critical or empirical. Although public addresses, like bargaining, do not constitute the whole of presidential communication, they seem a reasonable place to begin our search for rule systems. These selections reflect the fact that broadcast technologies and professional speechwriters have greatly magnified the role of presidential speeches during the twentieth century.

Third, we have rejected the traditional notion of organizing these speeches chronologically by presidencies. This is not accidental. Consistent with the CMM approach we think it necessary to study groups of speeches for various sets of rules. Because we already have a good start at understanding both historical changes and individual presidents, we chose to focus upon episodic and relational rules. Units I and IV present, respectively, Inaugural and Farewell Addresses—important transitional statements in which these presidents provided their constituents with a framework for interpreting their administrations. Unit II offers glimpses of various presidents concentrating on three important constituent relationships: Congress, Critics, and the World. Finally, Unit III examines recurrent presidential responsibilities so that we may better understand the similarities and differences in their Civil Rights, and Economic spheres, as well as their handling of domestic and foreign crises. Of course, the reader interested in studying the rhetoric of individual presidents can pull together the appropriate speeches from the various sections. Finally, we have offered introductory comments on the speeches at the beginning of each section. While necessarily brief, they provide the contextual essentials and sketch the nature of some operative rules. Yet we have tried to suggest the general nature of these rules without asserting any eternal truths. Hopefully, the reader will find the approach and speeches a useful addition to the study of presidential behavior.

REFERENCES

Barber, James David. *The Presidential Character: Predicting Performance in the White House*, 2nd ed. Englewood Cliffs, NJ: Prentice-Hall, 1977.

Bitzer, Lloyd. The Rhetorical Situation. *Philosophy and Rhetoric*, 1968, 1–14.

Bitzer, Lloyd. Functional Communication: A Situational Perspective. in Eugene E. White (ed.), *Rhetoric in Transition: Studies in the Nature and Uses of Rhetoric*. University Park: Penn State University Press, 1980.

Burns, James MacGregor. *Leadership*. New York: Harper Colophon, 1978.

Cronen, Vernon E., Pearce, W. Barnett, and Harris, Linda M. The Coordinated Management of Meaning: A Theory of Communication. in Frank E. X. Dance (ed.), *Human Communication Theory*. New York: Harper and Row, 1982.

Hargrove, Erwin. *Presidential Leadership: Personality and Political Style*. London: Macmillan, 1966.

Harris, Linda, and Cronen, Vernon. A Rules-Based Model for the Analysis and Evaluation of Organizational Communication. *Communication Quarterly*, 1979, 12–28.

Mueller, John E. Presidential Popularity from Truman to Johnson. *The American Political Science Review*, 1970, 18–34.

Neustadt, Richard. *Presidential Power: The Politics of Leadership from FDR to Carter*. New York: John Wiley, 1980 (original published in 1960).

Pearce, W. Barnett, and Conklin, Forest. A Model of Hierarchical Meanings in Coherent Conversation and a Study of Indirect Responses. *Communication Monographs*, 1976, 75–87.

Pearce, W. Barnett, Cronen, Vernon E., Conklin, Forest. What to Look at When Analyzing Communication: A Hierarchical Model of Actors' Meanings. *Communication*. 1979, 179–203.

Seymour-Ure, Colin. *The American Presidency: Power and Communication*. New York: St. Martin's, 1982.

Smith, Craig Allen. The Audiences of the 'Rhetorical Presidency': An Analysis of Presidential-Constituent Interactions, 1963–1981. *Presidential Studies Quarterly*, 1983, 613–622.

Smith, Craig Allen, and Smith, Kathy B. Presidential Values and Public Priorities: Recurrent Patterns in Addresses to the Nation, 1963–1984. *Presidential Studies Quarterly*, in press.

Vatz, Richard E. The Myth of the Rhetorical Situation. *Philosophy and Rhetoric*, 1973, 154–161.

UNIT ONE

Presidential Prospects

Chapter 1 Inaugural Addresses

Leadership involves the articulation of goals and the motivation of followers. In a very real sense anything that any president does is, or should be, leadership. Our presidents typically use the inaugural address to establish the major themes of their administrations. Although each president faces different domestic and international issues, all presidents face recurrent challenges in their inaugural addresses. First, the president must begin to unify the country after a divisive campaign. Second, he must begin to spell out the themes of the rhetorical vision which will orient his administration. Thirdly, he speaks to posterity so that they will understand his place in history. Our presidents are usually able to respond to all three challenges, as Dante Germino observed in *The Inaugural Addresses of American Presidents*, by reinterpreting the American "Public Philosophy."

Speaking in the Senate chamber of the new Capitol, Thomas Jefferson made an eloquent plea for union. In this brief address he succinctly described what he held to be the purposes of government. His values and goals were clearly stated as he began his first presidential term.

President Lincoln faced the unenviable task of promoting unity as the Union quickly dissolved. In fact, by the time of his inaugural address six southern states had already seceded. This speech was one of his last rhetorical efforts to persuade fellow Americans to remain one nation, and his emphasis upon the enduring "Union" became the basis for his conduct of the War.

In contrast, Franklin Roosevelt's depression era audience was united by a common fear and uncertainty for their personal and

national safety. Roosevelt confronted this anxiety in his address
and offered energy, direction, and above all, hope to his people.

President John F. Kennedy was heralded as the "New Guard"
after the quiet years of the Eisenhower Administration. His
inaugural address reinforced this perception with its challenging
tone and its assertion that the torch of leadership was being passed
to a new generation of Americans.

When Lyndon Johnson was thrust into the presidency by the
assassination of President Kennedy he chose to address a joint
session of Congress (which was broadcast nationally). Johnson
articulated the national sadness, assured the world that we would
keep our treaty commitments, and pointed to important legislative
priorities. He argued that many of Kennedy's favorite projects
were left unfinished, and that together he and they could honor
their fallen leader by enacting those programs. This emotional
speech rallied the grief-stricken nation around their new president
and contributed to Johnson's tremendous legislative successes in
1964–65.

Finally, President Reagan became president during a period of
extreme inflation and government expansion. While he spoke, the
television audience watched the plane carrying our hostages
prepare to take-off for the trip home from Iran. Reagan's inaugural
address articulates a state of crisis existing in the nation. Reagan
skillfully transferred the crisis mentality associated with the
hostage episode to the less fearsome problems of inflation and
government expansion that had highlighted his campaign. His
speech is resplendent with the images, symbols, and values of our
shared political culture. As is common in inaugural addresses,
President Reagan portrayed an unsettled present before calling for
action to move toward a better tomorrow.

Thomas Jefferson
First Inaugural Address
March 4, 1801

FRIENDS AND FELLOW CITIZENS:

Called upon to undertake the duties of the first executive office of our country, I avail myself of the presence of that portion of my fellow-citizens which is here assembled to express my grateful thanks for the favor with which they have been pleased to look toward me, to declare a sincere consciousness that the task is above my talents, and that I approach it with those anxious and awful presentiments which the greatness of the charge and the weakness of my powers so justly inspire. A rising nation, spread over a wide and fruitful land, traversing all the seas with the rich productions of their industry, engaged in commerce with nations who feel power and forget right, advancing rapidly to destinies beyond the reach of mortal eye—when I contemplate these transcendent objects, and see the honor, the happiness, and the hopes of this beloved country committed to the issue and the auspices of this day, I shrink from the contemplation, and humble myself before the magnitude of the undertaking. Utterly, indeed, should I despair did not the presence of many whom I here see remind me that in the other high authorities provided by our Constitution I shall find resources of wisdom, of virtue, and of zeal on which to rely under all difficulties. To you, then, gentlemen, who are charged with the sovereign functions of legislation, and to those associated with you, I look with encouragement for that guidance and support which may enable us to steer with safety the vessel in which we are all embarked amidst the conflicting elements of a troubled world.

During the contest of opinion through which we have passed the animation of discussions and of exertions has sometimes worn an aspect which might impose on strangers unused to think freely and to speak and to write what they think; but this being now decided by the voice of the nation, announced according to the rules of the Constitution, all will, of course, arrange themselves under the will of the law, and unite in common efforts for the common good. All, too, will bear in mind this sacred principle, that though the will of the majority is in all cases to prevail, that will to be rightful must be reasonable; that the minority possess their equal rights, which equal law must protect, and to violate would be oppression. Let us, then, fellow-citizens, unite with one heart and one mind. Let us restore to social intercourse that harmony and affection without which liberty and even life itself are but dreary things. And let us reflect that, having banished from our land that religious intolerance under which mankind so long bled and suffered, we have yet gained little if we countenance a political intolerance as despotic, as wicked, and capable of as bitter and bloody persecutions. During the throes and convulsions of the ancient world, during the agonizing spasms of infuriated man, seeking through blood and slaughter his long-lost liberty, it was not wonderful that the agitation of the billows should reach even this distant and peaceful shore; that this should be more felt and feared by some and less by others, and should divide opinions as to measures of safety. But every difference of opinion is not a difference of principle. We have called by different names brethren of the same principle. We are all Republicans, we are all Federalists. If there be any among us who would wish to dissolve this Union or to change its republican form, let them stand undisturbed as monuments of the safety with which error of opinion may be tolerated where reason is left free to combat it. I know, indeed, that some honest men fear that a republican government can not be strong, that this Government is not strong enough; but would the honest patriot, in the full tide of successful experiment, abandon a government which has so far kept us free and firm on the theoretic and visionary fear that this Government, the world's best hope, may by possibility want energy to preserve itself? I trust not. I believe this, on the contrary, the strongest Government on earth. I believe it is the only one where every man, at the call of the law, would fly to the standard of the law, and would meet invasions of the public order as his own personal concern. Sometimes it is said that man can not be trusted with the government of himself. Can he, then, be trusted with the government of others? Or have we found angels in the forms of kings to govern him? Let history answer this question.

Let us, then, with courage and confidence pursue our own Federal and Republican principles, our attachment to union and representative government. Kindly separated by nature and a wide ocean from the exterminating havoc of one quarter of the globe; too high-minded to endure the degradations of the others; possessing a chosen country, with room enough for our descendants to the thousandth and thousandth generation; entertaining a due sense of our equal rights to the use of our own faculties, to the acquisitions of our own industry, to honor and confidence from our fellow-citizens, resulting not from birth, but from our actions and their sense of them; enlightened by a benign religion, professed, indeed, and practiced in various forms, yet all of them inculcating honesty, truth, temperance, gratitude, and the love of man; acknowledging and adoring an overruling Providence, which by all its dispensations proves that it delights in the happiness of man here and his greater happiness hereafter—with all these blessings, what more is necessary to make us a happy and a prosperous people? Still one thing more, fellow-citizens—a wise and frugal Government, which shall restrain men from injuring one another, shall leave them otherwise free to regulate their own pursuits of industry and improvement, and shall not take from the mouth of labor the bread it has earned. This is the sum of good government, and this is necessary to close the circle of our felicities.

About to enter, fellow-citizens, on the exercise of duties which comprehend everything dear and valuable to you, it is proper you should understand what I deem the essential principles of our Government, and consequently those which ought to shape its Administration. I will compress them within the narrowest compass they will bear, stating the general principle, but not all its limitations. Equal and exact justice to all men, of whatever state or persuasion, religious or political; peace, commerce, and honest friendship with all nations, entangling alliances with none; the support of the State governments in all their rights, as the most competent administrations for our domestic concerns and the surest bulwarks against antirepublican tendencies; the preservation of the General Government in its whole constitutional vigor, as the sheet anchor of our peace at home and safety abroad; a jealous care of the right of election by the people—a mild and safe corrective of abuses which are lopped by the sword of revolution where peaceable remedies are unprovided; absolute acquiescence in the decisions of the majority, the vital principle of republics, from which is no appeal but to force, the vital principle and immediate parent of despotism; a well-disciplined militia, our best reliance in peace and for the first moments of war, till regulars may relieve them; the supremacy of the civil over the military authority; economy in the public expense, that labor may be lightly bur- thened; the honest payment of our debts and sacred preservation of the public faith; encouragement of agriculture, and of commerce as its handmaid; the diffusion of information and arraignment of all abuses at the bar of the public reason; freedom of religion; freedom of the press, and freedom of person under the protection of the habeas corpus, and trial by juries impartially selected. These principles form the bright constellation which has gone before us and guided our steps through an age of revolution and reforma- tion. The wisdom of our sages and blood of our heroes have been devoted to their attainment. They should be the creed of our political faith, the text of civic instruction, the touchstone by which to try the services of those we trust; and should we wander from them in moments of error or of alarm, let us hasten to retrace our steps and to regain the road which alone leads to peace, liberty, and safety.

I repair, then, fellow-citizens, to the post you have assigned me. With experience enough in subordinate offices to have seen the difficulties of this the greatest of all, I have learnt to expect that it will rarely fall to the lot of imperfect man to retire from this station with the reputation and the favor which bring him into it. Without pretensions to that high confidence you reposed in our first and greatest revolutionary character, whose preeminent services had entitled him to the first place in his country's love and destined for him the fairest page in the volume of faithful history, I ask so much confidence only as may give firmness and effect to the legal administration of your affairs. I shall often go wrong through defect of judgment. When right, I shall often be thought wrong by those whose positions will not command a view of the whole ground. I ask you indulgence for my own errors, which will never be intentional, and your support against the errors of others, who may condemn what they would not if seen in all its parts. The approbation implied by your suffrage is a great consolation to me for the past, and my future solicitude will be to retain the good opinion of those who have bestowed it in advance, to conciliate that of others by doing them all the good in my power, and to be instrumental to the happiness and freedom of all.

Relying, then, on the patronage of your good will, I advance with obedience to the work, ready to retire from it whenever you become sensible how much better choice it is in your power to make. And may that Infinite Power which rules the destinies of the universe lead our councils to what is best, and give them a favorable issue for your peace and prosperity.

Abraham Lincoln
First Inaugural Address—
Final Text
March 4, 1861

FELLOW CITIZENS OF THE UNITED STATES:

In compliance with a custom as old as the government itself, I appear before you to address you briefly, and to take, in your presence, the oath prescribed by the Constitution of the United States, to be taken by the President "before he enters on the execution of his office."

I do not consider it necessary, at present, for me to discuss those matters of administration about which there is no special anxiety, or excitement.

Apprehension seems to exist among the people of the Southern States, that by the accession of a Republican Administration, their property, and their peace, and personal security, are to be endangered. There has never been any reasonable cause for such apprehension. Indeed, the most ample evidence to the contrary has all the while existed, and been open to their inspection. It is found in nearly all the published speeches of him who now addresses you. I do but quote from one of those speeches when I declare that "I have no purpose, directly or indirectly, to interfere with the institution of slavery in the States where it exists. I believe I have no lawful right to do so, and I have no inclination to do so." Those who nominated and elected me did so with full knowledge that I had made this, and many similar declarations, and had never recanted them. And more than this, they placed in the platform, for my acceptance, and as a law to themselves, and to me, the clear and emphatic resolution which I now read:

"*Resolved*, That the maintenance inviolate of the rights of the

States, and especially the right of each State to order and control its own domestic institutions according to its own judgment exclusively, is essential to that balance of power on which the perfection and endurance of our political fabric depend; and we denounce the lawless invasion by armed force of the soil of any State or Territory, no matter under what pretext, as among the gravest of crimes."

I now reiterate these sentiments: and in doing so, I only press upon the public attention the most conclusive evidence of which the case is susceptible, that the property, peace and security of no section are to be in anywise endangered by the now incoming Administration. I add too, that all the protection which, consistently with the Constitution and the laws, can be given, will be cheerfully given to all the States when lawfully demanded, for whatever cause—as cheerfully to one section, as to another.

There is much controversy about the delivering up of fugitives from service or labor. The clause I now read is as plainly written in the Constitution as any other of its provisions:

"No person held to service or labor in one State, under the laws thereof, escaping into another, shall, in consequence of any law or regulation therein, be discharged from such service or labor, but shall be delivered up on claim of the party to whom such service or labor may be due."

It is scarcely questioned that this provision was intended by those who made it, for the reclaiming of what we call fugitive slaves; and the intention of the law-giver is the law. All members of Congress swear their support to the whole Constitution—to this provision as much as to any other. To the proposition, then, that slaves whose cases come within the terms of this clause, "shall be delivered up," their oaths are unanimous. Now, if they would make the effort in good temper, could they not, with nearly equal unanimity, frame and pass a law, by means of which to keep good that unanimous oath?

There is some difference of opinion whether this clause should be enforced by national or by state authority; but surely that difference is not a very material one. If the slave is to be surrendered, it can be of but little consequence to him, or to others, by which authority it is done. And should any one, in any case, be content that his oath shall go unkept, on a merely unsubstantial controversy as to *how* it shall be kept?

Again, in any law upon this subject, ought not all the safeguards of liberty known in civilized and humane jurisprudence to be introduced, so that a free man be not, in any case, surrendered as a slave? And might it not be well, at the same time, to provide by law for the enforcement of that clause in the Constitution which guarranties that "The citizens of each State shall be entitled to all privileges and immunities of citizens in the several States?"

I take the official oath to-day, with no mental reservations, and with no purpose to construe the Constitution or laws, by any hypercritical rules. And while I do not choose now to specify particular acts of Congress as proper to be enforced, I do suggest, that it will be much safer for all, both in official and private stations, to conform to, and abide by, all those acts which stand unrepealed, than to violate any of them, trusting to find impunity in having them held to be unconstitutional.

It is seventy-two years since the first inauguration of a President under our national Constitution. During that period fifteen different and greatly distinguished citizens, have, in succession, administered the executive branch of the government. They have conducted it through many perils; and, generally, with great success. Yet, with all this scope for precedent, I now enter upon the same task for the brief constitutional term of four years, under great and peculiar difficulty. A disruption of the Federal Union heretofore only menaced, is now formidably attempted.

I hold, that in contemplation of universal law, and of the Constitution, the Union of these States is perpetual. Perpetuity is implied, if not expressed, in the fundamental law of all national governments. It is safe to assert that no government proper, ever had a provision in its organic law for its own termination. Continue to execute all the express provisions of our national Constitution, and the Union will endure forever—it being impossible to destroy it, except by some action not provided for in the instrument itself.

Again, if the United States be not a government proper, but an association of States in the nature of contract merely, can it, as a contract, be peaceably unmade, by less than all the parties who made it? One party to a contract may violate it—break it, so to speak; but does it not require all to lawfully rescind it?

Descending from these general principles, we find the proposition that, in legal contemplation, the Union is perpetual, confirmed by the history of the Union itself. The Union is much older than the Constitution. It was formed in fact, by the Articles of Association in 1774. It was matured and continued by the Declaration of Independence in 1776. It was further matured and the faith of all the then thirteen States expressly plighted and engaged that it should be perpetual, by the Articles of Confederation in 1778. And finally, in 1787, one of the declared objects for ordaining and establishing the Constitution, was "*to form a more perfect union.*"

But if destruction of the Union, by one, or by a part only, of the States, be lawfully possible, the Union is *less* perfect than before the Constitution, having lost the vital element of perpetuity.

It follows from these views that no State, upon its own mere motion, can lawfully get out of the Union—that *resolves* and *ordinances* to that effect are legally void; and that acts of violence, within any State or States, against the authority of the United States, are insurrectionary or revolutionary, according to circumstances.

I therefore consider that, in view of the Constitution and the laws, the Union is unbroken; and, to the extent of my ability, I shall take care, as the Constitution itself expressly enjoins upon me, that the laws of the Union be faithfully executed in all the States. Doing this I deem to be only a simple duty on my part; and I shall perform it, so far as practicable, unless my rightful masters, the American people, shall withold the requisite means, or, in some authoritative manner, direct the contrary. I trust this will not be regarded as a menace, but only as the declared purpose of the Union that it *will* constitutionally defend, and maintain itself.

In doing this there needs to be no bloodshed or violence; and there shall be none, unless it be forced upon the national authority. The power confided to me, will be used to hold, occupy, and possess the property, and places belonging to the government, and to collect the duties and imposts; but beyond what may be necessary for these objects, there will be no invasion—no using of force against, or among the people anywhere. Where hostility to the United States, in any interior locality, shall be so great and so universal, as to prevent competent resident citizens from holding the Federal offices, there will be no attempt to force obnoxious strangers among the people for that object. While the strict legal right may exist in the government to enforce the exercise of these offices, the attempt to do so would be so irritating, and so nearly impracticable with all, that I deem it better to forego, for the time, the uses of such offices.

The mails, unless repelled, will continue to be furnished in all parts of the Union. So far as possible, the people everywhere shall have that sense of perfect security which is most favorable to calm thought and reflection. The course here indicated will be followed, unless current events, and experience, shall show a modification, or change, to be proper; and in every case and exigency, my best discretion will be exercised, according to circumstances actually existing, and with a view and a hope of a peaceful solution of the national troubles, and the restoration of fraternal sympathies and affections.

That there are persons in one section, or another who seek to destroy the Union at all events, and are glad of any pretext to do it, I will neither affirm or deny; but if there be such, I need address no word to them. To those, however, who really love the Union, may I not speak?

Before entering upon so grave a matter as the destruction of our national fabric, with all its benefits, its memories, and its hopes, would it not be wise to ascertain precisely why we do it? Will you hazard so desperate a step, while there is any possibility that any portion of the ills you fly from, have no real existence? Will you, while the certain ills you fly to, are greater than all the real ones you fly from? Will you risk the commission of so fearful a mistake?

All profess to be content in the Union, if all constitutional rights can be maintained. Is it true, then, that any right, plainly written in the Constitution, has been denied? I think not. Happily the human mind is so constituted, that no party can reach to the audacity of doing this. Think, if you can, of a single instance in which a plainly written provision of the Constitution has ever been denied. If, by the mere force of numbers, a majority should deprive a minority of any clearly written constitutional right, it might, in a moral point of view, justify revolution—certainly would, if such right were a vital one. But such is not our case. All the vital rights of minorities, and of individuals, are so plainly assured to them, by affirmations and negations, guarranties and prohibitions, in the Constitution, that controversies never arise concerning them. But no organic law can ever be framed with a provision specifically applicable to every question which may occur in practical administration. No foresight can anticipate, nor any document of reasonable length contain express provisions for all possible questions. Shall fugitives from labor be surrendered by national or by State authority? The Constitution does not expressly say. *May* Congress prohibit slavery in the territories? The Constitution does not expressly say. *Must* Congress protect slavery in the territories? The Constitution does not expressly say.

From questions of this class spring all our constitutional controversies, and we divide upon them into majorities and minorities. If the minority will not acquiesce, the majority must, or the government must cease. There is no other alternative; for continuing the government, is acquiescence on one side or the other. If a minority, in such case, will secede rather than acquiesce, they make a precedent which, in turn, will divide and ruin them; for a minority of their own will secede from them, whenever a majority refuses to be controlled by such minority. For instance, why may not any portion of a new confederacy, a year or two hence, arbitrarily secede again, precisely as portions of the present Union now claim to secede from it. All who cherish disunion sentiments, are now being educated to the exact temper of doing this. Is there such perfect identity of interests among the States to compose a new Union, as to produce harmony only, and prevent renewed secession?

Plainly, the central idea of secession, is the essence of anarchy. A majority, held in restraint by constitutional checks, and limitations, and always changing easily, with deliberate changes of popular opinions and sentiments, is the only true sovereign of a free people. Whoever rejects it, does, of necessity, fly to anarchy or to despotism. Unanimity is impossible; the rule of a minority, as a permanent arrangement, is wholly inadmissable; so that, rejecting the majority principle, anarchy, or despotism in some form, is all that is left.

I do not forget the position assumed by some, that constitutional questions are to be decided by the Supreme Court; nor do I deny that such decisions must be binding in any case, upon the parties to a suit, as to the object of that suit, while they are also entitled to very high respect and consideration, in all parallel cases, by all other departments of the government. And while it is obviously possible that such decision may be erroneous in any given case, still the evil effect following it, being limited to that particular case, with the chance that it may be over-ruled, and never become a precedent for other cases, can better be borne than could the evils of a different practice. At the same time the candid citizen must confess that if the policy of the government, upon vital questions, affecting the whole people, is to be irrevocably fixed by decisions of the Supreme Court, the instant they are made, in ordinary litigation between parties, in personal actions, the people will have ceased, to be their own rulers, having, to that extent, practically resigned their government, into the hands of that eminent tribunal. Nor is there, in this view, any assault upon the court, or the judges. It is a duty, from which they may not shrink, to decide cases properly brought before them; and it is no fault of theirs, if others seek to turn their decisions to political purposes.

One section of our country believes slavery is *right*, and ought to be extended, while the other believes it is *wrong*, and ought not to be extended. This is the only substantial dispute. The fugitive slave clause of the Constitution, and the law for the suppression of the foreign slave trade, are each as well enforced, perhaps, as any law can ever be in a community where the moral sense of the people imperfectly supports the law itself. The great body of the people abide by the dry legal obligation in both cases, and a few break over in each. This, I think, cannot be perfectly cured; and it would be worse in both cases *after* the separation of the sections, than before. The foreign slave trade, now imperfectly suppressed, would be ultimately revived without restriction, in one section; while fugitive slaves, now only partially surrendered, would not be surrendered at all, by the other.

Physically speaking, we cannot separate. We cannot remove our respective sections from each other, nor build an impassable wall between them. A husband and wife may be divorced, and go out of the presence, and beyond the reach of each other; but the different parts of our country cannot do this. They cannot but remain face to face; and intercourse, either amicable or hostile, must continue between them. Is it possible then to make that intercourse more advantageous, or more satisfactory, *after* separation than *before*? Can aliens make treaties easier than friends can make laws? Can treaties be more faithfully enforced between aliens, than laws can among friends? Suppose you go to war, you cannot fight always; and when, after much loss on both sides, and no gain on either, you cease fighting, the identical old questions, as to terms of intercourse, are again upon you.

This country, with its institutions, belongs to the people who inhabit it. Whenever they shall grow weary of the existing government, they can exercise their *constitutional* right of amending it, or their *revolutionary* right to dismember, or overthrow it. I can not be ignorant of the fact that many worthy, and patriotic citizens are desirous of having the national constitution amended. While I make no recommendation of amendments, I fully recognize the rightful authority of the people over the whole subject, to be exercised in either of the modes prescribed in the instrument itself; and I should, under existing circumstances, favor, rather than oppose, a fair opportunity being afforded the people to act upon it.

I will venture to add that, to me, the convention mode seems preferable, in that it allows amendments to originate with the people themselves, instead of only permitting them to take, or reject, propositions, originated by others, not especially chosen for the purpose, and which might not be precisely such, as they would wish to either accept or refuse. I understand a proposed amendment to the Constitution—which amendment, however, I have not seen, has passed Congress, to the effect that the federal government, shall never interfere with the domestic institutions of the States, including that of persons held to service. To avoid misconstruction of what I have said, I depart from my purpose not to speak of particular amendments, so far as to say that, holding such a provision to now be implied constitutional law, I have no objection to its being made express, and irrevocable.

The Chief Magistrate derives all his authority from the people, and they have conferred none upon him to fix terms for the separation of the States. The people themselves can do this also if they choose; but the executive, as such, has nothing to do with it. His duty is to administer the present government, as it came to his hands, and to transmit it, unimpaired by him, to his successor.

Why should there not be a patient confidence in the ultimate justice of the people? Is there any better, or equal hope, in the world? In our present differences, is either party without faith of being in the right? If the Almighty Ruler of nations, with his eternal truth and justice, be on your side of the North, or on yours of the South, that truth, and that justice, will surely prevail, by the judgment of this great tribunal, the American people.

By the frame of the government under which we live, this same people have wisely given their public servants but little power for mischief; and have, with equal wisdom, provided for the return of that little to their own hands at very short intervals.

While the people retain their virtue, and vigilence, no administration, by any extreme of wickedness or folly, can very seriously injure the government in the short space of four years.

My countrymen, one and all, think calmly and *well*, upon this whole subject. Nothing valuable can be lost by taking time. If there be an object to *hurry* any of you, in hot haste, to a step which you would never take *deliberately*, that object will be frustrated by taking time; but no good object can be frustrated by it. Such of you as are now dissatisfied, still have the old Constitution unimpaired, and, on the sensitive point, the laws of your own framing under it; while the new administration will have no immediate power, if it would, to change either. If it were admitted that you who are dissatisfied, hold the right side in the dispute, there still is no single good reason for precipitate action. Intelligence, patriotism, Christianity, and a firm reliance on Him, who has never yet forsaken this favored land, are still competent to adjust, in the best way, all our present difficulty.

In *your* hands, my dissatisfied fellow countrymen, and not in *mine*, is the momentous issue of civil war. The government will not assail *you*. You can have no conflict, without being yourselves the aggressors. *You* have no oath registered in Heaven to destroy the government, while *I* shall have the most solemn one to "preserve, protect and defend" it.

I am loth to close. We are not enemies, but friends. We must not be enemies. Though passion may have strained, it must not break our bonds of affection. The mystic chords of memory, stretching from every battle-field, and patriot grave, to every living heart and hearthstone, all over this broad land, will yet swell the chorus of the Union, when again touched, as surely they will be, by the better angels of our nature.

Franklin D. Roosevelt
Inaugural Address
March 4, 1933

I am certain that my fellow Americans expect that on my induction into the Presidency I will address them with a candor and a decision which the present situation of our Nation impels. This is preeminently the time to speak the truth, the whole truth, frankly and boldly. Nor need we shrink from honestly facing conditions in our country today. This great Nation will endure as it has endured, will revive and will prosper. So, first of all, let me assert my firm belief that the only thing we have to fear it fear itself—nameless, unreasoning, unjustified terror which paralyzes needed efforts to convert retreat into advance. In every dark hour of our national life a leadership of frankness and vigor has met with that understanding and support of the people themselves which is essential to victory. I am convinced that you will again give that support to leadership in these critical days.

In such a spirit on my part and on yours we face our common difficulties. They concern, thank God, only material things. Values have shrunken to fantastic levels; taxes have risen; our ability to pay has fallen; government of all kinds is faced by serious curtailment of income; the means of exchange are frozen in the currents of trade; the withered leaves of industrial enterprise lie on every side; farmers find no markets for their produce; the savings of many years in thousands of families are gone.

More important, a host of unemployed citizens face the grim problem of existence, and an equally great number toil with little return. Only a foolish optimist can deny the dark realities of the moment.

Yet our distress comes from no failure of substance. We are stricken by no plague of locusts. Compared with the perils which our forefathers conquered because they believed and were not afraid, we have still much to be thankful for. Nature still offers her bounty and human efforts have multiplied it. Plenty is at our doorstep, but a generous use of it languishes in the very sight of the supply. Primarily this is because rulers of the exchange of mankind's goods have failed through their own stubbornness and their own incompetence, have admitted their failure, and have abdicated. Practices of the unscrupulous money changers stand indicted in the court of public opinion, rejected by the hearts and minds of men.

True they have tried, but their efforts have been cast in the pattern of an outworn tradition. Faced by failure of credit they have proposed only the lending of more money. Stripped of the lure of profit by which to induce our people to follow their false leadership, they have resorted to exhortations, pleading tearfully for restored confidence. They know only the rules of a generation of self-seekers. They have no vision, and when there is no vision the people perish.

The money changers have fled from their high seats in the temple of our civilization. We may now restore that temple to the ancient truths. The measure of the restoration lies in the extent to which we apply social values more noble than mere monetary profit.

Happiness lies not in the mere possession of money; it lies in the joy of achievement, in the thrill of creative effort. The joy and moral stimulation of work no longer must be forgotten in the mad chase of evanescent profits. These dark days will be worth all they cost us if they teach us that our true destiny is not to be ministered unto but to minister to ourselves and to our fellow men.

Recognition of the falsity of material wealth as the standard of success goes hand in hand with the abandonment of the false belief that public office and high political position are to be valued only by the standards of pride of place and personal profit; and there must be an end to a conduct in banking and in business which too often has given to a sacred trust the likeness of callous and selfish wrongdoing. Small wonder that confidence languishes, for it thrives only on honesty, on honor, on the sacredness of obligations, on faithful protection, on unselfish performance; without them it cannot live.

Restoration calls, however, not for changes in ethics alone. This Nation asks for action, and action now.

Our greatest primary task is to put people to work. This is no unsolvable problem if we face it wisely and courageously. It can be accomplished in part by direct recruiting by the Government itself, treating the task as we would treat the emergency of a war, but at the same time, through this employment, accomplishing greatly needed projects to stimulate and reorganize the use of our natural resources.

Hand in hand with this we must frankly recognize the overbalance of population in our industrial centers and, by engaging on a national scale in a redistribution, endeavor to provide a better use of the land for those best fitted for the land. The task can be helped by definite efforts to raise the values of agricultural products and with this the power to purchase the output of our cities. It can be helped by preventing realistically the tragedy of the growing loss through foreclosure of our small homes and our farms. It can be helped by insistence that the Federal, State, and local governments act forthwith on the demand that their cost be drastically reduced. It can be helped by the unifying of relief activities which today are often scattered, uneconomical, and unequal. It can be helped by national planning for and supervision of all forms of transportation and of communications and other utilities which have a definitely public character. There are many ways in which it can be helped, but it can never be helped merely by talking about it. We must act and act quickly.

Finally, in our progress toward a resumption of work we require two safeguards against a return of the evils of the old order: there must be a strict supervision of all banking and credits and investments, so that there will be an end to speculation with other people's money, and there must be provision for an adequate but sound currency.

These are the lines of attack. I shall presently urge upon a new Congress, in special session, detailed measures for their fulfillment, and I shall seek the immediate assistance of the several States.

Through this program of action we address ourselves to putting our own national house in order and making income balance outgo. Our international trade relations, though vastly important, are in point of time and necessity secondary to the establishment of a sound national economy. I favor as a practical policy the putting of first things first. I shall spare no effort to restore world trade by international economic readjustment, but the emergency at home cannot wait on that accomplishment.

The basic thought that guides these specific means of national recovery is not narrowly nationalistic. It is the insistence, as a first consideration, upon the interdependence of the various elements in and parts of the United States—a recognition of the old and permanently important manifestation of the American spirit of the pioneer. It is the way to recovery. It is the immediate way. It is the strongest assurance that the recovery will endure.

In the field of world policy I would dedicate this Nation to the policy of the good neighbor—the neighbor who resolutely respects himself and, because he does so, respects the rights of others—the neighbor who respects his obligations and respects the sanctity of his agreements in and with a world of neighbors.

If I read the temper of our people correctly, we now realize as we have never realized before our interdependence on each other; that we cannot merely take but we must give as well; that if we are to go forward, we must move as a trained and loyal army willing to sacrifice for the good of a common discipline, because without such discipline no progress is made, no leadership becomes effective. We are, I know, ready and willing to submit our lives and property to such discipline, because it makes possible a leadership which aims at a larger good. This I propose to offer, pledging that the larger purposes will bind upon us all as a sacred obligation with a unity of duty hitherto evoked only in time of armed strife.

With this pledge taken, I assume unhesitatingly the leadership of this great army of our people dedicated to a disciplined attack upon our common problems.

Action in this image and to this end is feasible under the form of government which we have inherited from our ancestors. Our Constitution is so simple and practical that it is possible always to meet extraordinary needs by changes in emphasis and arrangement without loss of essential form. That is why our constitutional system has proved itself the most superbly enduring political mechanism the modern world has produced. It has met every stress of vast expansion of territory, of foreign wars, of bitter internal strife, of world relations.

It is to be hoped that the normal balance of Executive and

legislative authority may be wholly adequate to meet the unprecedented task before us. But it may be that an unprecedented demand and need for undelayed action may call for temporary departure from that normal balance of public procedure.

I am prepared under my constitutional duty to recommend the measures that a stricken Nation in the midst of a stricken world may require. These measures, or such other measures as the Congress may build out of its experience and wisdom, I shall seek, within my constitutional authority, to bring to speedy adoption.

But in the event that the Congress shall fail to take one of these two courses, and in the event that the national emergency is still critical, I shall not evade the clear course of duty that will then confront me. I shall ask the Congress for the one remaining instrument to meet the crisis—broad Executive power to wage a war against the emergency, as great as the power that would be given to me if we were in fact invaded by a foreign foe.

For the trust reposed in me I will return the courage and the devotion that befit the time. I can do no less.

We face the arduous days that lie before us in the warm courage of national unity; with the clear consciousness of seeking old and precious moral values; with the clean satisfaction that comes from the stern performance of duty by old and young alike. We aim at the assurance of a rounded and permanent national life.

We do not distrust the future of essential democracy. The people of the United States have not failed. In their need they have registered a mandate that they want direct, vigorous action. They have asked for discipline and direction under leadership. They have made me the present instrument of their wishes. In the spirit of the gift I take it.

In this dedication of a Nation we humbly ask the blessing of God. May He protect each and every one of us. May He guide me in the days to come.

John F. Kennedy
Inaugural Address
January 20, 1961

VICE PRESIDENT JOHNSON, MR. SPEAKER, MR. CHIEF JUSTICE, PRESIDENT EISENHOWER, VICE PRESIDENT NIXON, PRESIDENT TRUMAN, REVEREND CLERGY, FELLOW CITIZENS:

We observe today not a victory of party but a celebration of freedom—symbolizing an end as well as a beginning—signifying renewal as well as change. For I have sworn before you and Almighty God the same solemn oath our forebears prescribed nearly a century and three quarters ago.

The world is very different now. For man holds in his mortal hands the power to abolish all forms of human poverty and all forms of human life. And yet the same revolutionary beliefs for which our forebears fought are still at issue around the globe—the belief that the rights of man come not from the generosity of the state but from the hand of God.

We dare not forget today that we are the heirs of that first revolution. Let the word go forth from this time and place, to friend and foe alike, that the torch has been passed to a new generation of Americans—born in this century, tempered by war, disciplined by a hard and bitter peace, proud of our ancient heritage—and unwilling to witness or permit the slow undoing of those human rights to which this nation has always been committed, and to which we are committed today at home and around the world.

Let every nation know, whether it wishes us well or ill, that we shall pay any price, bear any burden, meet any hardship, support any friend, oppose any foe to assure the survival and the success of liberty.

This much we pledge—and more.

To those old allies whose cultural and spiritual origins we share, we pledge the loyalty of faithful friends. United, there is little we cannot do in a host of cooperative ventures. Divided, there is little we can do—for we dare not meet a powerful challenge at odds and split asunder.

To those new states whom we welcome to the ranks of the free, we pledge our word that one form of colonial control shall not have passed away merely to be replaced by a far more iron tyranny. We shall not always expect to find them supporting our view. But we shall always hope to find them strongly supporting their own freedom—and to remember that, in the past, those who foolishly sought power by riding the back of the tiger ended up inside.

To those peoples in the huts and villages of half the globe struggling to break the bonds of mass misery, we pledge our best efforts to help them help themselves, for whatever period is required—not because the communists may be doing it, not because we seek their votes, but because it is right. If a free society cannot help the many who are poor, it cannot save the few who are rich.

To our sister republics south of our border, we offer a special pledge—to convert our good words into good deeds—in a new alliance for progress—to assist free men and free governments in casting off the chains of poverty. But this peaceful revolution of hope cannot become the prey of hostile powers. Let all our neighbors know that we shall join with them to oppose aggression or subversion anywhere in the Americas. And let every other power know that this Hemisphere intends to remain the master of its own house.

To that world assembly of sovereign states, the United Nations, our last best hope in an age where the instruments of war have far outpaced the instruments of peace, we renew our pledge of support—to prevent it from becoming merely a forum for invective—to strengthen its shield of the new and the weak—and to enlarge the area in which its writ may run.

Finally, to those nations who would make themselves our adversary, we offer not a pledge but a request: that both sides begin anew the quest for peace, before the dark powers of destruction unleashed by science engulf all humanity in planned or accidental self-destruction.

We dare not tempt them with weakness. For only when our arms are sufficient beyond doubt can we be certain beyond doubt that they will never be employed.

But neither can two great and powerful groups of nations take comfort from our present course—both sides overburdened by the cost of modern weapons, both rightly alarmed by the steady spread of the deadly atom, yet both racing to alter that uncertain balance of terror that stays the hand of mankind's final war.

So let us begin anew—remembering on both sides that civility is not a sign of weakness, and sincerity is always subject to proof. Let us never negotiate out of fear. But let us never fear to negotiate.

Let both sides explore what problems unite us instead of belaboring those problems which divide us.

Let both sides, for the first time, formulate serious and precise proposals for the inspection and control of arms—and bring the absolute power to destroy other nations under the absolute control of all nations.

Let both sides seek to invoke the wonders of science instead of its terrors. Together let us explore the stars, conquer the deserts, eradicate disease, tap the ocean depths and encourage the arts and commerce.

Let both sides unite to heed in all corners of the earth the command of Isaiah—to "undo the heavy burdens . . . (and) let the oppressed go free."

And if a beach-head of cooperation may push back the jungle of suspicion, let both sides join in creating a new endeavor, not a new balance of power, but a new world of law, where the strong are just and the weak secure and the peace preserved.

All this will not be finished in the first one hundred days. Nor will it be finished in the first one thousand days, nor in the life of this Administration, nor even perhaps in our lifetime on this planet. But let us begin.

In your hands, my fellow citizens, more than mine, will rest the final success or failure of our course. Since this country was founded, each generation of Americans has been summoned to give testimony to its national loyalty. The graves of young Americans who answered the call to service surround the globe.

Now the trumpet summons us again—not as a call to bear arms, though arms we need—not as a call to battle, though embattled we are—but a call to bear the burden of a long twilight struggle, year in and year out, "rejoicing in hope, patient in tribulation"—a struggle against the common enemies of man: tyranny, poverty, disease and war itself.

Can we forge against these enemies a grand and global alliance, North and South, East and West, that can assure a more fruitful life for all mankind? Will you join in that historic effort?

In the long history of the world, only a few generations have been granted the role of defending freedom in its hour of maximum danger. I do not shrink from this responsibility—I welcome it. I do not believe that any of us would exchange places with any other people or any other generation. The energy, the faith, the devotion which we bring to this endeavor will light our country and all who serve it—and the glow from that fire can truly light the world.

And so, my fellow Americans: ask not what your country can do for you—ask what you can do for your country.

My fellow citizens of the world: ask not what America will do for you, but what together we can do for the freedom of man.

Finally, whether you are citizens of America or citizens of the world, ask of us here the same high standards of strength and sacrifice which we ask of you. With a good conscience our only sure reward, with history the final judge of our deeds, let us go forth to lead the land we love, asking His blessing and His help, but knowing that here on earth God's work must truly be our own.

NOTE

The President spoke at 12:52 p.m. from a platform erected at the east front of the Capitol. Immediately before the address the oath of office was administered by Chief Justice Warren.

The President's opening words "Reverend Clergy" referred to His Eminence Richard Cardinal Cushing, Archbishop of Boston; His Eminence Archbishop Iakovos, head of the Greek Archdiocese of North and South America; the Reverend Dr. John Barclay, pastor of the Central Christian Church, Austin, Tex.; and Rabbi Dr. Nelson Glueck, President of the Hebrew Union College, Cincinnati, Ohio.

Lyndon B. Johnson
Address Before a Joint Session
of the Congress
November 27, 1963

MR. SPEAKER, MR. PRESIDENT, MEMBERS OF THE HOUSE, MEMBERS OF THE SENATE, MY FELLOW AMERICANS:

All I have I would have given gladly not to be standing here today.

The greatest leader of our time has been struck down by the foulest deed of our time. Today John Fitzgerald Kennedy lives on in the immortal words and works that he left behind. He lives on in the mind and memories of mankind. He lives on in the hearts of his countrymen.

No words are sad enough to express our sense of loss. No words are strong enough to express our determination to continue the forward thrust of America that he began.

The dream of conquering the vastness of space—the dream of partnership across the Atlantic—and across the Pacific as well—the dream of a Peace Corps in less developed nations—the dream of education for all of our children—the dream of jobs for all who seek them and need them—the dream of care for our elderly—the dream of an all-out attack on mental illness—and above all, the dream of equal rights for all Americans, whatever their race or color—these and other American dreams have been vitalized by his drive and by his dedication.

And now the ideas and the ideals which he so nobly represented must and will be translated into effective action.

Under John Kennedy's leadership, this Nation has demonstrated that it has the courage to seek peace, and it has the fortitude to risk war. We have proved that we are a good and reliable friend to those who seek peace and freedom. We have shown that we can also be a formidable foe to those who reject the path of peace and those who seek to impose upon us or our allies the yoke of tyranny.

This Nation will keep its commitments from South Viet-Nam to West Berlin. We will be unceasing in the search for peace; resourceful in our pursuit of areas of agreement even with those with whom we differ; and generous and loyal to those who join with us in common cause.

In this age when there can be no losers in peace and no victors in war, we must recognize the obligation to match national strength with national restraint. We must be prepared at one and the same time for both the confrontation of power and the limitation of power. We must be ready to defend the national interest and to negotiate the common interest. This is the path that we shall continue to pursue. Those who test our courage will find it strong, and those who seek our friendship will find it honorable. We will demonstrate anew that the strong can be just in the use of strength; and the just can be strong in the defense of justice.

And let all know we will extend no special privilege and impose no persecution. We will carry on the fight against poverty and misery, and disease and ignorance, in other lands and in our own.

We will serve all the Nation, not one section or one sector, or one group, but all Americans. These are the United States—a united people with a united purpose.

Our American unity does not depend upon unanimity. We have differences; but now, as in the past, we can derive from those differences strength, not weakness, wisdom, not despair. Both as a people and a government, we can unite upon a program, a program which is wise and just, enlightened and constructive.

For 32 years Capitol Hill has been my home. I have shared many moments of pride with you, pride in the ability of the Congress of the United States to act, to meet any crisis, to distill from our differences strong programs of national action.

An assassin's bullet has thrust upon me the awesome burden of the Presidency. I am here today to say I need your help; I cannot bear this burden alone. I need the help of all Americans, and all America. This Nation has experienced a profound shock, and in this critical moment, it is our duty, yours and mine, as the Government of the United States, to do away with uncertainty and doubt and delay, and to show that we are capable of decisive action; that from the brutal loss of our leader we will derive not weakness, but strength; that we can and will act and act now.

From this chamber of representative government, let all the world know and none misunderstand that I rededicate this Government to the unswerving support of the United Nations, to the honorable and determined execution of our commitments to our allies, to the maintenance of military strength second to none, to the defense of the strength and the stability of the dollar, to the expansion of our foreign trade, to the reinforcement of our programs of mutual assistance and cooperation in Asia and Africa, and to our Alliance for Progress in this hemisphere.

On the 20th day of January, in 1961, John F. Kennedy told his countrymen that our national work would not be finished "in the first thousand days, nor in the life of this administration, nor even perhaps in our lifetime on this planet. But," he said, "let us begin."

Today, in this moment of new resolve, I would say to all my fellow Americans, let us continue.

This is our challenge—not to hesitate, not to pause, not to turn about and linger over this evil moment, but to continue on our course so that we may fulfill the destiny that history has set for us. Our most immediate tasks are here on this Hill.

First, no memorial oration or eulogy could more eloquently honor President Kennedy's memory than the earliest possible passage of the civil rights bill for which he fought so long. We have talked long enough in this country about equal rights. We have talked for one hundred years or more. It is time now to write the next chapter, and to write it in the books of law.

I urge you again, as I did in 1957 and again in 1960, to enact a civil rights law so that we can move forward to eliminate from this Nation every trace of discrimination and oppression that is based upon race or color. There could be no greater source of strength to this Nation both at home and abroad.

And second, no act of ours could more fittingly continue the work of President Kennedy than the early passage of the tax bill for which he fought all this long year. This is a bill designed to increase our national income and Federal revenues, and to provide insurance against recession. That bill, if passed without delay, means more security for those now working, more jobs for those now without them, and more incentive for our economy.

In short, this is no time for delay. It is a time for action—strong, forward-looking action on the pending education bills to help bring the light of learning to every home and hamlet in America—strong, forward-looking action on youth employment opportunities; strong, forward-looking action on the pending foreign aid bill, making clear that we are not forfeiting our responsibilities to this hemisphere or to the world, nor erasing Executive flexibility in the conduct of our foreign affairs—and strong, prompt, and forward-looking action on the remaining appropriation bills.

In this new spirit of action, the Congress can expect the full cooperation and support of the executive branch. And in particular, I pledge that the expenditures of your Government will be administered with the utmost thrift and frugality. I will insist that the Government get a dollar's value for a dollar spent. The Government will set an example of prudence and economy. This does not mean that we will not meet our unfilled needs or that we will not honor our commitments. We will do both.

As one who has long served in both Houses of the Congress, I firmly believe in the independence and the integrity of the legislative branch. And I promise you that I shall always respect this. It is deep in the marrow of my bones. With equal firmness, I believe in the capacity and I believe in the ability of the Congress, despite the divisions of opinions which characterize our Nation, to act—to act wisely, to act vigorously, to act speedily when the need arises.

The need is here. The need is now. I ask your help.

We meet in grief, but let us also meet in renewed dedication and renewed vigor. Let us meet in action, in tolerance, and in mutual understanding. John Kennedy's death commands what his life conveyed—that America must move forward. The time has come for Americans of all races and creeds and political beliefs to understand and to respect one another. So let us put an end to the teaching and the preaching of hate and evil and violence. Let us turn away from the fanatics of the far left and the far right, from the apostles of bitterness and bigotry, from those defiant of law, and those who pour venom into our Nation's bloodstream.

I profoundly hope that the tragedy and the torment of these

terrible days will bind us together in new fellowship, making us one people in our hour of sorrow. So let us here highly resolve that John Fitzgerald Kennedy did not live—or die—in vain. And on this Thanksgiving eve, as we gather together to ask the Lord's blessing, and give Him our thanks, let us unite in those familiar and cherished words:

America, America,
God shed His grace on thee,
And crown thy good
With brotherhood
From sea to shining sea.

Ronald W. Reagan
Inaugural Address
January 20, 1981

SENATOR HATFIELD, MR. CHIEF JUSTICE, MR. PRESIDENT, VICE PRESIDENT BUSH, VICE PRESIDENT MONDALE, SENATOR BAKER, SPEAKER O'NEILL, REVEREND MOOMAW, AND MY FELLOW CITIZENS:

To a few of us here today this is a solemn and most momentous occasion, and yet in the history of our nation it is a commonplace occurrence. The orderly transfer of authority as called for in the Constitution routinely takes place, as it has for almost two centuries, and few of us stop to think how unique we really are. In the eyes of many in the world, this every-4-year ceremony we accept as normal is nothing less than a miracle.

Mr. President, I want our fellow citizens to know how much you did to carry on this tradition. By your gracious cooperation in the transition process, you have shown a watching world that we are a united people pledged to maintaining a political system which guarantees individual liberty to a greater degree than any other, and I thank you and your people for all your help in maintaining the continuity which is the bulwark of our Republic.

The business of our nation goes forward. These United States are confronted with an economic affliction of great proportions. We suffer from the longest and one of the worst sustained inflations in our national history. It distorts our economic decisions, penalizes thrift, and crushes the struggling young and the fixed-income elderly, alike. It threatens to shatter the lives of millions of our people.

33

Idle industries have cast workers into unemployment, human misery, and personal indignity. Those who do work are denied a fair return for their labor by a tax system which penalizes successful achievement and keeps us from maintaining full productivity.

But great as our tax burden is, it has not kept pace with public spending. For decades we have piled deficit upon deficit, mortgaging our future and our children's future for the temporary convenience of the present. To continue this long trend is to guarantee tremendous social, cultural, political, and economic upheavals.

You and I, as individuals, can, by borrowing, live beyond our means, but for only a limited period of time. Why, then, should we think that collectively, as a nation, we're not bound by that same limitation? We must act today in order to preserve tomorrow. And let there be no misunderstanding: We are going to begin to act, beginning today.

The economic ills we suffer have come upon us over several decades. They will not go away in days, weeks, or months, but they will go away. They will go away because we as Americans have the capacity now, as we've had in the past, to do whatever needs to be done to preserve this last and greatest bastion of freedom.

In this present crisis, government is not the solution to our problem; government is the problem. From time to time we've been tempted to believe that society has become too complex to be managed by self-rule, that government by an elite group is superior to government for, by, and of the people. Well, if no one among us is capable of governing himself, then who among us has the capacity to govern someone else? All of us together, in and out of government, must bear the burden. The solutions we seek must be equitable, with no one group singled out to pay a higher price.

We hear much of special interest groups. Well, our concern must be for a special interest group that has been too long neglected. It knows no sectional boundaries or ethnic and racial divisions, and it crosses political party lines. It is made up of men and women who raise our food, patrol our streets, man our mines and factories, teach our children, keep our homes, and heal us when we're sick—professionals, industrialists, shopkeepers, clerks, cabbies, and truckdrivers. They are, in short, "We the people," this breed called Americans.

Well, this administration's objective will be a healthy, vigorous, growing economy that provides equal opportunities for all Americans, with no barriers born of bigotry or discrimination. Putting America back to work means putting all Americans back to work. Ending inflation means freeing all Americans from the terror of runaway living costs. All must share in the productive work of this "new beginning," and all must share in the bounty of a revived economy. With the idealism and fair play which are the core of our system and our strength, we can have a strong and prosperous America, at peace with itself and the world.

So, as we begin, let us take inventory. We are a nation that has a government—not the other way around. And this makes us special among the nations of the Earth. Our government has no power except that granted it by the people. It is time to check and reverse the growth of government, which shows signs of having grown beyond the consent of the governed.

It is my intention to curb the size and influence of the Federal establishment and to demand recognition of the distinction between the powers granted to the Federal Government and those reserved to the States or to the people. All of us need to be reminded that the Federal Government did not create the States; the States created the Federal Government.

Now, so there will be no misunderstanding, it's not my intention to do away with government. It is rather to make it work—work with us, not over us; to stand by our side, not ride on our back. Government can and must provide opportunity, not smother it; foster productivity, not stifle it.

If we look to the answer as to why for so many years we achieved so much, prospered as no other people on Earth, it was because here in this land we unleashed the energy and individual genius of man to a greater extent than has ever been done before. Freedom and the dignity of the individual have been more available and assured here than in any other place on Earth. The price for this freedom at times has been high, but we have never been unwilling to pay that price.

It is no coincidence that our present troubles parallel and are proportionate to the intervention and intrusion in our lives that result from unnecessary and excessive growth of government. It is time for us to realize that we're too great a nation to limit ourselves to small dreams. We're not, as some would have us believe, doomed to an inevitable decline. I do not believe in a fate that will fall on us no matter what we do. I do believe in a fate that will fall on us if we do nothing. So, with all the creative energy at our command, let us begin an era of national renewal. Let us renew our determination, our courage, and our strength. And let us renew our faith and our hope.

We have every right to dream heroic dreams. Those who say that we're in a time when there are no heroes, they just don't know where to look. You can see heroes every day going in and out of factory gates. Others, a handful in number, produce enough food to feed all of us and then the world beyond. You meet heroes across a counter, and they're on both sides of that counter. There are entrepreneurs with faith in themselves and faith in an idea who create new jobs, new wealth and opportunity. They're individuals and families whose taxes support the government and whose voluntary gifts support church, charity, culture, art, and education. Their patriotism is quiet, but deep. Their values sustain our national life.

Now, I have used the words "they" and "their" in speaking of these heroes. I could say "you" and "your," because I'm addressing the heroes of whom I speak—you, the citizens of this blessed land. Your dreams, your hopes, your goals are going to be the dreams, the hopes, and the goals of this administration, so help me God.

We shall reflect the compassion that is so much a part of your makeup. How can we love our country and not love our countrymen; and loving them, reach out a hand when they fall, heal them when they're sick, and provide opportunity to make them self-sufficient so they will be equal in fact and not just in theory?

Can we solve the problems confronting us? Well, the answer is an unequivocal and emphatic "yes." To paraphrase Winston Churchill, I did not take the oath I've just taken with the intention of presiding over the dissolution of the world's strongest economy.

In the days ahead I will propose removing the roadblocks that have slowed our economy and reduced productivity. Steps will be taken aimed at restoring the balance between the various levels of government. Progress may be slow, measured in inches and feet, not miles, but we will progress. It is time to reawaken this industrial giant, to get government back within its means, and to lighten our punitive tax burden. And these will be our first priorities, and on these principles there will be no compromise.

On the eve of our struggle for independence a man who might have been one of the greatest among the Founding Fathers, Dr. Joseph Warren, president of the Massachusetts Congress, said to his fellow Americans, "Our country is in danger, but not to be despaired of. . . . On you depend the fortunes of America. You are to decide the important questions upon which rests the happiness and the liberty of millions yet unborn. Act worthy of yourselves."

Well, I believe we, the Americans of today, are ready to act worthy of ourselves, ready to do what must be done to ensure happiness and liberty for ourselves, our children, and our children's children. And as we renew ourselves here in our own land, we will be seen as having greater strength throughout the world. We will again be the exemplar of freedom and a beacon of hope for those who do not now have freedom.

To those neighbors and allies who share our freedom, we will strengthen our historic ties and assure them of our support and firm commitment. We will match loyalty with loyalty. We will strive for mutually beneficial relations. We will not use our friendship to impose on their sovereignty, for our own sovereignty is not for sale.

As for the enemies of freedom, those who are potential adversaries, they will be reminded that peace is the highest aspiration of the American people. We will negotiate for it, sacrifice for it; we will not surrender for it, now or ever.

Our forbearance should never be misunderstood. Our reluctance for conflict should not be misjudged as a failure of will. When action is required to preserve our national security, we will act. We will maintain sufficient strength to prevail if need be, knowing that if we do so we have the best chance of never having to use that strength.

Above all, we must realize that no arsenal or no weapon in the arsenals of the world is so formidable as the will and moral courage of free men and women. It is a weapon our adversaries in today's world do not have. It is a weapon that we as Americans do have. Let that be understood by those who practice terrorism and prey upon their neighbors.

I'm told that tens of thousands of prayer meetings are being held on this day, and for that I'm deeply grateful. We are a nation under God, and I believe God intended for us to be free. It would be fitting and good, I think, if on each Inaugural Day in future years it should be declared a day of prayer.

This is the first time in our history that this ceremony has been held, as you've been told, on this West Front of the Capitol. Standing here, one faces a magnificent vista, opening up on this city's special beauty and history. At the end of this open mall are those shrines to the giants on whose shoulders we stand.

Directly in front of me, the monument to a monumental man, George Washington, father of our country. A man of humility who came to greatness reluctantly. He led America out of revolutionary victory into infant nationhood. Off to one side, the stately memorial to Thomas Jefferson. The Declaration of Independence flames with his eloquence. And then, beyond the Reflecting Pool, the dignified columns of the Lincoln Memorial. Whoever would understand in his heart the meaning of America will find it in the life of Abraham Lincoln.

Beyond those monuments to heroism is the Potomac River, and on the far shore the sloping hills of Arlington National Cemetery, with its row upon row of simple white markers bearing crosses or Stars of David. They add up to only a tiny fraction of the price that has been paid for our freedom.

Each one of those markers is a monument to the kind of hero I spoke of earlier. Their lives ended in places called Belleau Wood, The Argonne, Omaha Beach, Salerno, and halfway around the world on Guadalcanal, Tarawa, Pork Chop Hill, the Chosin Reservoir, and in a hundred rice paddies and jungles of a place called Vietnam.

Under one such marker lies a young man, Martin Treptow, who left his job in a small town barbershop in 1917 to go to France with the famed Rainbow Division. There, on the western front, he was killed trying to carry a mesage between battalions under heavy artillery fire.

We're told that on his body was found a diary. On the flyleaf under the heading, "My Pledge," he had written these words: "America must win this war. Therefore I will work, I will save, I will sacrifice, I will endure, I will fight cheerfully and do my utmost, as if the issue of the whole struggle depended on me alone."

The crisis we are facing today does not require of us the kind of sacrifice that Martin Treptow and so many thousands of others were called upon to make. It does require, however, our best effort and our willingness to believe in ourselves and to believe in our capacity to perform great deeds, to believe that together with God's help we can and will resolve the problems which now confront us.

And, after all, why shouldn't we believe that? We are Americans.

God bless you, and thank you.

NOTE

The President spoke at 12 noon from a platform erected at the West Front of the Capitol. Immediately before the address, the oath of office was administered by Chief Justice Warren E. Burger.

In his opening remarks, the President referred to Rev. Donn D. Moomaw, senior pastor, Bel Air Presbyterian Church, Los Angeles, Calif.

The address was broadcast live on radio and television.

UNIT TWO

Presidents and
Their Constituencies

Chapter 2 The President and Congress

All presidents have major goals or objectives that they hope to accomplish during their administrations. But because the Constitution created a system in which most powers are shared by the three branches of government, these goals can rarely be realized without the cooperation of a congressional majority. The constitution specifies few powers which the president can use to strong-arm a reluctant Congress. Instead, our successful presidents have used diverse personal strategies in their efforts to influence Congress. The selections in this section look at both Constitutional and personal techniques applied over a period of years.

The Republican-controlled House of Representatives easily passed a 1796 resolution by Rep. Edward Livingstone of New York requesting that the president provide the House with papers related to the Jay Treaty. Since the Constitution mentions only the President and the Senate with respect to treaty-making, President Washington refused to comply. His refusal asserted the principle of "Executive Privilege" which has been used often (most notably with regard to the Watergate Tapes).

Unlike the Washington case, where presidential actions expanded the powers of the presidency and withstood the onslaught of contemporary critics, President Roosevelt's proposed judicial reform was far less successful. The Supreme Court had been declaring important pieces of New Deal legislation unconstitutional since 1935. But it was only after what Roosevelt perceived as a great public mandate in his 1936 re-election that he decided to "deal with the court." Excluding most of his talented advisors and influentials from the planning, Roosevelt developed a reform plan that surprised, shocked, and angered many Americans. Roosevelt promoted his cause by explaining his plan to the American public in a "Fireside Chat." But the final outcome in the Senate was a resounding rejection of the plan. Even for this skillful and popular president there were limits of acceptable action in relation to the principles of checks and balances and separation of powers.

With a Republican majority in Congress, Democratic President Harry Truman faced a very difficult time. After thirteen years of the popular Roosevelt and his liberal reforms, the Republicans saw in Truman, the Kansas City haberdasher turned machine politician, a beatable Democratic president. When the 80th Congress produced less legislation than criticism of Truman during the election year of 1948, Truman took the offensive. Accepting his party's presidential nomination at 2:00 AM, Truman electrified his partisans with an unusual challenge. He called Congress into special session to pass the promises of the Republican Party platform into law. As expected, after two weeks nothing had been passed and a disgruntled and politically scarred Congress went home to campaign. And Truman, long regarded as a certain loser to New York Governor Thomas Dewey, was elected to a full term as president.

Although Lyndon Johnson faced a friendly Congress, he presented them with the then highly explosive issue of voting rights for black Americans. Many congressmen realized that the addition of large numbers of voters to their districts and states might well mean the end of their congressional careers. Johnson's major legislative success—the Civil Rights Act of 1965—can be partially attributed to the moral fervor fueled by his emphasis upon simple justice and common decency, exemplified by his address to Congress. By redefining the issue as a national rather than a southern or black concern, and by portraying opposition to the Act as unfair, immoral, and unjust, Johnson transcended electoral implications of voting for (or against) Civil Rights legislation.

President Ford's assumption of the office upon the resignation of Richard Nixon placed him in an uncomfortable position as the first president never elected to either national office. Although this rendered him vulnerable to a Congress that had just forced an elected president from office, Ford hoped that his background as a recent congressional leader would tilt the balance in his favor. In his first speech to Congress Ford emphasized their common bonds and alluded to the use of another presidential tool, the veto, should he not agree with their legislation. Of course, congressmen who study, campaign for, and meet endlessly to hammer our legislation do not like to have it come to naught because of the veto. Ford's implicit message was: either produce my kind of legislation or you will be wasting your time. In addition to stating goals he would like to accomplish, Ford also discusses the areas that he would disapprove if passed by Congress. Thus both "the carrot" and "the stick" are discussed in this address.

Finally, President Reagan's address to the American people exemplified yet another important presidential technique for influencing congress—the direct appeal to the public. This speech thanks the public for past help, explains what still must be done, and urges people to petition their congressmen in support of the President's tax reduction legislation. Presidential appeals directly to a congressman's constituents can be a powerful executive strategy (as in this case) because it is the president's popularity in their own district—not in the nation at large—that is likely to influence a congressman. The implicit danger is that congressmen, like the rest of us, resent people who go behind their backs rather than dealing with them directly. This strategy has been popular at least since Woodrow Wilson's campaign for the League of Nations, and it was used extensively by Richard Nixon who called it "going over [Congress's] heads to the people." But it is a short-term strategy which often strains long-term executive-congressional relations: neither Wilson nor Nixon is noted for his congressional victories.

George Washington
Assertion of Executive Privilege
March 30, 1796

Gentlemen of the House of Representatives: With the utmost attention I have considered your resolution of the 24th. instant, requesting me to lay before your House, a copy of the instructions to the Minister of the United States who negotiated the Treaty with the King of Great Britain, together with the correspondence and other documents relative to that Treaty, excepting such of the said papers as any existing negotiation may render improper to be disclosed.

In deliberating upon this subject, it was impossible for me to lose sight of the principle which some have avowed in its discussion; or to avoid extending my views to the consequences which must flow from the admission of that principle.

I trust that no part of my conduct has ever indicated a disposition to withhold any information which the Constitution has enjoined upon the President as a duty to give, or which could be required of him by either House of Congress as a right; And with truth I affirm, that it has been, as it will continue to be, while I have the honor to preside in the Government, my constant endeavour to harmonize with the other branches thereof; so far as the trust delegated to me by the People of the United States, and my sense of the obligation it imposes to "preserve, protect and defend the Constitution" will permit.

The nature of foreign negotiations requires caution; and their success must often depend on secrecy: and even when brought to a conclusion, a full disclosure of all the measures, demands, or eventual concessions, which may have been proposed or contemplated, would be extremely impolitic: for this might have a pernicious influence on future negotiations; or produce immediate inconveniences, perhaps danger and mischief, in relation to other powers. The necessity of such caution and secrecy was one cogent reason for vesting the power of making Treaties in the President, with the advice and consent of the Senate, the principle on which that body was formed confining it to a small number of Members.

To admit then a right in the House of Representatives to demand, and to have as a matter of course, all the Papers respecting a negotiation with a foreign power, would be to establish a dangerous precedent.

It does not occur that the inspection of the papers asked for, can be relative to any purpose under the cognizance of the House of Representatives, except that of an impeachment, which the resolution has not expressed. I repeat, that I have no disposition to withhold any information which the duty of my station will permit, or the public good shall require to be disclosed: and in fact, all the Papers affecting the negotiation with Great Britain were laid before the Senate, when the Treaty itself was communicated for their consideration and advice.

The course which the debate has taken, on the resolution of the House, leads to some observations on the mode of making treaties under the Constitution of the United States.

Having been a member of the General Convention, and knowing the principles on which the Constitution was formed, I have ever entertained but one opinion on this subject; and from the first establishment of the Government to this moment, my conduct has exemplified that opinion, that the power of making treaties is exclusively vested in the President, by and with the advice and consent of the Senate, provided two thirds of the Senators present concur, and that every treaty so made, and promulgated, thenceforward became the Law of the land. It is thus that the treaty making power has been understood by foreign Nations: and in all the treaties made with them, *we* have declared, and *they* have believed, than when ratified by the President with the advice and consent of the Senate, they became obligatory. In this construction of the Constitution every House of Representatives has heretofore acquiesced; and until the present time, not a doubt or suspicion has appeared to my knowledge that this construction was not the true one. Nay, they have more than acquiesced: for till now, without controverting the obligation of such treaties, they have made all the requisite provisions for carrying them into effect.

There is also reason to believe that this construction agrees with the opinions entertained by the State Conventions, when they were deliberating on the Constitution; especially by those who objected to it, because there was not required, in *commercial treaties*, the consent of two thirds of the whole number of the members of the Senate, instead of two thirds of the Senators present; and because in treaties respecting territorial and certain other rights and claims, the concurrence of three fourths of the whole number of the members of both houses respectively, was not made necessary.

It is a fact declared by the General Convention, and universally understood, that the Constitution of the United States was the result of a spirit of amity and mutual concession. And it is well known that under this influence the smaller States were admitted to an equal representation in the Senate with the larger States; and that this branch of the government was invested with great powers: for on the equal participation of those powers, the sovereignty and political safety of the smaller States were deemed essentially to depend.

If other proofs than these, and the plain letter of the Constitution itself, be necessary to ascertain the point under consideration, they may be found in the journals of the General Convention, which I have deposited in the office of the department of State. In these journals it will appear that a proposition was made, "that no Treaty should be binding on the United States which was not ratified by a Law"; and that the proposition was explicitly rejected.

As therefore it is perfectly clear to my understanding, that the assent of the House of Representatives is not necessary to the validity of a treaty: as the treaty with Great Britain exhibits in itself all the objects requiring legislative provision; And on these the papers called for can throw no light: And as it is essential to the due administration of the government, that the boundaries fixed by the constitution between the different departments should be preserved: A just regard to the Constitution and to the duty of my Office, under all the circumstances of this case, forbids a compliance with your request.

Franklin D. Roosevelt
A "Fireside Chat" Discussing the
Plan for Reorganization of
the Judiciary
March 9, 1937

Last Thursday I described in detail certain economic problems which everyone admits now face the Nation. For the many messages which have come to me after that speech, and which it is physically impossible to answer individually, I take this means of saying "thank you."

Tonight, sitting at my desk in the White House, I make my first radio report to the people in my second term of office.

I am reminded of that evening in March, four years ago, when I made my first radio report to you. We were then in the midst of the great banking crisis.

Soon after, with the authority of the Congress, we asked the Nation to turn over all of its privately held gold, dollar for dollar, to the Government of the United States.

Today's recovery proves how right that policy was.

But when, almost two years later, it came before the Supreme Court its constitutionality was upheld only by a five-to-four vote. The change of one vote would have thrown all the affairs of this great Nation back into hopeless chaos. In effect, four Justices ruled that the right under a private contract to exact a pound of flesh was more sacred than the main objectives of the Constitution to establish an enduring Nation.

In 1933 you and I knew that we must never let our economic system get completely out of joint again—that we could not afford to take the risk of another great depression.

We also became convinced that the only way to avoid a repetition of those dark days was to have a government with power to prevent and to cure the abuses and the inequalities which had thrown that system out of joint.

We then began a program of remedying those abuses and inequalities—to give balance and stability to our economic system—to make it bomb-proof against the causes of 1929.

Today we are only part-way through that program—and recovery is speeding up to a point where the dangers of 1929 are again becoming possible, not this week or month perhaps, but within a year or two.

National laws are needed to complete that program. Individual or local or state effort alone cannot protect us in 1937 any better than ten years ago.

It will take time—and plenty of time—to work out our remedies administratively even after legislation is passed. To complete our program of protection in time, therefore, we cannot delay one moment in making certain that our National Government has power to carry through.

Four years ago action did not come until the eleventh hour. It was almost too late.

If we learned anything from the depression we will not allow ourselves to run around in new circles of futile discussion and debate, always postponing the day of decision.

The American people have learned from the depression. For in the last three national elections an overwhelming majority of them voted a mandate that the Congress and the President begin the task of providing that protection—not after long years of debate, but now.

The Courts, however, have cast doubts on the ability of the elected Congress to protect us against catastrophe by meeting squarely our modern social and economic conditions.

We are at a crisis in our ability to proceed with that protection. It is a quiet crisis. There are no lines of depositors outside closed banks. But to the far-sighted it is far-reaching in its possibilities of injury to America.

I want to talk with you very simply about the need for present action in this crisis—the need to meet the unanswered challenge of one-third of a Nation ill-nourished, ill-clad, ill-housed.

Last Thursday I described the American form of Government as a three horse team provided by the Constitution to the American people so that their field might be plowed. The three horses are, of course, the three branches of government—the Congress, the Executive and the Courts. Two of the horses are pulling in unison today; the third is not. Those who have intimated that the President of the United States is trying to drive that team, overlook the simple fact that the President, as Chief Executive, is himself one of the three horses.

It is the American people themselves who are in the driver's seat.

It is the American people themselves who want the furrow plowed.

It is the American people themselves who expect the third horse to pull in unison with the other two.

I hope that you have re-read the Constitution of the United States in these past few weeks. Like the Bible, it ought to be read again and again.

It is an easy document to understand when you remember that it was called into being because the Articles of Confederation under which the original thirteen States tried to operate after the Revolution showed the need of a National Government with power enough to handle national problems. In its Preamble, the Constitution states that it was intended to form a more perfect Union and promote the general welfare; and the powers given to the Congress to carry out those purposes can be best described by saying that they were all the powers needed to meet each and every problem which then had a national character and which could not be met by merely local action.

But the framers went further. Having in mind that in succeeding generations many other problems then undreamed of would become national problems, they gave to the Congress the ample broad powers "to levy taxes ... and provide for the common defense and general welfare of the United States."

That, my friends, is what I honestly believe to have been the clear and underlying purpose of the patriots who wrote a Federal Constitution to create a National Government with national power, intended as they said, "to form a more perfect union ... for ourselves and our posterity."

For nearly twenty years there was no conflict between the Congress and the Court. Then Congress passed a statute which, in 1803, the Court said violated an express provision of the Constitution. The Court claimed the power to declare it unconstitutional and did so declare it. But a little later the Court itself admitted that it was an extraordinary power to exercise and through Mr. Justice Washington laid down this limitation upon it: "It is but a decent respect due to the wisdom, the integrity and the patriotism of the legislative body, by which any law is passed, to presume in favor of its validity until its violation of the Constitution is proved beyond all reasonable doubt."

But since the rise of the modern movement for social and economic progress through legislation, the Court has more and more often and more and more boldly asserted a power to veto laws passed by the Congress and State Legislatures in complete disregard of this original limitation.

In the last four years the sound rule of giving statutes the benefit of all reasonable doubt has been cast aside. The Court has been acting not as a judicial body, but as a policy-making body.

When the Congress has sought to stabilize national agriculture, to improve the conditions of labor, to safeguard business against unfair competition, to protect our national resources, and in many other ways, to serve our clearly national needs, the majority of the Court has been assuming the power to pass on the wisdom of these Acts of Congress—and to approve or disapprove the public policy written into these laws.

That is not only my accusation. It is the accusation of most distinguished Justices of the present Supreme Court. I have not the time to quote to you all the language used by dissenting Justices in many of these cases. But in the case holding the Railroad Retirement Act unconstitutional, for instance, Chief Justice Hughes said in a dissenting opinion that the majority opinion was "a departure from sound principles," and placed "an unwarranted limitation upon the commerce clause." And three other Justices agreed with him.

In the case holding the A.A.A. unconstitutional, Justice Stone said of the majority opinion that it was a "tortured construction of the Constitution." And two other Justices agreed with him.

In the case holding the New York Minimum Wage Law unconstitutional, Justice Stone said that the majority were actually reading into the Constitution their own "personal economic predilections," and that if the legislative power is not left free to choose the methods of solving the problems of poverty, subsistence and health of large numbers in the community, then "government is to be rendered impotent." And two other Justices agreed with him.

In the face of these dissenting opinions, there is no basis for the claim made by some members of the Court that something in the Constitution has compelled them regretfully to thwart the will of the people.

In the face of such dissenting opinions, it is perfectly clear, that as Chief Justice Hughes has said: "We are under a Constitution, but the Constitution is what the Judges say it is."

The Court in addition to the proper use of its judicial functions has improperly set itself up as a Third House of the Congress—a super-legislature, as one of the justices has called it—reading into the Constitution words and implications which are not there, and which were never intended to be there.

We have, therefore, reached the point as a Nation where we must take action to save the Constitution from the Court and the Court from itself. We must find a way to take an appeal from the Supereme Court to the Constitution itself. We want a Supreme Court which will do justice under the Constitution—not over it. In our Courts we want a government of laws and not of men.

I want—as all Americans want—an independent judiciary as proposed by the framers of the Constitution. That means a Supreme Court that will enforce the Constitution as written—that will refuse to amend the Constitution by the arbitrary exercise of judicial power—amendment by judicial say-so. It does not mean a judiciary so independent that it can deny the existence of facts universally recognized.

How then could we proceed to perform the mandate given us? It was said in last year's Democratic platform, "If these problems cannot be effectively solved within the Constitution, we shall seek such clarifying amendment as will assure the power to enact those laws, adequately to regulate commerce, protect public health and safety, and safeguard economic security." In other words, we said we would seek an amendment only if every other possible means by legislation were to fail.

When I commenced to review the situation with the problem squarely before me, I came by a process of elimination to the conclusion that, short of amendments, the only method which was clearly constitutional, and would at the same time carry out other much needed reforms, was to infuse new blood into all our Courts. We must have men worthy and equipped to carry out impartial justice. But, at the same time, we must have Judges who will bring to the Courts a present-day sense of the Constitution—Judges who will retain in the Courts the judicial functions of a court, and reject the legislative powers which the courts have today assumed.

In forty-five out of the forty-eight States of the Union, Judges are chosen not for life but for a period of years. In many States Judges must retire at the age of seventy. Congress has provided financial security by offering life pensions at full pay for Federal Judges on all Courts who are willing to retire at seventy. In the case of Supreme Court Justices, that pension is $20,000 a year. But all Federal Judges, once appointed, can, if they choose, hold office for life, no matter how old they may get to be.

What is my proposal? It is simply this: whenever a Judge or Justice of any Federal Court has reached the age of seventy and does not avail himself of the opportunity to retire on a pension, a new member shall be appointed by the President then in office, with the approval, as required by the Constitution, of the Senate of the United States.

That plan has two chief purposes. By bringing into the judicial system a steady and continuing stream of new and younger blood, I hope, first, to make the administration of all Federal justice speedier and, therefore, less costly; secondly, to bring to the decision of social and economic problems younger men who have had personal experience and contact with modern facts and circumstances under which average men have to live and work. This plan will save our national Constitution from hardening of the judicial arteries.

The number of Judges to be appointed would depend wholly on the decision of present Judges now over seventy, or those who would subsequently reach the age of seventy.

If, for instance, any one of the six Justices of the Supreme Court now over the age of seventy should retire as provided under the plan, no additional place would be created. Consequently, although there never can be more than fifteen, there may be only fourteen, or thirteen, or twelve. And there may be only nine.

There is nothing novel or radical about this idea. It seeks to maintain the Federal bench in full vigor. It has been discussed and approved by many persons of high authority ever since a similar proposal passed the House of Representatives in 1869.

Why was the age fixed at seventy? Because the laws of many

States, the practice of the Civil Service, the regulations of the Army and Navy, and the rules of many of our Universities and of almost every great private business enterprise, commonly fix the retirement age at seventy years or less.

The statute would apply to all the courts in the Federal system. There is general approval so far as the lower Federal courts are concerned. The plan has met opposition only so far as the Supreme Court of the United States itself is concerned. If such a plan is good for the lower courts it certainly ought to be equally good for the highest Court from which there is no appeal.

Those opposing this plan have sought to arouse prejudice and fear by crying that I am seeking to "pack" the Supreme Court and that a baneful precedent will be established.

What do they mean by the words "packing the Court"?

Let me answer this question with a bluntness that will end all *honest* misunderstandings of my purposes.

If by that phrase "packing the Court" it is charged that I wish to place on the bench spineless puppets who would disregard the law and would decide specific cases as I wished them to be decided, I make this answer: that no President fit for his office would appoint, and no Senate of honorable men fit for their offices would confirm, that kind of appointees to the Supreme Court.

But if by that phrase the charge is made that I would appoint and the Senate would confirm Justices worthy to sit beside present members of the Court who understand those modern conditions, that I will appoint Justices who will not undertake to override the judgment of the Congress on legislative policy, that I will appoint Justices who will act as Justices and not as legislators—if the appointment of such Justices can be called "packing the Courts," then I say that I and with me the vast majority of the American people favor doing just that thing—now.

Is it a dangerous precedent for the Congress to change the number of the Justices? The Congress has always had, and will have, that power. The number of Justices has been changed several times before, in the Administrations of John Adams and Thomas Jefferson—both signers of the Declaration of Independence—Andrew Jackson, Abraham Lincoln and Ulysses S. Grant.

I suggest only the addition of Justices to the bench in accordance with a clearly defined principle relating to a clearly defined age limit. Fundamentally, if in the future, America cannot trust the Congress it elects to refrain from abuse of our Constitutional usages, democracy will have failed far beyond the importance to it of any kind of precedent concerning the Judiciary.

We think it so much in the public interest to maintain a vigorous judiciary that we encourage the retirement of elderly Judges by offering them a life pension at full salary. Why then should we leave the fulfillment of this public policy to chance or make it dependent upon the desire or prejudice of any individual Justice?

It is the clear intention of our public policy to provide for a constant flow of new and younger blood into the Judiciary. Normally every President appoints a large number of District and Circuit Judges and a few members of the Supreme Court. Until my first term practically every President of the United States had appointed at least one member of the Supreme Court. President Taft appointed five members and named a Chief Justice; President Wilson, three; President Harding, four, including a Chief Justice; President Coolidge, one; President Hoover, three, including a Chief Justice.

Such a succession of appointments should have provided a Court well-balanced as to age. But chance and the disinclination of individuals to leave the Supreme bench have now given us a Court in which five Justices will be over seventy-five years of age before next June and one over seventy. Thus a sound public policy has been defeated.

I now propose that we establish by law an assurance against any such ill-balanced Court in the future. I propose that hereafter, when a Judge reaches the age of seventy, a new and younger Judge shall be added to the Court automatically. In this way I propose to enforce a sound public policy by law instead of leaving the composition of our Federal Courts, including the highest, to be determined by chance or the personal decision of individuals.

If such a law as I propose is regarded as establishing a new precedent, is it not a most desirable precedent?

Like all lawyers, like all Americans, I regret the necessity of this controversy. But the welfare of the United States, and indeed of the Constitution itself, is what we all must think about first. Our difficulty with the Court today rises not from the Court as an institution but from human beings within it. But we cannot yield our constitutional destiny to the personal judgment of a few men who, being fearful of the future, would deny us the necessary means of dealing with the present.

This plan of mine is no attack on the Court; it seeks to restore the Court to its rightful and historic place in our system of Constitutional Government and to have it resume its high task of building anew on the Constitution "a system of living law." The Court itself can best undo what the Court has done.

I have thus explained to you the reasons that lie behind our efforts to secure results by legislation within the Constitution. I hope that thereby the difficult process of constitutional amendment may be rendered unnecessary. But let us examine that process.

There are many types of amendment proposed. Each one is radically different from the other. There is no substantial group within the Congress or outside it who are agreed on any single amendment.

It would take months or years to get substantial agreement upon the type and language of an amendment. It would take months and years thereafter to get a two-thirds majority in favor of that amendment in *both* Houses of the Congress.

Then would come the long course of ratification by three-fourths of all the States. No amendment which any powerful economic interests or the leaders of any powerful political party have had reason to oppose has ever been ratified within anything like a reasonable time. And thirteen States which contain only five percent of the voting population can block ratification even though the thirty-five States with ninety-five percent of the population are in favor of it.

A very large percentage of newspaper publishers, Chambers of Commerce, Bar Associations, Manufacturers' Associations, who are trying to give the impression that they really do want a constitutional amendment would be the first to exclaim as soon as an amendment was proposed, "Oh! I was for an amendment all right, but this amendment that you have proposed is not the kind of an amendment that I was thinking about. I am, therefore, going to spend my time, my efforts and my money to block that amendment, although I would be awfully glad to help get some other kind of amendment ratified."

Two groups oppose my plan on the ground that they favor a constitutional amendment. The first includes those who funda-

mentally object to social and economic legislation along modern
lines. This is the same group who during the campaign last Fall
tried to block the mandate of the people.

Now they are making a last stand. And the strategy of that last
stand is to suggest the time-consuming process of amendment in
order to kill off by delay the legislation demanded by the
mandate.

To them I say: I do not think you will be able long to fool the
American people as to your purposes.

The other group is composed of those who honestly believe the
amendment process is the best and who would be willing to support
a reasonable amendment if they could agree on one.

To them I say: we cannot rely on an amendment as the
immediate or only answer to our present difficulties. When the time
comes for action, you will find that many of those who pretend to
support you will sabotage any constructive amendment which is
proposed. Look at these strange bed-fellows of yours. When before
have you found them really at your side in your fights for
progress?

And remember one thing more. Even if an amendment were
passed, and even if in the years to come it were to be ratified, its
meaning would depend upon the kind of Justices who would be
sitting on the Supreme Court bench. An amendment, like the rest
of the Constitution, is what the Justices say it is rather than what
its framers or you might hope it is.

This proposal of mine will not infringe in the slightest upon the
civil or religious liberties so dear to every American.

My record as Governor and as President proves my devotion
to those liberties. You who know me can have no fear that I would
tolerate the destruction by any branch of government of any part
of our heritage of freedom.

The present attempt by those opposed to progress to play upon
the fears of danger to personal liberty brings again to mind that
crude and cruel strategy tried by the same opposition to frighten
the workers of America in a pay-envelope propaganda against the
Social Security Law. The workers were not fooled by that
propaganda then. The people of America will not be fooled by such
propaganda now.

I am in favor of action through legislation:

First, because I believe it can be passed at this session of the Congress.

Second, because it will provide a reinvigorated, liberal-minded Judiciary necessary to furnish quicker and cheaper justice from bottom to top.

Third, because it will provide a series of Federal Courts willing to enforce the Constitution as written, and unwilling to assert legislative powers by writing into it their own political and economic policies.

During the past half century the balance of power between the three great branches of the Federal Government, has been tipped out of balance by the Courts in direct contradiction of the high purposes of the framers of the Constitution. It is my purpose to restore that balance. You who know me will accept my solemn assurance that in a world in which democracy is under attack, I seek to make American democracy succeed. You and I will do our part.

Harry S Truman
Address in Philadelphia Upon Accepting the Nomination of the Democratic National Convention July 15, 1948

I am sorry that the microphones are in the way, but I must leave them the way they are because I have got to be able to see what I am doing—as I am always able to see what I am doing.

I can't tell you how very much I appreciate the honor which you have just conferred upon me. I shall continue to try to deserve it.

I accept the nomination.

And I want to thank this convention for its unanimous nomination of my good friend and colleague, Senator Barkley of Kentucky. He is a great man, and a great public servant. Senator Barkley and I will win this election and make these Republicans like it—don't you forget that!

We will do that because they are wrong and we are right, and I will prove it to you in just a few minutes.

This convention met to express the will and reaffirm the beliefs of the Democratic Party. There have been differences of opinion, and that is the democratic way. Those differences have been settled by a majority vote, as they should be.

Now it is time for us to get together and beat the common enemy. And that is up to you.

We have been working together for victory in a great cause. Victory has become a habit of our party. It has been elected four times in succession, and I am convinced it will be elected a fifth time next November.

The reason is that the people know that the Democratic Party is the people's party, and the Republican Party is the party of special interest, and it always has been and always will be.

The record of the Democratic Party is written in the accomplishments of the last 16 years. I don't need to repeat them. They have been very ably placed before this convention by the keynote speaker, the candidate for Vice President, and by the permanent chairman.

Confidence and security have been brought to the people by the Democratic Party. Farm income has increased from less than $2½ billion in 1932 to more than $18 billion in 1947. Never in the world were the farmers of any republic or any kingdom or any other country as prosperous as the farmers of the United States; and if they don't do their duty by the Democratic Party, they are the most ungrateful people in the world!

Wages and salaries in this country have increased from 29 billion in 1933 to more than $128 billion in 1947. That's labor, and labor never had but one friend in politics, and that is the Democratic Party and Franklin D. Roosevelt.

And I say to labor what I have said to the farmers: they are the most ungrateful people in the world if they pass the Democratic Party by this year.

The total national income has increased from less than $40 billion in 1933 to $203 billion in 1947, the greatest in all the history of the world. These benefits have been spread to all the people, because it is the business of the Democratic Party to see that the people get a fair share of these things.

This last, worst 80th Congress proved just the opposite for the Republicans.

The record on foreign policy of the Democratic Party is that the United States has been turned away permanently from isolationism, and we have converted the greatest and best of the Republicans to our viewpoint on that subject.

The United States has to accept its full responsibility for leadership in international affairs. We have been the backers and the people who organized and started the United Nations, first started under that great Democratic President, Woodrow Wilson, as the League of Nations. The League was sabotaged by the Republicans in 1920. And we must see that the United Nations continues a strong and growing body, so we can have everlasting peace in the world.

We removed trade barriers in the world, which is the best asset we can have for peace. Those trade barriers must not be put back into operation again.

We have started the foreign aid program, which means the recovery of Europe and China, and the Far East. We instituted the program for Greece and Turkey, and I will say to you that all these things were done in a cooperative and bipartisan manner. The Foreign Relations Committees of the Senate and House were taken into the full confidence of the President in every one of these moves, and don't let anybody tell you anything else.

As I have said time and time again, foreign policy should be the policy of the whole Nation and not the policy of one party or the other. Partisanship should stop at the water's edge; and I shall continue to preach that through this whole campaign.

I would like to say a word or two now on what I think the Republican philosophy is; and I will speak from actions and from history and from experience.

The situation in 1932 was due to the policies of the Republican Party control of the Government of the United States. The Republican Party, as I said a while ago, favors the privileged few and not the common everyday man. Ever since its inception, that party has been under the control of special privilege; and they have completely proved it in the 80th Congress. They proved it by the things they did *to* the people, and not *for* them. They proved it by the things they failed to do.

Now, let's look at some of them—just a few.

Time and time again I recommended extension of price control before it expired June 30, 1946. I asked for that extension in September 1945, in November 1945, in a Message on the State of the Union in 1946; and that price control legislation did not come to my desk until June 30, 1946, on the day on which it was supposed to expire. And it was such a rotten bill that I couldn't sign it. And 30 days after that, they sent me one just as bad. I had to sign it, because they quit and went home.

They said, when OPA died, that prices would adjust themselves for the benefit of the country. They have been adjusting themselves all right! They have gone all the way off the chart in adjusting themselves, at the expense of the consumer and for the benefit of the people that hold the goods.

I called a special session of the Congress in November 1947— November 17, 1947—and I set out a 10-point program for the welfare and benefit of this country, among other things standby controls. I got nothing. Congress has still done nothing.

Way back 4½ years ago, while I was in the Senate, we passed a housing bill in the Senate known as the Wagner-Ellender-Taft bill. It was a bill to clear the slums in the big cities and to help to erect low-rent housing. That bill, as I said, passed the Senate 4 years ago. It died in the House. That bill was reintroduced in the 80th Congress as the Taft-Ellender-Wagner bill. The name was slightly changed, but it is practically the same bill. And it passed the Senate, but it was allowed to die in the House of Representatives; and they sat on that bill, and finally forced it out of the Banking and Currency Committee, and the Rules Committee took charge, and it still is in the Rules Committee.

But desperate pleas from Philadelphia in that convention that met here 3 weeks ago couldn't get that housing bill passed. They passed a bill they called a housing bill, which isn't worth the paper it's written on.

In the field of labor we need moderate legislation to promote labor-management harmony, but Congress passed instead that so-called Taft-Hartley Act, which has disrupted labor-management relations and will cause strife and bitterness for years to come if it is not repealed, as the Democratic platform says it ought to be repealed.

On the Labor Department, the Republican platform of 1944 said, if they were in power, that they would build up a strong Labor Department. They have simply torn it up. Only one bureau is left that is functioning, and they cut the appropriation of that so it can hardly function.

I recommended an increase in the minimum wage. What did I get? Nothing. Absolutely nothing.

I suggested that the schools in this country are crowded, teachers underpaid, and that there is a shortage of teachers. One of our greatest national needs is more and better schools. I urged the Congress to provide $300 million to aid the States in the present educational crisis. Congress did nothing about it. Time and again I have recommended improvements in the social security law, including extending protection to those not now covered, and increasing the amount of benefits, to reduce the eligibility age of women from 65 to 60 years. Congress studied the matter for 2 years, but couldn't find the time to extend or increase the benefits. But they did find time to take social security benefits away from 750,000 people, and they passed that over my veto.

I have repeatedly asked the Congress to pass a health program. The Nation suffers from lack of medical care. That situation can be remedied any time the Congress wants to act upon it.

Everybody knows that I recommended to the Congress the civil rights program. I did that because I believed it to be my duty under the Constitution. Some of the members of my own party disagree with me violently on this matter. But they stand up and do it openly! People can tell where they stand. But the Republicans all professed to be for these measures. But Congress failed to act. They had enough men to do it, they could have had cloture, they didn't have to have a filibuster. They had enough people in that Congress that would vote for cloture.

Now everybody likes to have low taxes, but we must reduce the national debt in times of prosperity. And when tax relief can be given, it ought to go to those who need it most, and not those who need it least, as this Republican rich man's tax bill did when they passed it over my veto on the third try.

The first one of these was so rotten that they couldn't even stomach it themselves. They finally did send one that was somewhat improved, but it still helps the rich and sticks a knife into the back of the poor.

Now the Republicans came here a few weeks ago, and they wrote a platform. I hope you have all read that platform. They adopted the platform, and that platform had a lot of promises and statements of what the Republican Party is for, and what they would do if they were in power. They promised to do in that platform a lot of things I have been asking them to do that they have refused to do when they had the power.

The Republican platform cries about cruelly high prices. I have been trying to get them to do something about high prices ever since they met the first time.

Now listen! This is equally as bad, and as cynical. The Republican platform comes out for slum clearance and low-rental housing. I have been trying to get them to pass that housing bill ever since they met the first time, and it is still resting in the Rules Committee, that bill.

The Republican platform favors educational opportunity and promotion of education. I have been trying to get Congress to do something about that ever since they came there, and that bill is at rest in the House of Representatives.

The Republican platform is for extending and increasing social security benefits. Think of that! Increasing social security benefits! Yet when they had the opportunity, they took 750,000 off the social security rolls!

I wonder if they think they can fool the people of the United States with such poppycock as that!

There is a long list of these promises in that Republican platform. If it weren't so late, I would tell you all about them. I have discussed a number of these failures of the Republican 80th Congress. Every one of them is important. Two of them are of major concern to nearly every American family. They failed to do anything about high prices, they failed to do anything about housing.

My duty as President requires that I use every means within my power to get the laws the people need on matters of such importance and urgency.

I am therefore calling this Congress back into session July 26th.

On the 26th day of July, which out in Missouri we call "Turnip Day," I am going to call Congress back and ask them to pass laws to halt rising prices, to meet the housing crisis—which they are saying they are for in their platform.

At the same time I shall ask them to act upon other vitally needed measures such as aid to education, which they say they are for; a national health program; civil rights legislation, which they say they are for; an increase in the minimum wage, which I doubt very much they are for; extension of the social security coverage and increased benefits, which they say they are for; funds for projects needed in our program to provide public power and cheap electricity. By indirection, this 80th Congress has tried to sabotage the power policies the United States has pursued for 14 years. That power lobby is as bad as the real estate lobby, which is sitting on the housing bill.

I shall ask for adequate and decent laws for displaced persons in place of this anti-Semitic, anti-Catholic law which this 80th Congress passed.

Now, my friends, if there is any reality behind that Republican platform, we ought to get some action from a short session of the 80th Congress. They can do this job in 15 days, if they want to do it. They will still have time to go out and run for office.

They are going to try to dodge their responsibility. They are going to drag all the red herrings they can across this campaign, but I am here to say that Senator Barkley and I are not going to let them get away with it.

Now, what that worst 80th Congress does in this special session will be the test. The American people will not decide by listening to mere words, or by reading a mere platform. They will decide on the record, the record as it has been written. And in the record is the stark truth, that the battle lines of 1948 are the same as they were in 1932, when the Nation lay prostrate and helpless as a result of Republican misrule and inaction.

In 1932 we were attacking the citadel of special privilege and greed. We were fighting to drive the money changers from the temple. Today, in 1948, we are now the defenders of the stronghold of democracy and of equal opportunity, the haven of the ordinary people of this land and not of the favored classes or the powerful few. The battle cry is just the same now as it was in 1932, and I paraphrase the words of Franklin D. Roosevelt as he issued the challenge, in accepting nomination in Chicago: "This is more than a political call to arms. Give me your help, not to win votes alone, but to win in this new crusade to keep America secure and safe for its own people."

Now my friends, with the help of God and the wholehearted push which you can put behind this campaign, we can save this country from a continuation of the 80th Congress, and from misrule from now on.

I must have your help. You must get in and push, and win this election. The country can't afford another Republican Congress.

NOTE

The President spoke at 2 a.m. in Convention Hall in Philadelphia. The address was carried on a nationwide radio broadcast.

Lyndon B. Johnson
Special Message to the Congress:
The American Promise
March 15, 1965

MR. SPEAKER, MR. PRESIDENT, MEMBERS OF THE CONGRESS:

I speak tonight for the dignity of man and the destiny of democracy.

I urge every member of both parties, Americans of all religions and of all colors, from every section of this country, to join me in that cause.

At times history and fate meet at a single time in a single place to shape a turning point in man's unending search for freedom. So it was at Lexington and Concord. So it was a century ago at Appomattox. So it was last week in Selma, Alabama.

There, long-suffering men and women peacefully protested the denial of their rights as Americans. Many were brutally assaulted. One good man, a man of God, was killed.

There is no cause for pride in what has happened in Selma. There is no cause for self-satisfaction in the long denial of equal rights of millions of Americans. But there is cause for hope and for faith in our democracy in what is happening here tonight.

For the cries of pain and the hymns and protests of oppressed people have summoned into convocation all the majesty of this great Government—the Government of the greatest Nation on earth.

Our mission is at once the oldest and the most basic of this country: to right wrong, to do justice, to serve man.

In our time we have come to live with moments of great crisis. Our lives have been marked with debate about great issues; issues of war and peace, issues of prosperity and depression. But rarely in any time does an issue lay bare the secret heart of America itself. Rarely are we met with a challenge, not to our growth or abundance, our welfare or our security, but rather to the values and the purposes and the meaning of our beloved Nation.

The issue of equal rights for American Negroes is such an issue. And should we defeat every enemy, should we double our wealth and conquer the stars, and still be unequal to this issue, then we will have failed as a people and as a nation.

For with a country as with a person, "What is a man profited, if he shall gain the whole world, and lose his own soul?"

There is no Negro problem. There is no Southern problem. There is no Northern problem. There is only an American problem. And we are met here tonight as Americans—not as Democrats or Republicans—we are met here as Americans to solve that problem.

This was the first nation in the history of the world to be founded with a purpose. The great phrases of that purpose still sound in every American heart, North and South: "All men are created equal"—"government by consent of the governed"—"give me liberty or give me death." Well, those are not just clever words, or those are not just empty theories. In their name Americans have fought and died for two centuries, and tonight around the world they stand there as guardians of our liberty, risking their lives.

Those words are a promise to every citizen that he shall share in the dignity of man. This dignity cannot be found in a man's possessions; it cannot be found in his power, or in his position. It really rests on his right to be treated as a man equal in opportunity to all others. It says that he shall share in freedom, he shall choose his leaders, educate his children, and provide for his family according to his ability and his merits as a human being.

To apply any other test—to deny a man his hopes because of his color or race, his religion or the place of his birth—is not only to do injustice, it is to deny America and to dishonor the dead who gave their lives for American freedom.

THE RIGHT TO VOTE

Our fathers believed that if this noble view of the rights of man was to flourish, it must be rooted in democracy. The most basic right of all was the right to choose your own leaders. The history of this country, in large measure, is the history of the expansion of that right to all of our people.

Many of the issues of civil rights are very complex and most difficult. But about this there can and should be no argument. Every American citizen must have an equal right to vote. There is no reason which can excuse the denial of that right. There is no duty which weighs more heavily on us than the duty we have to ensure that right.

Yet the harsh fact is that in many places in this country men and women are kept from voting simply because they are Negroes.

Every device of which human ingenuity is capable has been used to deny this right. The Negro citizen may go to register only to be told that the day is wrong, or the hour is late, or the official in charge is absent. And if he persists, and if he manages to present himself to the registrar, he may be disqualified because he did not spell out his middle name or because he abbreviated a word on the application.

And if he manages to fill out an application he is given a test. The registrar is the sole judge of whether he passes this test. He may be asked to recite the entire Constitution, or explain the most complex provisions of State law. And even a college degree cannot be used to prove that he can read and write.

For the fact is that the only way to pass these barriers is to show a white skin.

Experience has clearly shown that the existing process of law cannot overcome systematic and ingenious discrimination. No law that we now have on the books—and I have helped to put three of them there—can ensure the right to vote when local officials are determined to deny it.

In such a case our duty must be clear to all of us. The Constitution says that no person shall be kept from voting because of his race or his color. We have all sworn an oath before God to support and to defend that Constitution. We must now act in obedience to that oath.

GUARANTEEING THE RIGHT TO VOTE

Wednesday I will send to Congress a law designed to eliminate illegal barriers to the right to vote.

The broad principles of that bill will be in the hands of the Democratic and Republican leaders tomorrow. After they have reviewed it, it will come here formally as a bill. I am grateful for this opportunity to come here tonight at the invitation of the leadership to reason with my friends, to give them my views, and to visit with my former colleagues.

I have had prepared a more comprehensive analysis of the legislation which I had intended to transmit to the clerk tomorrow but which I will submit to the clerks tonight. But I want to really discuss with you now briefly the main proposals of this legislation.

This bill will strike down restrictions to voting in all elections— Federal, State, and local—which have been used to deny Negroes the right to vote.

This bill will establish a simple, uniform standard which cannot be used, however ingenious the effort, to flout our Constitution.

It will provide for citizens to be registered by officials of the United States Government if the State officials refuse to register them.

It will eliminate tedious, unnecessary lawsuits which delay the right to vote.

Finally, this legislation will ensure that properly registered individuals are not prohibited from voting.

I will welcome the suggestions from all of the Members of Congress—I have no doubt that I will get some—on ways and means to strengthen this law and to make it effective. But experience has plainly shown that this is the only path to carry out the command of the Constitution.

To those who seek to avoid action by their National Government in their own communities; who want to and who seek to maintain purely local control over elections, the answer is simple:

Open your polling places to all your people.

Allow men and women to register and vote whatever the color of their skin.

Extend the rights of citizenship to every citizen of this land.

THE NEED FOR ACTION

There is no constitutional issue here. The command of the Constitution is plain.

There is no moral issue. It is wrong—deadly wrong—to deny any of your fellow Americans the right to vote in this country.

There is no issue of States rights or national rights. There is only the struggle for human rights.

I have not the slightest doubt what will be your answer.

The last time a President sent a civil rights bill to the Congress it contained a provision to protect voting rights in Federal elections. That civil rights bill was passed after 8 long months of debate. And when that bill came to my desk from the Congress for my signature, the heart of the voting provision had been eliminated.

This time, on this issue, there must be no delay, no hesitation and no compromise with our purpose.

We cannot, we must not, refuse to protect the right of every American to vote in every election that he may desire to participate in. And we ought not and we cannot and we must not wait another 8 months before we get a bill. We have already waited a hundred years and more, and the time for waiting is gone.

So I ask you to join me in working long hours—nights and weekends, if necessary—to pass this bill. And I don't make that request lightly. For from the window where I sit with the problems of our country I recognize that outside this chamber is the outraged conscience of a nation, the grave concern of many nations, and the harsh judgment of history on our acts.

WE SHALL OVERCOME

But even if we pass this bill, the battle will not be over. What happened in Selma is part of a far larger movement which reaches into every section and State of America. It is the effort of American Negroes to secure for themselves the full blessings of American life.

Their cause must be our cause too. Because it is not just Negroes, but really it is all of us, who must overcome the crippling legacy of bigotry and injustice.

And we shall overcome.

As a man whose roots go deeply into Southern soil I know how agonizing racial feelings are. I know how difficult it is to reshape the attitudes and the structure of our society.

But a century has passed, more than a hundred years, since the Negro was freed. And he is not fully free tonight.

It was more than a hundred years ago that Abraham Lincoln, a great President of another party, signed the Emancipation Proclamation, but emancipation is a proclamation and not a fact.

A century has passed, more than a hundred years, since equality was promised. And yet the Negro is not equal.

A century has passed since the day of promise. And the promise is unkept.

The time of justice has now come. I tell you that I believe sincerely that no force can hold it back. It is right in the eyes of man and God that it should come. And when it does, I think that day will brighten the lives of every American.

For Negroes are not the only victims. How many white children have gone uneducated, how many white families have lived in stark poverty, how many white lives have been scarred by fear, because we have wasted our energy and our substance to maintain the barriers of hatred and terror?

So I say to all of you here, and to all in the Nation tonight, that those who appeal to you to hold on to the past do so at the cost of denying you your future.

This great, rich, restless country can offer opportunity and education and hope to all: black and white, North and South, sharecropper and city dweller. These are the enemies: poverty, ignorance, disease. They are the enemies and not our fellow man, not our neighbor. And these enemies too, poverty, disease and ignorance, we shall overcome.

AN AMERICAN PROBLEM

Now let none of us in any sections look with prideful righteousness on the troubles in another section, or on the problems of our neighbors. There is really no part of America where the promise of equality has been fully kept. In Buffalo as well as in Birmingham, in Philadelphia as well as in Selma, Americans are struggling for the fruits of freedom.

This is one Nation. What happens in Selma or in Cincinnati is a matter of legitimate concern to every American. But let each of us look within our own hearts and our own communities, and let each of us put our shoulder to the wheel to root out injustice wherever it exists.

As we meet here in this peaceful, historic chamber tonight, men from the South, some of whom were at Iwo Jima, men from the North who have carried Old Glory to far corners of the world and brought it back without a stain on it, men from the East and from the West, are all fighting together without regard to religion, or color, or region, in Viet-Nam. Men from every region fought for us across the world 20 years ago.

And in these common dangers and these common sacrifices the South made its contribution of honor and gallantry no less than any other region of the great Republic—and in some instances, a great many of them, more.

And I have not the slightest doubt that good men from everywhere in this country, from the Great Lakes to the Gulf of Mexico, from the Golden Gate to the harbors along the Atlantic, will rally together now in this cause to vindicate the freedom of all Americans. For all of us owe this duty; and I believe that all of us will respond to it.

Your President makes that request of every American.

PROGRESS THROUGH THE DEMOCRATIC PROCESS

The real hero of this struggle is the American Negro. His actions and protests, his courage to risk safety and even to risk his life, have awakened the conscience of this Nation. His demonstrations have been designed to call attention to injustice, designed to provoke change, designed to stir reform.

He has called upon us to make good the promise of America. And who among us can say that we would have made the same progress were it not for his persistent bravery, and his faith in American democracy.

For at the real heart of battle for equality is a deep-seated belief in the democratic process. Equality depends not on the force of arms or tear gas but upon the force of moral right; not on recourse to violence but on respect for law and order.

There have been many pressures upon your President and there will be others as the days come and go. But I pledge you tonight that we intend to fight this battle where it should be fought: in the courts and in the Congress, and in the hearts of men.

We must preserve the right of free speech and the right of free assembly. But the right of free speech does not carry with it, as has been said, the right to holler fire in a crowded theater. We must preserve the right to free assembly, but free assembly does not carry with it the right to block public thoroughfares to traffic.

We do have a right to protest, and a right to march under conditions that do not infringe the constitutional rights of our neighbors. And I intend to protect all those rights as long as I am permitted to serve in this office.

We will guard against violence, knowing it strikes from our hands the very weapons which we seek—progress, obedience to law, and belief in American values.

In Selma as elsewhere we seek and pray for peace. We seek order. We seek unity. But we will not accept the peace of stifled rights, or the order imposed by fear, or the unity that stifles protest. For peace cannot be purchased at the cost of liberty.

In Selma tonight, as in every—and we had a good day there— as in every city, we are working for just and peaceful settlement. We must all remember that after this speech I am making tonight, after the police and the FBI and the Marshals have all gone, and after you have promptly passed this bill, the people of Selma and the other cities of the Nation must still live and work together. And when the attention of the Nation has gone elsewhere they must try to heal the wounds and to build a new community.

This cannot be easily done on a battleground of violence, as the history of the South itself shows. It is in recognition of this that men of both races have shown such an outstandingly impressive responsibility in recent days—last Tuesday, again today.

RIGHTS MUST BE OPPORTUNITIES

The bill that I am presenting to you will be known as a civil rights bill. But, in a larger sense, most of the program I am recommending is a civil rights program. Its object is to open the city of hope to all people of all races.

Because all Americans just must have the right to vote. And we are going to give them that right.

All Americans must have the privileges of citizenship regardless of race. And they are going to have those privileges of citizenship regardless of race.

But I would like to caution you and remind you that to exercise these privileges takes much more than just legal right. It requires a trained mind and a healthy body. It requires a decent home, and the chance to find a job, and the opportunity to escape from the clutches of poverty.

Of course, people cannot contribute to the Nation if they are never taught to read or write, if their bodies are stunted from hunger, if their sickness goes untended, if their life is spent in hopeless poverty just drawing a welfare check.

So we want to open the gates to opportunity. But we are also going to give all our people, black and white, the help that they need to walk through those gates.

THE PURPOSE OF THIS GOVERNMENT

My first job after college was as a teacher in Cotulla, Tex., in a small Mexican-American school. Few of them could speak English, and I couldn't speak much Spanish. My students were poor and they often came to class without breakfast, hungry. They knew even in their youth the pain of prejudice. They never seemed to know why people disliked them. But they knew it was so, because I saw it in their eyes. I often walked home late in the afternoon, after the classes were finished, wishing there was more that I could do. But all I knew was to teach them the little that I knew, hoping that it might help them against the hardships that lay ahead.

Somehow you never forget what poverty and hatred can do when you see its scars on the hopeful face of a young child.

I never thought then, in 1928, that I would be standing here in 1965. It never even occurred to me in my fondest dreams that I might have the chance to help the sons and daughters of those students and to help people like them all over this country.

But now I do have that chance—and I'll let you in on a secret—I mean to use it. And I hope that you will use it with me.

This is the richest and most powerful country which ever occupied the globe. The might of past empires is little compared to ours. But I do not want to be the President who built empires, or sought grandeur, or extended dominion.

I want to be the President who educated young children to the wonders of their world. I want to be the President who helped to feed the hungry and to prepare them to be taxpayers instead of taxeaters.

I want to be the President who helped the poor to find their own way and who protected the right of every citizen to vote in every election.

I want to be the President who helped to end hatred among his fellow men and who promoted love among the people of all races and all regions and all parties.

I want to be the President who helped to end war among the brothers of this earth.

And so at the request of your beloved Speaker and the Senator from Montana; the majority leader, the Senator from Illinois; the minority leader, Mr. McCulloch, and other Members of both parties, I came here tonight—not as President Roosevelt came down one time in person to veto a bonus bill, not as President Truman came down one time to urge the passage of a railroad bill—but I came down here to ask you to share this task with me and to share it with the people that we both work for. I want this to be the Congress, Republicans and Democrats alike, which did all these things for all these people.

Beyond this great chamber, out yonder in 50 States, are the people that we serve. Who can tell what deep and unspoken hopes are in their hearts tonight as they sit there and listen. We all can guess, from our own lives, how difficult they often find their own pursuit of happiness, how many problems each little family has. They look most of all to themselves for their futures. But I think that they also look to each of us.

Above the pyramid on the great seal of the United States it says—in Latin—"God has favored our undertaking."

God will not favor everything that we do. It is rather our duty to divine His will. But I cannot help believing that He truly understands and that He really favors the undertaking that we begin here tonight.

Gerald Ford
Address to a Joint Session of the Congress
August 12, 1974

MR. SPEAKER, MR. PRESIDENT, DISTINGUISHED GUESTS, AND MY VERY DEAR FRIENDS:

My fellow Americans, we have a lot of work to do. My former colleagues, you and I have a lot of work to do. Let's get on with it.

Needless to say, I am deeply grateful for the wonderfully warm welcome. I can never express my gratitude adequately.

I am not here to make an inaugural address. The Nation needs action, not words. Nor will this be a formal report of the state of the Union. God willing, I will have at least three more chances to do that.

It is good to be back in the People's House. But this cannot be a real homecoming. Under the Constitution, I now belong to the executive branch. The Supreme Court has even ruled that I *am* the executive branch—head, heart, and hand.

With due respect to the learned Justices—and I greatly respect the judiciary—part of my heart will always be here on Capitol Hill. I know well the coequal role of the Congress in our constitutional process. I love the House of Representatives. I revere the traditions of the Senate despite my too-short internship in that great body. As President, within the limits of basic principles, my motto toward the Congress is communication, conciliation, compromise, and cooperation.

This Congress, unless it has changed, I am confident, will be my working partner as well as my most constructive critic. I am not asking for conformity. I am dedicated to the two-party system, and you know which party I belong to.

I do not want a honeymoon with you. I want a good marriage.

I want progress, and I want problemsolving which requires my best efforts and also your best efforts.

I have no need to learn how Congress speaks for the people. As President, I intend to listen.

But I also intend to listen to the people themselves—all the people—as I promised last Friday. I want to be sure that we are all tuned in to the real voice of America.

My Administration starts off by seeking unity in diversity. My office door has always been open, and that is how it is going to be at the White House. Yes, Congressmen will be welcomed—if you don't overdo it. [Laughter]

The first seven words of the Constitution and the most important are these: "We the People of the United States. . . . " *We the people* ordained and established the Constitution and reserved to themselves all powers not granted to Federal and State government. I respect and will always be conscious of that fundamental rule of freedom.

Only 8 months ago, when I last stood here, I told you I was a Ford, not a Lincoln. Tonight I say I am still a Ford, but I am not a Model T.

I do have some old-fashioned ideas, however. I believe in the very basic decency and fairness of America. I believe in the integrity and patriotism of the Congress. And while I am aware of the House rule that no one ever speaks to the galleries, I believe in the first amendment and the absolute necessity of a free press.

But I also believe that over two centuries since the First Continental Congress was convened, the direction of our Nation's movement has been forward. I am here to confess that in my first campaign for President—of my senior class in South High School in Grand Rapids, Michigan—I headed the Progressive Party ticket, and lost. Maybe that is why I became a Republican. [*Laughter*]

Now I ask you to join with me in getting this country revved up and moving.

My instinctive judgment is that the state of the Union is excellent. But the state of our economy is not so good. Everywhere

I have been as Vice President, some 118,000 miles in 40 States and some 55 press conferences, the unanimous concern of Americans is inflation.

For once all the polls seem to agree. They also suggest that the people blame Government far more than either management or labor for the high cost of everything they have to buy.

You who come from 50 States, three territories, and the District of Columbia, know this better than I do. That is why you have created, since I left, your new Budget Reform Committee. I welcome it, and I will work with its members to bring the Federal budget into balance in fiscal year 1976.

The fact is that for the past 25 years that I had the honor of serving in this body, the Federal budget has been balanced in only six.

Mr. Speaker, I am a little late getting around to it, but confession is good for the soul. I have sometimes voted to spend more taxpayer's money for worthy Federal projects in Grand Rapids, Michigan, while I vigorously opposed wasteful spending boondoggles in Oklahoma. [*Laughter*]

Be that as it may, Mr. Speaker, you and I have always stood together against unwarranted cuts in national defense. This is no time to change that nonpartisan policy.

Just as escalating Federal spending has been a prime cause of higher prices over many years, it may take some time to stop inflation. But we must begin right now.

For a start, before your Labor Day recess, Congress should reactivate the Cost of Living Council through passage of a clean bill, without reimposing controls, that will let us monitor wages and prices to expose abuses.

Whether we like it or not, the American wage earner and the American housewife are a lot better economists than most economists care to admit. They know that a government big enough to give you everything you want is a government big enough to take from you everything you have.

If we want to restore confidence in ourselves as working politicians, the first thing we all have to do is to learn to say no.

The first specific request by the Ford Administration is not to Congress but to the voters in the upcoming November elections. It is this, very simple: Support your candidates, Congressmen and Senators, Democrats or Republicans, conservatives or liberals, who consistently vote for tough decisions to cut the cost of government, restrain Federal spending, and bring inflation under control.

I applaud the initiatives Congress has already taken. The only fault I find with the Joint Economic Committee's study on inflation, authorized last week, is that we need its expert findings in 6 weeks instead of 6 months.

A month ago, the distinguished majority leader of the United States Senate asked the White House to convene an economic conference of Members of Congress, the President's economic consultants, and some of the best economic brains from labor, industry, and agriculture.

Later, this was perfected by resolution [S. Res. 363] to assemble a domestic summit meeting to devise a bipartisan action for stability and growth in the American economy. Neither I nor my staff have much time right now for letterwriting. So, I will respond. I accept the suggestion, and I will personally preside.

Furthermore, I propose that this summit meeting be held at an early date, in full view of the American public. They are as anxious as we are to get the right answers.

My first priority is to work with you to bring inflation under control. Inflation is domestic enemy number one. To restore economic confidence, the Government in Washington must provide some leadership. It does no good to blame the public for spending too much when the Government is spending too much.

I began to put my Administration's own economic house in order starting last Friday. I instructed my Cabinet officers and Counsellors and my White House Staff to make fiscal restraint their first order of business, and to save every taxpayer's dollar the safety and genuine welfare of our great Nation will permit. Some economic activities will be affected more by monetary and fiscal restraint than other activities. Good government clearly requires that we tend to the economic problems facing our country in a spirit of equity to all of our citizens in all segments of our society.

Tonight, obviously, is no time to threaten you with vetoes. But I do have the last recourse, and I am a veteran of many a veto fight right here in this great chamber. Can't we do a better job by reasonable compromise? I hope we can.

Minutes after I took the Presidential oath, the joint leadership of Congress told me at the White House they would go more than halfway to meet me. This was confirmed in your unanimous concurrent resolution of cooperation, for which I am deeply grateful. If, for my part, I go more than halfway to meet the Congress, maybe we can find a much larger area of national agreement.

I bring no legislative shopping list here this evening. I will deal with specifics in future messages and talks with you, but here are a few examples of how seriously I feel about what we must do together.

Last week, the Congress passed the elementary and secondary education bill, and I found it on my desk. Any reservations I might have about some of its provisions—and I do have—fade in comparison to the urgent needs of America for quality education. I will sign it in a few days.

I must be frank. In implementing its provisions, I will oppose excessive funding during this inflationary crisis.

As Vice President, I studied various proposals for better health care financing. I saw them coming closer together and urged my friends in the Congress and in the Administration to sit down and sweat out a sound compromise. The comprehensive health insurance plan goes a long ways toward providing early relief to people who are sick.

Why don't we write—and I ask this with the greatest spirit of cooperation—why don't we write a good health bill on the statute books in 1974, before this Congress adjourns?

The economy of our country is critically dependent on how we interact with the economies of other countries. It is little comfort that our inflation is only a part of a worldwide problem or that American families need less of their paychecks for groceries than most of our foreign friends.

As one of the building blocks of peace, we have taken the lead in working toward a more open and a more equitable world economic system. A new round of international trade negotiations started last September among 105 nations in Tokyo. The others are waiting for the United States Congress to grant the necessary authority to the executive branch to proceed.

With modifications, the trade reform bill passed by the House last year would do a good job. I understand good progress has been made in the Senate Committee on Finance. But I am optimistic, as always, that the Senate will pass an acceptable bill quickly as a key part of our joint prosperity campaign.

I am determined to expedite other international economic plans. We will be working together with other nations to find better ways to prevent shortages of food and fuel. We must not let last winter's energy crisis happen again. I will push Project Independence for our own good and the good of others. In that, too, I will need your help.

Successful foreign policy is an extension of the hopes of the whole American people for a world of peace and orderly reform and orderly freedom. So, I would say a few words to our distinguished guests from the governments of other nations where, as at home, it is my determination to deal openly with allies and adversaries.

Over the past 5½ years in Congress and as Vice President, I have fully supported the outstanding foreign policy of President Nixon. This policy I intend to continue.

Throughout my public service, starting with wartime naval duty under the command of President Franklin D. Roosevelt, I have upheld all our Presidents when they spoke for my country to the world. I believe the Constitution commands this. I know that in this crucial area of international policy I can count on your firm support.

Now, let there be no doubt or any misunderstanding anywhere, and I emphasize anywhere: There are no opportunities to exploit, should anyone so desire. There will be no change of course, no relaxation of vigilance, no abandonment of the helm of our ship of state as the watch changes.

We stand by our commitments and we will live up to our responsibilities in our formal alliances, in our friendships, and in our improving relations with potential adversaries.

On this, Americans are united and strong. Under my term of leadership, I hope we will become more united. I am certain America will remain strong.

A strong defense is the surest way to peace. Strength makes détente attainable. Weakness invites war, as my generation—my generation—knows from four very bitter experiences.

Just as America's will for peace is second to none, so will America's strength be second to none.

We cannot rely on the forbearance of others to protect this Nation. The power and diversity of the Armed Forces, active Guard and Reserve, the resolve of our fellow citizens, the flexibility in our command to navigate international waters that remain troubled are all essential to our security.

I shall continue to insist on civilian control of our superb military establishment. The Constitution plainly requires the President to be Commander in Chief, and I will be.

Our job will not be easy. In promising continuity, I cannot promise simplicity. The problems and challenges of the world remain complex and difficult. But we have set out on a path of reason, of fairness, and we will continue on it.

As guideposts on that path, I offer the following:

—To our allies of a generation in the Atlantic community and Japan, I pledge continuity in the loyal collaboration on our many mutual endeavors.

—To our friends and allies in this hemisphere, I pledge continuity in the deepening dialogue to define renewed relationships of equality and justice.

—To our allies and friends in Asia, I pledge a continuity in our support for their security, independence, and economic development. In Indochina, we are determined to see the observance of the Paris agreement on Vietnam and the cease-fire and negotiated settlement in Laos. We hope to see an early compromise settlement in Cambodia.

—To the Soviet Union, I pledge continuity in our commitment to the course of the past 3 years. To our two peoples, and to all mankind, we owe a continued effort to live and, where possible, to work together in peace, for in a thermonuclear age there can be no alternative to a positive and peaceful relationship between our nations.

—To the People's Republic of China, whose legendary hospitality I enjoyed, I pledge continuity in our commitment to the principles of the Shanghai communique. The new relationship built on those principles has demonstrated that it serves serious and objective mutual interests and has become an enduring feature of the world scene.

—To the nations in the Middle East, I pledge continuity in our vigorous efforts to advance the progress which has brought hopes of peace to that region after 25 years as a hotbed of war. We shall carry out our promise to promote continuing negotiations among all parties for a complete, just, and lasting settlement.

—To all nations, I pledge continuity in seeking a common global goal: a stable international structure of trade and finance which reflects the interdependence of all peoples.

—To the entire international community—to the United Nations, to the world's nonaligned nations, and to all others—I pledge continuity in our dedication to the humane goals which throughout our history have been so much of America's contribution to mankind.

So long as the peoples of the world have confidence in our purposes and faith in our word, the age-old vision of peace on Earth will grow brighter.

I pledge myself unreservedly to that goal. I say to you in words that cannot be improved upon: "Let us never negotiate out of fear, but let us never fear to negotiate."

As Vice President, at the request of the President, I addressed myself to the individual rights of Americans in the area of privacy. There will be no illegal tappings (tapings), eavesdropping, buggings, or break-ins by my Administration. There will be hot pursuit of tough laws to prevent illegal invasion of privacy in both government and private activities.

On the higher plane of public morality, there is no need for me to preach tonight. We have thousands of far better preachers and millions of sacred scriptures to guide us on the path of personal right-living and exemplary official conduct. If we can make effective and earlier use of moral and ethical wisdom of the centuries in today's complex society, we will prevent more crime and more corruption than all the policemen and prosecutors governments can ever deter. If I might say so, this is a job that must begin at home, not in Washington.

I once told you that I am not a saint, and I hope never to see the day that I cannot admit having made a mistake. So I will close with another confession.

Frequently, along the tortuous road of recent months from this chamber to the President's House, I protested that I was my own man. Now I realize that I was wrong.

I am your man, for it was your carefully weighed confirmation that changed my occupation.

The truth is I am the people's man, for you acted in their name, and I accepted and began my new and solemn trust with a promise to serve all the people and do the best that I can for America. When I say all the people, I mean exactly that.

To the limits of my strength and ability, I will be the President of black, brown, red, and white Americans, of old and young, of women's liberationists and male chauvinists—[laughter]—and all the rest of us in-between, of the poor and the rich, of native sons and new refugees, of those who work at lathes or at desks or in mines or in the fields, of Christians, Jews, Moslems, Buddhists, and atheists, if there really are any atheists after what we have all been through.

Fellow Americans, one final word: I want to be a good President. I need your help. We all need God's sure guidance. With it, nothing can stop the United States of America.

Thank you very much.

NOTE

The President spoke at 9:06 p.m. in the House Chamber at the Capitol, after being introduced by Carl Albert, Speaker of the House of Representatives. The address was broadcast live on radio and television.

Ronald Reagan
Address to the Nation on Federal Tax Reduction Legislation
July 27, 1981

Good evening.

I'd intended to make some remarks about the problem of social security tonight, but the immediacy of congressional action on the tax program, a key component of our economic package, has to take priority. Let me just say, however, I've been deeply disturbed by the way those of you who are dependent on social security have been needlessly frightened by some of the inaccuracies which have been given wide circulation. It's true that the social security system has financial problems. It's also true that these financial problems have been building for more than 20 years, and nothing has been done. I hope to address you on this entire subject in the near future.

In the meantime, let me just say this: I stated during the campaign and I repeat now, I will not stand by and see those of you who are dependent on social security deprived of the benefits you've worked so hard to earn. I make that pledge to you as your President. You have no reason to be frightened. You will continue to receive your checks in the full amount due you. In any plan to restore fiscal integrity of social security, I personally will see that the plan will not be at the expense of you who are now dependent on your monthly social security checks.

Now, let us turn to the business at hand. It's been nearly 6 months since I first reported to you on the state of the nation's economy. I'm afraid my message that night was grim and disturbing. I remember telling you we were in the worst economic mess since the Great Depression. Prices were continuing to spiral upward, unemployment was reaching intolerable levels, and all because government was too big and spent too much of our money.

We're still not out of the woods, but we've made a start. And we've certainly surprised those longtime and somewhat cynical observers of the Washington scene, who looked, listened, and said, "It can never be done; Washington will never change its spending habits." Well, something very exciting has been happening here in Washington, and you're responsible.

Your voices have been heard—millions of you, Democrats, Republicans, and Independents, from every profession, trade and line of work, and from every part of this land. You sent a message that you wanted a new beginning. You wanted to change one little, two little word—two letter word, I should say. It doesn't sound like much, but it sure can make a difference changing "by government" "control *by* government" to "control *of* government."

In that earlier broadcast, you'll recall I proposed a program to drastically cut back government spending in the 1982 budget, which begins October 1st, and to continue cutting in the '83 and '84 budgets. Along with this I suggested an across-the-board tax cut, spread over those same 3 years, and the elimination of unnecessary regulations which were adding billions to the cost of things we buy.

All the lobbying, the organized demonstrations, and the cries of protest by those whose way of life depends on maintaining government's wasteful ways were no match for your voices, which were heard loud and clear in these marble halls of government. And you made history with your telegrams, your letters, your phone calls and, yes, personal visits to talk to your elected representatives. You reaffirmed the mandate you delivered in the election last November—a mandate that called for an end to government policies that sent prices and mortgage rates skyrocketing while millions of Americans went jobless

Because of what you did, Republicans and Democrats in the Congress came together and passed the most sweeping cutbacks in the history of the Federal budget. Right now, Members of the House and Senate are meeting in a conference committee to reconcile the differences between the two budget-cutting bills passed by the House and Senate. When they finish, all Americans will benefit from savings of approximately $140 billion in reduced government costs over just the next 3 years. And that doesn't include the additional savings from the hundreds of burdensome regulations already cancelled or facing cancellation.

For 19 out of the last 20 years, the Federal Government has spent more than it took in. There will be another large deficit in this present year which ends September 30th, but with our program in place, it won't be quite as big as it might have been. And starting next year, the deficits will get smaller until in just a few years the budget can be balanced. And we hope we can begin whittling at that almost $1 trillion debt that hangs over the future of our children.

Now, so far, I've been talking about only one part of our program for economic recovery—the budget-cutting part. I don't minimize its importance. Just the fact that Democrats and Republicans could work together as they have, proving the strength of our system, has created an optimism in our land. The rate of inflation is no longer in double-digit figures. The dollar has regained strength in the international money markets, and businessmen and investors are making decisions with regard to industrial development, modernization and expansion—all of this based on anticipation of our program being adopted and put into operation.

A recent poll shows that where a year and a half ago only 24 percent of our people believed things would get better, today 46 percent believe they will. To justify their faith, we must deliver the other part of our program. Our economic package is a closely knit, carefully constructed plan to restore America's economic strength and put our nation back on the road to prosperity.

Each part of this package is vital. It cannot be considered piecemeal. It was proposed as a package, and it has been supported as such by the American people. Only if the Congress passes all of its major components does it have any real chance of success. This is absolutely essential if we are to provide incentives and make capital available for the increased productivity required to provide real, permanent jobs for our people.

And let us not forget that the rest of the world is watching America carefully to see how we'll act at this critical moment.

I have recently returned from a summit meeting with world leaders in Ottawa, Canada, and the message I heard from them was quite clear. Our allies depend on a strong and economically sound America. And they're watching events in this country, particularly those surrounding our program for economic recovery, with close attention and great hopes. In short, the best way to have a strong foreign policy abroad is to have a strong economy at home.

The day after tomorrow, Wednesday, the House of Representatives will begin debate on two tax bills. And once again, they need to hear from you. I know that doesn't give you much time, but a great deal is at stake. A few days ago I was visited here in the office by a Democratic Congressman from one of our southern States. He'd been back in his distrct. And one day one of his constituents asked him where he stood on our economic recovery program—I outlined that program in an earlier broadcast—particularly the tax cut. Well, the Congressman, who happens to be a strong leader in support of our program, replied at some length with a discussion of the technical points involved, but he also mentioned a few reservations he had on certain points. The constituent, a farmer, listened politely until he'd finished, and then he said, "Don't give me an essay. What I want to know is are you for 'im or agin 'im?"

Well, I appreciate the gentleman's support and suggest his question is a message your own representatives should hear. Let me add, those representatives honestly and sincerely want to know your feelings. They get plenty of input from the special interest groups. They'd like to hear from their home folks.

Now, let me explain what the situation is and what's at issue. With our budget cuts, we've presented a complete program of reduction in tax rates. Again, our purpose was to provide incentive for the individual, incentives for business to encourage production and hiring of the unemployed, and to free up money for investment. Our bill calls for a 5-percent reduction in the income tax rates by October 1st, a 10-percent reduction beginning July 1st, 1982, and another 10-percent cut a year later, a 25-percent total reduction over 3 years.

But then to ensure the tax cut is permanent, we call for indexing the tax rates in 1985, which means adjusting them for inflation. As it is now, if you get a cost-of-living raise that's intended to keep you even with inflation, you find that the increase in the number of dollars you get may very likely move you into a higher tax bracket, and you wind up poorer than you would. This is called bracket creep.

Bracket creep is an insidious tax. Let me give an example. If you earned $10,000 a year in 1972, by 1980 you had to earn $19,700 just to stay even with inflation. But that's before taxes. Come April 15th, you'll find your tax rates have increased 30 percent. Now, if you've been wondering why you don't seem as well-off as you were a few years back, it's because government makes a profit on inflation. It gets an automatic tax increase without having to vote on it. We intend to stop that.

Time won't allow me to explain every detail. But our bill includes just about everything to help the economy. We reduce the marriage penalty, that unfair tax that has a working husband and wife pay more tax than if they were single. We increase the exemption on the inheritance or estate tax to $600,000, so that farmers and family-owned businesses don't have to sell the farm or store in the event of death just to pay the taxes. Most important, we wipe out the tax entirely for a surviving spouse. No longer, for example, will a widow have to sell the family source of income to pay a tax on her husband's death.

There are deductions to encourage investment and savings. Business gets realistic depreciation on equipment and machinery. And there are tax breaks for small and independent businesses which create 80 percent of all our new jobs.

This bill also provides major credits to the research and development industry. These credits will help spark the high technology breakthroughs that are so critical to America's economic leadership in the world. There are also added incentives for small businesses, including a provision that will lift much of the burden of costly paperwork that government has imposed on small business.

In addition, there's short-term but substantial assistance for the hard pressed thrift industry, as well as reductions in oil taxes that will benefit new or independent oil producers and move our nation a step closer to energy self-sufficiency. Our bill is, in short, the first real tax cut for everyone in almost 20 years.

Now, when I first proposed this—incidentally, it has now become a bipartisan measure coauthored by Republican Barber Conable and Democrat Kent Hance—the Democratic leadership said a tax cut was out of the question. It would be wildly inflationary. And that was before my inauguration. And then your voices began to be heard and suddenly, in February, the leadership discovered that, well, a 1-year tax cut was feasible. Well, we kept on pushing our 3-year tax cut and by June, the opposition found that a 2-year tax cut might work. Now it's July, and they find they could even go for a third year cut provided there was a trigger arrangement that would only allow it to go into effect if certain economic goals had been met by 1983.

But by holding the people's tax reduction hostage to future economic events, they will eliminate the people's ability to plan ahead. Shopkeepers, farmers, and individuals will be denied the certainty they must have to begin saving or investing more of their money. And encouraging more savings and investment is precisely what we need now to rebuild our economy.

There's also a little sleight of hand in that trigger mechanism. You see, their bill, the committee bill, ensures that the 1983 deficit will be $6½ billion greater than their own trigger requires. As it stands now, the design of their own bill will not meet the trigger they've put in; therefore, the third year tax cut will automatically never take place.

If I could paraphrase a well-known statement by Will Rogers that he had never met a man he didn't like, I'm afraid we have some people around here who never met a tax they didn't hike. Their tax proposal, similar in a number of ways to ours but differing in some very vital parts, was passed out of the House Ways and Means Committee, and from now on I'll refer to it as the committee bill and ours as the bipartisan bill. They'll be the bills taken up Wednesday.

The majority leadership claims theirs gives a greater break to the worker than ours, and it does—that is, if you're only planning to live 2 more years. The plain truth is, our choice is not between two plans to reduce taxes; it's between a tax cut or a tax increase. There is now built into our present system, including payroll social security taxes and the bracket creep I've mentioned, a 22-percent tax increase over the next 3 years. The committee bill offers a 15-percent cut over 2 years; our bipartisan bill gives a 25-percent reduction over 3 years.

Now, as you can see by this chart,[1] there is the 22-percent tax increase. Their cut is below that line. But ours wipes out that increase and with a little to spare. And there it is, as you can see. The red column—that is the 15-percent tax cut, and it still leaves you with an increase. The green column is our bipartisan bill which wipes out the tax increase and gives you an ongoing cut.

Incidentally, their claim that cutting taxes for individuals for as much as 3 years ahead is risky, rings a litle hollow when you realize that their bill calls for business tax cuts each year for 7 years ahead. It rings even more hollow when you consider the fact the majority leadership routinely endorses Federal spending bills that project years into the future, but objects to a tax bill that will return your money over a 3-year period.

Now, here is another chart which illustrates what I said about their giving a better break if you only intend to live for 2 more years. Their tax cut, so called, is the dotted line. Ours is the solid line. As you can see, in an earning bracket of $20,000, their tax cut is slightly more generous than ours for the first 2 years. Then, as you can see, their tax bill, the dotted line, starts going up and up and up. On the other hand, in our bipartisan tax bill, the solid line, our tax cut keeps on going down, and then stays down permanently. This is true of all earning brackets—not just the $20,000 level that I've used as an example—from the lowest to the highest. This red space between the two lines is the tax money that will remain in your pockets if our bill passes; and it's the amount that will leave your pockets if their tax bill is passed.

Now, I take no pleasure in saying this, but those who will seek to defeat our Conable-Hance bipartisan bill as debate begins Wednesday are the ones who have given us five "tax cuts" in the last 10 years. But, our taxes went up $400 billion in those same 10 years. The lines on these charts say a lot about who's really fighting for whom. On the one hand, you see a genuine and lasting commitment to the future of working Americans; on the other, just another empty promise.

Those of us in the bipartisan coalition want to give this economy and the future of this Nation back to the people, because putting people first has always been America's secret weapon. The House majority leadership seems less concerned about protecting your family budget than with spending more on the Federal budget.

Our bipartisan tax bill targets three-quarters of its tax relief to middle-income wage earners who presently pay almost three-quarters of the total income tax. It also then indexes the tax brackets to ensure that you can keep that tax reduction in the years ahead. There also is, as I said, estate tax relief that will keep family farms and family-owned businesses in the family, and there are provisions for personal retirement plans and individual savings accounts.

Because our bipartisan bill is so clearly drawn and broadly based, it provides the kind of predictability and certainty that the financial segments of our society need to make investment decisions that stimulate productivity and make our economy grow. Even more important, if the tax cut goes to you, the American people, in the third year, that money returned to you won't be available to the Congress to spend, and that, in my view, is what this whole controversy comes down to. Are you entitled to the fruits of your own labor or does government have some presumptive right to spend and spend and spend?

I'm also convinced our business tax cut is superior to theirs because it's more equitable, and it will do a much better job promoting the surge in investment we so badly need to rebuild our industrial base.

There's something else I want to tell you. Our bipartisan coalition worked out a tax bill we felt would provide incentive and stimulate productivity, thus reducing inflation and providing jobs for the unemployed. That was our only goal. Our opponents in the beginning didn't want a tax bill at all. So what is the purpose behind their change of heart? They've put a tax program together for one reason only: to provide themselves with a political victory. Never mind that it won't solve the economic problems confronting our country. Never mind that it won't get the wheels of industry turning again or eliminate the inflation which is eating us alive.

This is not the time for political fun and games. This is the time for a new beginning. I ask you now to put aside any feelings of frustration or helplessness about our political institutions and join me in this dramatic but responsible plan to reduce the enormous burden of Federal taxation on you and your family.

During recent months many of you have asked what can you do to help make America strong again. I urge you again to contact your Senators and Congressmen. Tell them of your support for this bipartisan proposal. Tell them you believe this is an unequalled opportunity to help return America to prosperity and make government again the servant of the people.

In a few days the Congress will stand at the fork of two roads. One road is all too familiar to us. It leads ultimately to higher taxes. It merely brings us full circle back to the source of our economic problems, where the government decides that it knows better than you what should be done with your earnings and, in fact, how you should conduct your life. The other road promises to renew the American spirit. It's a road of hope and opportunity. It places the direction of your life back in your hands where it belongs.

I've not taken your time this evening merely to ask you to trust me. Instead, I ask you to trust yourselves. That's what America is all about. Our struggle for nationhood, our unrelenting fight for freedom, our very existence—these have all rested on the assurance that you must be free to shape your life as you are best able to, that no one can stop you from reaching higher or take from you the creativity that has made America the envy of mankind.

One road is timid and fearful; the other bold and hopeful.

In these 6 months, we've done so much and have come so far. It's been the power of millions of people like you who have determined that we will make America great again. You have made the difference up to now. You will make the difference again. Let us not stop now.

Thank you. God bless you, and good night.

NOTE

The President spoke at 8:01 p.m. from the Oval Office at the White House. His remarks were broadcast live on radio and television.

1. At this point, the President referred to two charts which were shown on the televised broadcast of his address.

Chapter 3 The President and Critics

The speeches in chapters 1 and 2 illustrated presidential efforts to mobilize and sustain public support. But it is naive to expect unanimous public support of any administration. The important question is not *whether* a president is criticized. Instead, we should ask: *Who* opposes him, for what *reasons*, how *vehemently*, and with what potential for *undermining* others' support of the administration? This chapter will explore strategies for handling critics and strategies for self-defense.

Any president can expect at least nominal opposition from the other party, from Congress, and from the "watchdog constituencies" (intellectuals, the press, and some religious leaders). But criticism from generally *supportive* constituencies can prove much more damaging. The farmers' tractorcade protesting Jimmy Carter's agricultural policies, for instance, was especially poignant because of his own farming background, and the AFL-CIO's refusal to endorse George McGovern irreparably damaged his 1972 candidacy.

The vehemence of criticism is important because it reduces the possibilities for compromise and negotiation. Especially intense criticism "polarizes" society, and when the president and his critics advance their arguments moralistically even the most mundane policy matter can become an apocolyptic struggle between Good and Evil.

Thus president and critics are both concerned with persuading the "undecideds." If the president can contain criticism to his expected critics at a moderate level of intensity, he will usually enjoy success.

Presidents have four general strategies for dealing with their critics. The first of these is "avoidance." Richard Nixon managed to publicly ignore the Watergate controversy for the nine months between the break-in and the formation of the Senate Select Subcommittee on Campaign Practices; and several incumbents have adopted the "Rose Garden" campaign strategy. Avoidance is practical if the critics are unsophisticated and scattered. But it is an unwise approach when the critics can use presidential avoidance to advance their criticism.

The second strategy is "Ridicule." Franklin Roosevelt's campaign speech to the Teamsters exemplifies "friendly ridicule," as he uses humor with supporters to defuse criticism and reduce his opponents' objections to apparent absurdity. "Nasty ridicule," apparent in the speeches of former Vice-President Spiro Agnew for example, often increases hostility. Ridicule is most effective when it can draw a smile from the critics themselves and reduce, rather than increase, hostility.

The third strategy is "confrontation." President Nixon's Phoenix campaign speech is a double-barrelled attack on anti-war protesters. It is a good example of the "Rhetoric of Polarization" which virtually eliminates any possibility of subsequent accomodation.

The fourth strategy is "identification." Gerald Ford knew that the strongest opposition to his plan to allow draft evaders to earn a return to American society would come from veterans. Because he respected them, he announced the plan in a speech to the Veterans of Foreign Wars. Ford demonstrated his concern by visiting them and explaining his reasons. The President stressed his common ground with the veterans and differentiated his plan from the kind of blanket amnesty program that he and they all opposed.

Some attempts to deal with critics are notably unsuccessful. President Jimmy Carter initially responded to the seizure of the American Embassy in Iran through normal diplomatic channels. For months he steadfastly resisted those who urged him to "Bomb Iran," counselling a patient and careful approach. Then, suddenly, Americans awoke to learn that Carter had ordered a military rescue mission that failed completely when our helicopters collided in the desert. Carter was caught between his urgings of patience on the one hand and his demonstrated admission that force was necessary, all the while realizing that the gamble could goad the Iranians into executing the hostages.

Few presidents have consistently relied upon only one of these strategies to deal with their critics, and specific situations and relationships generally dictate the best combination of strategies. But the insightful President realizes that critics and undecideds will become more, or less, hostile in response to his choices.

Franklin D. Roosevelt
Address at Dinner of
International Brotherhood of
Teamsters, Chauffeurs,
Warehousemen and Helpers
of America
September 23, 1944

Well, here we are together again—after four years—and what years they have been! You know, I am actually four years older, which is a fact that seems to annoy some people. In fact, in the mathematical field there are millions of Americans who are more than eleven years older than when we started in to clear up the mess that was dumped in our laps in 1933.

We all know that certain people who make it a practice to depreciate the accomplishments of labor—who even attack labor as unpatriotic—they keep this up usually for three years and six months in a row. But then, for some strange reason they change their tune—every four years—just before election day. When votes are at stake, they suddenly discover that they really love labor and that they are anxious to protect labor from its old friends.

I got quite a laugh, for example—and I am sure that you did— when I read this plank in the Republican platform adopted at their National Convention in Chicago last July:

> "The Republican Party accepts the purposes of the National Labor Relations Act, the Wage and Hour Act, the Social Security Act and all other Federal statutes designed to promote and protect the welfare of American working men and women, and we promise a fair and just administration of these laws."

You know, many of the Republican leaders and Congressmen and candidates, who shouted enthusiastic approval of that plank in that Convention Hall would not even recognize these progressive laws if they met them in broad daylight. Indeed, they have personally spent years of effort and energy—and much money—in fighting every one of those laws in the Congress, and in the press, and in the courts, ever since this Administration began to advocate them and enact them into legislation. That is a fair example of their insincerity and of their inconsistency.

The whole purpose of Republican oratory these days seems to be to switch labels. The object is to persuade the American people that the Democratic Party was responsible for the 1929 crash and the depression, and that the Republican Party was responsible for all social progress under the New Deal.

Now, imitation may be the sincerest form of flattery—but I am afraid that in this case it is the most obvious common or garden variety of fraud.

Of course, it is perfectly true that there are enlightened, liberal elements in the Republican Party, and they have fought hard and honorably to bring the Party up to date and to get it in step with the forward march of American progress. But these liberal elements were not able to drive the Old Guard Republicans from their entrenched positions.

Can the Old Guard pass itself off as the New Deal?

I think not.

We have all seen many marvelous stunts in the circus but no performing elephant could turn a hand-spring without falling flat on his back.

I need not recount to you the centuries of history which have been crowded into these four years since I saw you last.

There were some—in the Congress and out—who raised their voices against our preparations for defense—before and after 1939—objected to them, raised their voices against them as hysterical war mongering, who cried out against our help to the Allies as provocative and dangerous. We remember the voices. They would like to have us forget them now. But in 1940 and 1941—my, it seems a long time ago—they were loud voices. Happily they were a minority and—fortunately for ourselves, and for the world—they could not stop America.

There are some politicians who kept their heads buried deep in the sand while the storms of Europe and Asia were headed our way, who said that the lend-lease bill "would bring an end to free government in the United States," and who said, "only hysteria entertains the idea that Germany, Italy, or Japan contemplates war on us." These very men are now asking the American people to intrust to them the conduct of our foreign policy and our military policy.

What the Republican leaders are now saying in effect is this: "Oh, just forget what we used to say, we have changed our minds now—we have been reading the public opinion polls about these things and now we know what the American people want." And they say: "Don't leave the task of making the peace to those old men who first urged it and who have already laid the foundations for it, and who have had to fight all of us inch by inch during the last five years to do it. Why, just turn it all over to us. We'll do it so skillfully—that we won't lose a single isolationist vote or a single isolationist campaign contribution."

I think there is one thing that you know: I am too old for that. I cannot talk out of both sides of my mouth at the same time.

The Government welcomes all sincere supporters of the cause of effective world collaboration in the making of a lasting peace. Millions of Republicans all over the Nation are with us—and have been with us—in our unshakable determination to build the solid structure of peace. And they too will resent this campaign talk by those who first woke up to the facts of international life a few short months ago when they began to study the polls of public opinion.

Those who today have the military responsibility for waging this war in all parts of the globe are not helped by the statements of men who, without responsibility and without the knowledge of the facts, lecture the Chiefs of Staff of the United States as to the best means of dividing our armed forces and our military resources between the Atlantic and Pacific, between the Army and the Navy, and among the commanding generals of the different theaters of war. And I may say that those commanding generals are making good in a big way.

When I addressed you four years ago, I said, "I know that America will never be disappointed in its expectation that labor will always continue to do its share of the job we now face and do it patriotically and effectively and unselfishly."

Today we know that America has not been disappointed. In his Order of the Day when the Allied armies first landed in Normandy two months ago, General Eisenhower said: "Our home fronts have given us overwhelming superiority in weapons and munitions of war."

The country knows that there is a breed of cats, luckily not too numerous, called labor-baiters. I know that there are labor-baiters among the opposition who, instead of calling attention to the achievements of labor in this war, prefer to pick on the occasional strikes that have occurred—strikes that have been condemned by every responsible national labor leader. I ought to say, parenthetically, all but one. And that one labor leader, incidentally, is certainly not conspicuous among my supporters.

Labor-baiters forget that at our peak American labor and management have turned out airplanes at the rate of 109,000 a year; tanks—57,000 a year; combat vessels—573 a year; landing vessels, to get the troops ashore—31,000 a year; cargo ships—19 million tons a year—and Henry Kaiser is here tonight, I am glad to say; and small arms ammunition—oh, I can't understand it, I don't believe you can either—23 billion rounds a year.

But a strike is news, and generally appears in shrieking headlines—and, of course, they say labor is always to blame. The fact is that since Pearl Harbor only one-tenth of one percent of manhours have been lost by strikes. Can you beat that?

But, you know, even those candidates who burst out in election-year affection for social legislation and for labor in general, still think that you ought to be good boys and stay out of politics. And above all, they hate to see any working man or woman contribute a dollar bill to any wicked political party. Of course, it is all right for large financiers and industrialists and monopolists to contribute tens of thousands of dollars—but their solicitude for that dollar which the men and women in the ranks of labor contribute is always very touching.

They are, of course, perfectly willing to let you vote—unless you happen to be a solidier or a sailor overseas, or a merchant seaman carrying the munitions of war. In that case they have made it pretty hard for you to vote at all—for there are some political candidates who think that they may have a chance of election, if only the total vote is small enough.

And while I am on the subject of voting, let me urge every

American citizen—man and woman—to use your sacred privilege of voting, no matter which candidate you expect to support. Our millions of soldiers and sailors and merchant seamen have been handicapped or prevented from voting by those politicians and candidates who think that they stand to lose by such votes. You here at home have the freedom of the ballot. Irrespective of party, you should register and vote this November. I think that is a matter of plain good citizenship.

Words come easily, but they do not change the record. You are, most of you, old enough to remember what things were like for labor in 1932.

You remember the closed banks and the breadlines and the starvation wages; the foreclosures of homes and farms, and the bankruptcies of business; the "Hoovervilles," and the young men and women of the Nation facing a hopeless, jobless future; the closed factories and mines and mills; the ruined and abandoned farms; the stalled railroads and the empty docks; the blank despair of a whole Nation—and the utter impotence of the Federal Government.

You remember the long, hard road, with its gains and its setbacks, which we have traveled together ever since those days.

Now there are some politicians who do not remember that far back, and there are some who remember but find it convenient to forget. No, the record is not to be washed away that easily.

The opposition in this year has already imported into this campaign a very interesting thing, because it is foreign. They have imported the propaganda technique invented by the dictators abroad. Remember, a number of years ago, there was a book, *Mein Kampf*, written by Hitler himself. The technique was all set out in Hitler's book—and it was copied by the aggressors of Italy and Japan. According to that technique, you should never use a small falsehood; always a big one, for its very fantastic nature would make it more credible—if only you keep repeating it over and over and over again.

Well, let us take some simple illustrations that come to mind. For example, although I rubbed my eyes when I read it, we have been told that it was not a Republican depression, but a Democratic depression from which this Nation was saved in 1933—that this Administration—this one—today—is responsible for all the suffering and misery that the history books and the American people have always thought had been brought about during the twelve ill-fated years when the Republican party was in power.

Now, there is an old and somewhat lugubrious adage which says: "Never speak of rope in the house of a man who has been hanged." In the same way, if I were a Republican leader speaking to a mixed audience, the last word in the whole dictionary that I think I would use is that word "depression."

You know, they pop up all the time. For another example, I learned—much to my amazement—that the policy of this Administration was to keep men in the Army when the war was over, because there might be no jobs for them in civil life.

Well, the very day that this fantastic charge was first made, a formal plan for the method of speedy discharge from the Army had already been announced by the War Department—a plan based on the wishes of the soldiers themselves.

This callous and brazen falsehood about demobilization did, of course, a very simple thing; it was an effort to stimulate fear among American mothers and wives and sweethearts. And, incidentally, it was hardly calculated to bolster the morale of our soldiers and sailors and airmen who are fighting our battles all over the world.

But perhaps the most ridiculous of these campaign falsifications is the one that this Administration failed to prepare for the war that was coming. I doubt whether even Goebbels would have tried that one. For even he would never have dared hope that the voters of America had already forgotten that many of the Republican leaders in the Congress and outside the Congress tried to thwart and block nearly every attempt that this Administration made to warn our people and to arm our Nation. Some of them called our 50,000 airplane program fantastic. Many of those very same leaders who fought every defense measure that we proposed are still in control of the Republican party—look at their names— were in control of its National Convention in Chicago, and would be in control of the machinery of the Congress and of the Republican party, in the event of a Republican victory this fall.

These Republican leaders have not been content with attacks on me, or my wife, or on my sons. No, not content with that, they now include my little dog, Fala. Well, of course, I don't resent attacks, and my family doesn't resent attacks, but Fala *does* resent them. You know, Fala is Scotch, and being a Scottie, as soon as he learned that the Republican fiction writers in Congress and out had concocted a story that I had left him behind on the Aleutian Islands and had sent a destroyer back to find him—at a cost to the taxpayers of two or three, or eight or twenty million dollars—his Scotch soul was furious. He has not been the same dog since. I am accustomed to hearing malicious falsehoods about myself—such as that old, worm-eaten chestnut that I have represented myself as indispensable. But I think I have a right to resent, to object to libelous statements about my dog.

Well, I think we all recognize the old technique. The people of this country know the past too well to be deceived into forgetting. Too much is at stake to forget. There are tasks ahead of us which we must now complete with the same will and the same skill and intelligence and devotion that have already led us so far along the road to victory.

There is the task of finishing victoriously this most terrible of all wars as speedily as possible and with the least cost in lives.

There is the task of setting up international machinery to assure that the peace, once established, will not again be broken.

And there is the task that we face here at home—the task of reconverting our economy from the purposes of war to the purposes of peace.

These peace-building tasks were faced once before, nearly a generation ago. They were botched by a Republican administration. That must not happen this time. We will not let it happen this time.

Fortunately, we do not begin from scratch. Much has been done. Much more is under way. The fruits of victory this time will not be apples sold on street corners.

Many months ago, this Administration set up the necessary machinery for an orderly peacetime demobilization. The Congress has passed much more legislation continuing the agencies needed for demobilization—with additional powers to carry out their functions.

I know that the American people—business and labor and agriculture—have the same will to do for peace what they have done for war. And I know that they can sustain a national income that will assure full production and full employment under our democratic system of private enterprise, with Government encouragement and aid whenever and wherever that is necessary.

The keynote of all that we propose to do in reconversion can be found in the one word *jobs*.

We shall lease or dispose of our Government-owned plants and facilities and our surplus war property and land, on the basis of how they can best be operated by private enterprise to give jobs to the greatest number.

We shall follow a wage policy that will sustain the purchasing power of labor—for that means more production and more jobs.

You and I know that the present policies on wages and prices were conceived to serve the needs of the great masses of the people. They stopped inflation. They kept prices on a relatively stable level. Through the demobilization period, policies will be carried out with the same objective in mind—to serve the needs of the great masses of the people.

This is not the time in which men can be forgotten as they were in the Republican catastrophe that we inherited. The returning soldiers, the workers by their machines, the farmers in the field, the miners, the men and women in offices and shops, do not intend to be forgotten.

No, they know that they are not surplus. Because they know that they are America.

We must set targets and objectives for the future which will seem impossible—like the airplanes—to those who live in and are weighted down by the dead past.

We are even now organizing the logistics of the peace, just as Marshall and King and Arnold, MacArthur, Eisenhower, and Nimitz are organizing the logistics of this war.

I think that the victory of the American people and their allies in this war will be far more than a victory against Fascism and reaction and the dead hand of despotism of the past. The victory of the American people and their allies in this war will be a victory for democracy. It will constitute such an affirmation of the strength and power and vitality of government by the people as history has never before witnessed.

And so, my friends, we have had affirmation of the vitality of democratic government behind us, that demonstration of its resilience and its capacity for decision and for action—we have that knowledge of our own strength and power—we move forward with God's help to the greatest epoch of free achievement by free men that the world has ever known.

NOTE

Because of the publication of an unfortunate photograph taken while the President was delivering his acceptance speech at San Diego (see Item 53 and note, this volume) and because of the poor quality of his speech at Bremerton, Washington (see Item 58 and note).

Richard M. Nixon
Remarks at Phoenix, Arizona
October 31, 1970

GOVERNOR WILLIAMS, SENATOR FANNIN, CONGRESSMAN RHODES, CONGRESSMAN STEIGER, ALL OF THE DISTINGUISHED GUESTS ON THE PLATFORM, AND ALL THE DISTINGUISHED MEMBERS OF THIS AUDIENCE:

I appreciate very much your wonderful reception. I understand, incidentally, that traffic is backed up for 3 miles. We saw it as we came in. I hope, incidentally, that our friends in radio and television that they have this on the radio, so the people in the cars can hear on the radio, and my greetings to you.

I am very happy to be back in Arizona. I remember my very young years when I was in Prescott on three different summers. I have very warm feelings about this State. As Barry Goldwater says, too, I was raised on Arizona's water, so we share something in common.

I am particularly impressed by the size of this crowd when I realize what we are competing with today, the homecoming at the University of Arizona at Tucson. I understand the Arizona State Fair—is that right?—is it going on now, and the opening of deer season.

And also, I am very appreciative of the fact that we have had some wonderful musical organizations that have been entertaining us and entertaining you before we were here. If I could just mention them briefly. I want all those who are listening on television and radio to hear it, too. I understand we have had from the choral groups—and let's give them all a hand—the Phoenix Boys' Club chorus, the Coronado High School choral group, The Phoenicians barbershop chorus, the Scottsdale High School Band, and the Arizona State University Band.

After that reception from that band, I can't resist just saying something to you that is going to get me in trouble someplace else. When I was in Texas a few days ago, they told me that Texas was number one. When I was in Ohio the other day, they told me that Ohio State was going to be number one. When I was in Indiana, they told me Notre Dame was going to be number one. When I was in northern California, they told me that Stanford was number one.

But, boy, when I am in Arizona, Arizona State is number one.

I am glad to be in the State of champions, a champion United States Senator and a man who belongs not only to Arizona but the whole Nation—Barry Goldwater.

And a champion in the form of the man that I am proud here to endorse, a very great Governor, one who has served this State and one who is among the top ranks among the Governors of the nation, Governor Williams, of Arizona.

And champion Congressman, too, Johnny Rhodes, who serves in the leadership with me, and Congressman Steiger. Let me say for our congressional candidates, let's give them the hand that they deserve, too.

And finally, your United States Senator, the man who is up for reelection, the man who is among those for whom I am particularly campaigning across this country, because what happens in the Senate this year is perhaps the most important Senate race in the 190-year history of this country.

I simply want to say this about Paul Fannin: I have known him as you have known him for a number of years. I have known him as a fine Senator and as a fine man.

I also know this: that he is a man on whom I depend. I value his advice. I know that he fights for Arizona, but I also know that he fights for the defense of the United States of America, and we need that, too, in the United States Senate.

I am proud to endorse him. I don't know what I would do without him. Give him back, will you? How about it? We want him back.

Now, ladies and gentlemen, you are all standing here and I know you have been standing for a long time, jammed up, and I don't want you to get tired. But I have selected this particular occasion for a major statement. A major statement that needs to be made, needs to be made now; not because it is the end of a political campaign, but because this problem has been building up in America.

It is time for the President of the United States to speak out clearly to the American people, not because he personally has been affected by it but because all of America is affected by what happened a couple of days ago in my home State of California, in San Jose.

You saw some of it on television. You saw the crowd inside, a crowd like this, 3,000 people, listening, cheering, indicating their interest in who might be the Governor, who might be the Senator, and, of course, showing respect for the office of the President of the United States. You saw also the crowd outside.

The crowd inside were exercising their right to peaceable assembly, as you are today. They were listening to political speakers. They were weighing the issues in the campaign of 1970.

And outside the hall there was a mob of about 1,000, maybe a few more. We could see the hate in their faces as we drove into the hall, and the obscene signs they waved. We could hear the hate in their voices as they chanted their obscenities.

And inside the hall, we could hear them pounding on the doors as if they could not bear the thought of people listening respectfully to the Governor of the State of California, the senior Senator, and the President of the United States.

Along the campaign trail we have seen and heard demonstrators, but never before in this campaign was there such an atmosphere of hatred. As we came out of the hall and entered the motorcade, the haters surged past the barricades.

They began throwing rocks. These were not small stones; they were large rocks. They were heavy enough to smash windows, windows in the press bus, windows in the staff cars. They weren't directed at me, though some did hit the Presidential car. Most of the rocks hit the buses and the other cars behind.

What is the reaction of the people who came—people like you? They are at a rally, peaceably at a rally. Many who brought their children were terrified. Others were incensed at the insult to their elected leaders. And all were repelled by the atmosphere of violence and hatred that marred the event. And they thought to themselves, "Is this America? Is this the land where reason and peaceful discussion is the hallmark of a free society?"

Some say that the violent dissent is caused by the war in Vietnam. Well, ladies and gentlemen, my fellow Americans, it is about time we branded this line of thinking, this alibi for violence, for what it is: pure nonsense.

Those who carry a "peace" sign in one hand and throw a bomb or a brick with the other are the super hypocrites of our time.

My friends, the war is ending. Instead of sending men to Vietnam, we are bringing them home. Instead of casualties going up, they are coming down. A peace plan is on the table. And we are ending the war in a way that will discourage aggressors so that we can have not just peace for the next election, but peace for the next generation. That is what is happening, and that is what Americans are for.

And yet, as the war ends, the violence continues, and this is proof that these abilis are worthless.

Others say that the cause of violence is repression, but the people who came peaceably to the rally in San Jose—they were not repressing the haters outside. There is more freedom in the United States than anywhere else in the world, and it is about time that we cut out the nonsense—it is simply pure nonsense that repression is the cause of violence in the United States of America.

Violence in America today is not caused by the war; it is not caused by repression. There is no romantic ideal involved. Let's recognize these people for what they are. They are not romantic revolutionaries. They are the same thugs and hoodlums that have always plagued the good people.

And now the reason, a major reason, that they have gained such prominence in our national life, the major reason they dominate our television screens as they do night after night, the reason that they increasingly terrorize decent citizens, can be summed up in a single word: appeasement. When you permit an imbalance to exist that favors the accused over the victim, you are inviting more violence and breeding more bullies.

For too long, and this needs to be said and said now and here, the strength of freedom in our society has been eroded by a creeping permissiveness in our legislatures, in our courts, in our family life, and in our colleges and universities.

For too long, we have appeased aggression here at home, and, as with all appeasement, the result has been more aggression and more violence. The time has come to draw the line. The time has come for the great silent majority of Americans of all ages, of every political persuasion, to stand up and be counted against appeasement of the rock throwers and the obscenity shouters in America.

My fellow Americans, let us understand this is not a partisan issue. There is no candidate of either party that is for crime, that is for violence. The choice before the American people next week is not so simple as picking between the proviolent and the antiviolent. Everyone denounces violence.

The choice is between approaches to the same goal. One approach holds that violence will end as we end the war; that violence will end as we give more power to those who demand more power; that violence will end as we end hunger and poverty in America.

The people who believe in this approach are sincere Americans. They have every right to this point of view. But I believe that their approach has led us down a path of appeasement that has resulted in the very thing that they abhor most: the increase in violence, the limiting of personal freedom.

For years now, it has been fashionable to portray ours, this great country of America, as a sick society; to belittle its successes and breastbeat about its shortcomings; to make automatic heroes out of those who protest as if the act of protest—regardless of what was being protested, or how it was done, or whose rights were being infringed, or even whether the protesters had anything better to offer—as if this act itself were the mark of some higher virtue, and when rituals of protest began establishing a tyranny of their own, there were many who somehow forgot that tyranny is wrong, whatever its form—whether the tyranny of government, or the tyranny of terrorists, or the tyranny of those who shout down speakers, or the tyranny of those who would shut down colleges or blockade streets in an effort to impose their own views on others.

That way is not the American way and that way will not be the American way as long as those who care about freedom and decency and respect for the rights of one another stand up and be counted.

For a decade, now, this approach dominated America. It has obviously failed. The time has come to try a new approach.

Let me first point out what this new approach, our approach, is not. The answer to bluster is not more bluster. The answer to bluster is firmness. The answer to a wave of violence is not a wave of repression. That is exactly what the violent few want so that they can enlist the sympathies of the moderates.

The answer to violence is the strong application of fair American justice.

And the answer to violent dissent is not oppression of legitimate dissent. The great danger to dissent today comes not from the forces of law, but from the organized tyranny of some dissenters.

Now, let me spell out what the new approach, our approach, is:

First, the new approach to violence calls for new and strong laws that will give the peace forces new muscle to deal with the criminal forces in the United States of America. And in the United States Senate, Paul Fannin, and in the House of Representatives, Johnny Rhodes and Sam Steiger, have stood firmly with the President for that proposition and we need them back.

I have called for a whole series of laws. But because we have not had enough support in the House and the Senate, Congress has dillydallied; Congress has bottled them up in committee; Congress has passed only part of a program I asked for; and then they waited until just before the election.

The new approach to violence requires men in Congress who will work for and fight for laws that will put the terrorists where they belong—not roaming around civil society, but behind bars. That is where they belong.

And our new approach calls for a new approach to the interpretation of the laws we already have. I will continue to appoint judges to the Supreme Court and to all the courts who have an awareness of the rights of the victim as well as the rights of the accused.

And I need men in the United States Senate like Paul Fannin who will back me up when I send those recommendations for such judges to the United States Senate.

Third, our new approach to violence calls for a new attitude on the part of the American people—on your part, all of us. "Law and order" are not code words for racism or repression. "Law and order" are code words for freedom from fear in America.

This new attitude means that parents must exercise their responsibility for moral guidance. It means that college administrators and college faculties must stop caving in to the demands of a radical few. It means that moderate students must take a position that says to the violent: "Hit the books or hit the road."

This new attiude means that all Americans should stand with the men who are assigned to carry out the laws. After all, my friends, the first step toward respect for law is respect for the lawman. Let's give him the respect that he deserves.

Today I have been describing two approaches to violence in America. While the goal of ending violence is the same, the two approaches are very different. But don't let anybody tell you everybody is against violence, it is not an issue. The two approaches are deeply different. It is an issue, one of the central issues in America today.

If we do not act now to protect our freedom, we will lose our freedom. If we do not choose the tough-minded approach to violence, we will allow violence to gain a terrible momentum. If a man chooses to dress differently, to wear his hair differently—if he has any—or to talk in a way that repels decent people, that is his business. But when he picks up a rock, then it becomes your business and my business to stop him. Because, you see, that is what American freedom is all about.

When a man cannot bring his child—and I see so many wonderful children here today—when he can't bring his child to a political rally for fear that the person in the next seat is going to start yelling some filthy obscenity; when a man can't bring his wife to a rally for fear she is going to be pushed around by an unruly mob; and when any American faces the risk of a rock being thrown at him when he rises to speak, that I say appeasement has gone too far and it is time to draw the line.

Since 1776, this great Nation of ours has never knuckled under to the tactics of terror, abroad or at home, and we are not about to start in the year 1970.

And now could I add a personal note? The terrorists, the far left, would like nothing better than to make the President of the

United States a prisoner in the White House. Well, let me just set them straight. As long as I am President, no band of violent thugs is going to keep me from going out and speaking with the American people wherever they want to hear me and wherever I want to go. This is a free country, and I fully intend to share that freedom with my fellow Americans. This President is not going to be cooped up in the White House.

To keep this country free, to adopt the new approach to violence, to answer those who shout their four-letter words and abuse the right of free speech, what can you do, particularly you of voting age, as an individual? I will tell you what.

You don't have to shout back the same obscenities. You don't have to pick up a rock or a stone or a bomb. You have your vote. That is more powerful than any obscenity, any word; more powerful than a bomb. That vote of yours is what makes this Government respond. That vote of yours can bring about the new toughminded approach to violence that threatens freedom.

Many people have asked me why I have been campaigning so hard in the past few weeks when my own name isn't on the ballot. "You are risking your prestige," they say. "After all, if some of the people you campaign for lose, you are going to be hurt." I am a lot less interested in my prestige than I am in the future of this country that we all love.

The American people, and the people of Arizona joined with them, elected me 2 years ago to do a job. I am trying to do that job, and I need help. I need help in the Congress to put across the programs that will make America strong enough to bring a full generation of peace abroad and strong enough to turn back the threat to peace and order at home.

My fellow Americans, America is a great country. Americans are a great people. And Americans together share a great future. I have seen this. I have felt this from an airplane hangar in Vermont to the warmth and good will of that vast majority of the people in San Jose.

I want to say, too, to young Americans, as I said last night and I repeat it here with so many young Americans: Night after night on the television screen you get an inaccurate picture of young Americans. You see the bomb throwers, the rock throwers, those shouting out the filthy words, trying to shout down speakers. And you get the impression that they are a majority of young Americans or maybe the leaders of the future.

Well, I have news for you. I have seen young Americans all over the country and those that appear on the television screens night after night, they are not a majority of young Americans today and they will not be the leaders of America tomorrow.

My fellow Americans, the message in the campaign of 1970 is very simple. It is this: Have faith in this great country. Have faith in your ability to improve this country with your vote. And have faith in a system that has resisted attack from the violent few for almost two centuries.

Nobody is going to tear this country down as long as you are ready to cast your vote to build this country up.

NOTE

The President spoke at 11:54 a.m. at Sky Harbor Airport. His remarks were videotaped and portions were broadcast on television on the evening of November 2, 1970, on time purchased by the Republican National Committee. An advance text was released on October 31.

Gerald R. Ford
Remarks to the Veterans of Foreign Wars Annual Convention August 19, 1974

COMMANDER RAY SODEN, GOVERNOR WALKER, MY FORMER MEMBERS OR FORMER COLLEAGUES OF THE UNITED STATES CONGRESS, MY FELLOW MEMBERS OF THE VETERANS OF FOREIGN WARS:

Let me express my deepest gratitude for your extremely warm welcome, and may I say to Mayor Daley and to all the wonderful people of Chicago who have done an unbelievable job in welcoming Betty and myself to Chicago, we are most grateful.

I have a sneaking suspicion that Mayor Daley and the people of Chicago knew that Betty was born in Chicago. Needless to say, I deeply appreciate your medal and the citation on my first trip out of Washington as your President. I hope that in the months ahead I can justify your faith in making the citation and the award available to me.

It is good to be back in Chicago, among people from all parts of our great Nation, to take part in this 75th annual convention of the Veterans of Foreign Wars.

As a proud member of Old Kent Post VFW 830, let me talk today about some of the work facing veterans—and all Americans—the issues of world peace and national unity.

Speaking of national unity, let me quickly point out that I am also a proud member of the American Legion and the AMVETS.

In a more somber note, this morning we heard the tragic news of the killiing of our American Ambassador to Cyprus.[1] He, too, gave his life in foreign wars. Let us offer our prayers and our condolences to his loved ones for his supreme sacrifice on behalf of all Americans.

As President and as a veteran, I want good relations with all veterans. We all proudly wore the same Nation's uniform and patriotically saluted the same flag. During my Administration, the door of my office will be open to veterans just as it was all my 25 years as a member of the Congress.

Today, I am happy to announce my intention to send the Senate the nomination of my personal friend and former Congressional colleague Dick Roudebush of Indiana—it seems to me you know what I am going to say—[laughter]—but I will finish the sentence—to be Administrator of the Veterans Administration.

As past national commander of the VFW, Roudy has served well as Deputy Administrator of the VA. He is a man who gets things done and, I am confident, will do a first-class job.

It seems to me that we should recognize the veteran is a human being, not just a "C" number to be processed by a computer system. We all know that the Government knew our name when we were called into service. This Administration is going to see to it that we still know your name and your problems. A veteran is a person, not just a digit in a computer system which more often than not goofs up.

I propose the VA take the best of our technology and the very best of our human capabilities and combine them. As President, I want no arrogance or indifference to any individual, veteran or not. Our Government's machinery exists to serve people, not to frustrate or humiliate them.

I don't like redtape. As a matter of fact, I don't like any kind of tapes.

Our great veterans hospitals, which will not lose their identity, must be the very best that medical skill and dedication can create. VA hospitals have made many great medical breakthroughs in the past. One of America's great challenges today is the older veteran. The VA medical and nursing care system for older people must become a showcase for the entire Nation. We can work together to achieve that end and humanize the VA.

But to achieve such progress, I intend to improve the management of the VA. We must get the most for our tax dollars. While supporting the new Administrator in maximum efforts to make the best use of funds available, I want Roudy to take a constructive new look at the VA's structure and the services that it renders to our veterans.

I think it is about time that we should stop thinking of veterans in terms of different wars. Some may march at a different pace than others. But we all march to the same drummer in the service of our Nation. I salute the men of many campaigns—of World War I, World War II, Korea, and Vietnam.

As minority leader of the House and recently as Vice President, I stated my strong conviction that unconditional, blanket amnesty for anyone who illegally evaded or fled military service is wrong. It *is* wrong.

Yet, in my first words as President of all the people, I acknowledged a Power, higher than the people, Who commands not only righteousness but love, not only justice but mercy.

Unlike my last two predecessors, I did not enter this office facing the terrible decisions of a foreign war, but like President Truman and President Lincoln before him, I found on my desk, where the buck stops, the urgent problem of how to bind up the Nation's wounds. And I intend to do that.

As a lawyer, I believe our American system of justice is fundamentally sound. As President, I will work within it.

As a former naval reservist, I believe our system of military justice is fundamentally sound. As Commander in Chief, I will work within it.

As a former Congressman who championed it, I believe the concept of an all-volunteer armed force is fundamentally sound and will work much better than peacetime conscription.

Accordingly, in my first week at the White House, I requested the Attorney General of the United States and the Secretary of Defense to report to me personally, before September 1, on the status of some 50,000 of our countrymen convicted, charged or under investigation, or still sought for violations of [the] Selective Service [Act] or the Uniform Code of Military Justice—offenses loosely described as desertion and draft-dodging.

These two Cabinet officers are to consult with other Government officials concerned and communicate me their unvarnished views and those of the full spectrum of American opinion on this controversial question, consolidating the known facts and legal precedents.

I will then decide how best to deal with the different kinds of cases—and there are differences. Decisions of my Administration will make any future penalties fit the seriousness of the individual's mistake.

Only a fraction of such cases I find in a quick review relate directly to Vietnam, from which the last American combatant was withdrawn over a year ago by President Nixon.

But all, in a sense, are casualties, still abroad or absent without leave from the real America.

I want them to come home if they want to *work* their way back.

One of the last of my official duties as Vice President, perhaps the hardest of all, was to present posthumously 14 Congressional Medals of Honor to the parents, widows, and children of fallen Vietnam heroes.

As I studied their records of supreme sacrifice, I kept thinking how young they were.

The few citizens of our country who, in my judgment, committed the supreme folly of shirking their duty at the expense of others, were also very young.

All of us who served in one war or another know very well that all wars are the glory and the agony of the young. In my judgment, these young Americans should have a second chance to contribute their fair share to the rebuilding of peace among ourselves and with all nations.

So, I am throwing the weight of my Presidency into the scales of justice on the side of leniency. I foresee their earned re-entry— *earned* re-entry—into a new atmosphere of hope, hard work, and mutual trust.

I will act promptly, fairly, and very firmly in the same spirit that guided Abraham Lincoln and Harry Truman. As I reject amnesty, so I reject revenge.

As men and women whose patriotism has been tested and proved—and yours has—I want your help and understanding. I ask all Americans who ever asked for goodness and mercy in their lives, who ever sought forgiveness for their trespasses, to join in rehabilitating all the casualties of the tragic conflict of the past.

Naturally, I am glad to see the VFW at this convention install a veteran of the Korean war, John Stang, as your new national commander-in-chief. And I compliment you and congratulate you as well as John.

We have struggled for years in America to overcome discrimination against younger Americans, against older Americans, against Americans of various creeds, religions, races and, yes, against women. I will not tolerate any discrimination against veterans, especially those who served honorably in the war in Vietnam.

I am deeply concerned about employment opportunities for the Vietnam-era veterans. We have had some success in placing veterans in the age span of 20 to 34, but the facts and figures show us that there are some tough problems in this category.

As of last month, the rate of unemployment for veterans between 20 and 24 was nearly 10 percent, much too high. The rate of unemployment for these young veterans who are members of minority groups was 19 percent. And far, far too many disabled veterans are still without jobs.

I can assure you, without hesitation or reservation, that this Administration puts a very high priority on aiding the men who bore the brunt of battle. If we can send men thousands and thousands of miles from home to fight in the rice paddies, certainly we can send them back to school and better jobs at home.

I am consequently considering the veterans education bill in this light. But your Government, of necessity, has to be constrained by other considerations as well. We are all soldiers in a war against brutal inflation. The veterans education bill more than likely will come before me very shortly for action. It comes when I am working hard, along with others from the Congress, labor, management, and otherwise, on a nonpartisan battle against excessive Government spending.

America today is fighting for its economic life. The facts are that uncontrolled inflation could destroy the fabric and the foundation of America, and I will not hesitate to veto any legislation to try and control inflationary excesses. I am open to conciliation and compromise on the total amount authorized so that we can protect [veteran] trainees and all other Americans against the rising cost of living.

I commend not only the past service of veterans but also the continuing involvement of many of you in the National Guard and Reserve forces. With current manpower reductions in the active duty Army, Navy, Air Force, and Marines, the Commander in Chief must, of necessity, place continuing reliance on the readiness of our National Guard and Reserves. And I intend to put muscle into this program.

Peace—it depends upon the strength and readiness of our defenses. And I will support every sensible measure to enhance the morale and the combat readiness of our Armed Forces.

The United States, our allies, and our friends around the world must maintain strength and resolve. Potential adversaries obviously watch the state of our readiness and the strength of our will. I will offer them no temptations.

America is not the policeman of the world, but we continue to be the backbone of a free world collective security setup.

Just as America will maintain its nuclear deterrent strength, we will never fall behind in negotiations to control—and hopefully reduce—this threat to mankind. A great nation is not only strong but wise, not only principled but purposeful. A fundamental purpose of our Nation must be to achieve peace through strength and meaningful negotiations.

Our good will must never be construed as a lack of will. And I know that I can count on you and the families of each and every one of you. Peace and security require preparedness and dedication.

You have experienced war firsthand. I want to make certain and positive that Washington never sends another tragic telegram. The list of mourners is already far too long. So is the list of those who wait and wonder—the families of those missing in action. I will never forget them.

Together we are going forward to tackle future problems, including the scourge of inflation which is today our Nation's public enemy number one. Our task is not easy. But I have faith in America. Through our system of democracy and free enterprise, the United States has achieved remarkable, unbelievable progress. We have shared our plenty with all mankind.

This is the same Nation that transcended inflations and recessions, slumps and booms, to move forward to even higher levels of prosperity and productivity. This is the same Nation that emerged from the smoke of Pearl Harbor on December 7, 1941, to change its own destiny and the history of the world—and for the better.

During the first few months that I was Vice President, I traveled some 118,000 miles and visited 40 of our great States. What I saw and what I heard gave me renewed inspiration. It made me proud, proud of my country. It sustains me now.

Our great Republic is nearly 200 years old, but in many, many ways we are just getting started. Most Americans have faith in the American system. Let us now work for America, in which all Americans can take an even greater pride. I am proud of America. You are proud of America. We should be proud to be Americans.

Thank you very much.

NOTE

The President spoke at 11:38 a.m. at the Conrad Hilton Hotel. Prior to his remarks, the President was presented the VFW Citizenship Gold Medal Award by Ray R. Soden, commander-in-chief of the Veterans of Foreign Wars.

1. Ambassador Rodger P. Davies was killed by a sniper during a demonstration at the American Embassy in Nicosia on August 19.

    On the same day, the White House issued the following statement by Press Secretary J. F. terHorst:

    "The President was shocked and deeply saddened by the death of Ambassador Davies in Nicosia today. This tragic incident emphasizes the urgent need for an end to the violence on Cyprus and an immediate return to negotiations for a peaceful settlement."

Jimmy Carter
Rescue Attempt for American Hostages in Iran
April 25, 1980

Late yesterday, I cancelled a carefully planned operation which was underway in Iran to position our rescue team for later withdrawal of American hostages, who have been held captive there since November 4. Equipment failure in the rescue helicopters made it necessary to end the mission.

As our team was withdrawing, after my order to do so, two of our American aircraft collided on the ground following a refueling operation in a remote desert location in Iran. Other information about this rescue mission will be made available to the American people when it is appropriate to do so.

There was no fighting; there was no combat. But to my deep regret, eight of the crewmen of the two aircraft which collided were killed, and several other Americans were hurt in the accident. Our people were immediately airlifted from Iran. Those who were injured have gotten medical treatment, and all of them are expected to recover.

No knowledge of this operation by any Iranian officials or authorities was evident to us until several hours after all Americans were withdrawn from Iran.

Our rescue team knew and I knew that the operation was certain to be difficult and it was certain to be dangerous. We were all convinced that if and when the rescue operation had been commenced that it had an excellent chance of success. They were all volunteers; they were all highly trained. I met with their leaders before they went on this operation. They knew then what hopes of mine and of all Americans they carried with them.

To the families of those who died and who were wounded, I

want to express the admiration I feel for the courage of their loved ones and the sorrow that I feel personally for their sacrifice.

The mission on which they were embarked was a humanitarian mission. It was not directed against Iran; it was not directed against the people of Iran. It was not undertaken with any feeling of hostility toward Iran or its people. It has caused no Iranian casualties.

Planning for this rescue effort began shortly after our Embassy was seized, but for a number of reasons, I waited until now to put those rescue plans into effect. To be feasible, this complex operation had to be the product of intensive planning and intensive training and repeated rehearsal. However, a resolution of this crisis through negotiations and with voluntary action on the part of the Iranian officials was obviously then, has been, and will be preferable.

This rescue attempt had to wait my judgment that the Iranian authorities could not or would not resolve this crisis on their own initiative. With the steady unraveling of authority in Iran and the mounting dangers that were posed to the safety of the hostages themselves and the growing realization that their early release was highly unlikely, I made a decision to commence the rescue operations plans.

This attempt became a necessity and a duty. The readiness of our team to undertake the rescue made it completely practicable. Accordingly, I made the decision to set our long-developed plans into operation. I ordered this rescue mission prepared in order to safeguard American lives, to protect America's national interests, and to reduce the tensions in the world that have been caused among many nations as this crisis has continued.

It was my decision to attempt the rescue operation. It was my decision to cancel it when problems developed in the placement of our rescue team for a future rescue operation. The responsibility is fully my own.

In the aftermath of the attempt, we continue to hold the Government of Iran responsible for the safety and for the early release of the American hostages, who have been held so long. The United States remains determined to bring about their safe release at the earliest date possible.

As President, I know that our entire Nation feels the deep gratitude I feel for the brave men who were prepared to rescue their fellow Americans from captivity. And as President, I also know that the Nation shares not only my disappointment that the rescue effort could not be mounted, because of mechanical difficulties, but also my determination to persevere and to bring all of our hostages home to freedom.

We have been disappointed before. We will not give up in our efforts. Throughout this extraordinarily difficult period, we have pursued and will continue to pursue every possible avenue to secure the release of the hostages. In these efforts, the support of the American people and of our friends throughout the world has been a most crucial element. That support of other nations is even more important now.

We will seek to continue, along with other nations and with the officials of Iran, a prompt resolution of the crisis without any loss of life and through peaceful and diplomatic means.

Thank you very much.

NOTE

The President spoke at 7 a.m. from the Oval Office at the White House. His remarks were broadcast live on radio and television.

Chapter 4 The President and the World

Presidential leadership of domestic affairs is often confounded because the "good guys" and the "bad guys" are all represented in Congress. But foreign affairs provide a president with substantially more latitude, and many presidents have found that their lasting contributions (for better or worse) have been foreign rather than domestic. The six speeches in this section represent presidents' efforts to place their stamp upon international relations.

Less is remembered of the State of the Union in 1823 beyond the several paragraphs that would later become known as the Monroe Doctrine. President James Monroe was responding to persistent threats to the independence of nations in the Western Hemisphere. Although it was not originally intended as a sweeping doctrine of American foreign policy, later presidents have commonly interpreted his remarks to that end.

Woodrow Wilson believed that World War I was the war to end wars, and he proposed a League of Nations to make certain of it. Faced with strong congressional opposition, Wilson campaigned across the nation by rail in September of 1919 to mobilize public support for the League. While on the tour Wilson sufferred a crippling stroke, from which he never fully recovered. Although the League was formed, Wilson suffered the humiliation of having his country vote not to join his League of Nations.

President Kennedy's addresses about American-Soviet relations can seem like a rollercoaster to the contemporary reader. Nowhere is this more evident than in his two foreign policy speeches of June, 1963. In the first of these (a commencement address at American University), Kennedy outlined his hope for world peace, with an end to the cold war and the arms race.

Although regarded as a classic foreign policy statement, it was crowded off of the nation's front pages by the more dramatic desegregation activities at the University of Alabama. Only sixteen days later, Kennedy visited Berlin and addressed an audience at the newly-erected Wall. Emotionally affected by the wall, Kennedy delivered a brief, impassioned speech which was far from conciliatory toward the Kremlin.

Whereas Johnson needed to justify the escalation of American involvement in Vietnam, Richard Nixon needed to find a way out without seeming to give in to anti-war protestors. His plan was Vietnamization of the Vietnamese war. In the process he plainly spelled out the issues, the sides, and the alternatives—as he saw them. Most notable was his creation of the "Great Silent Majority" of support—anyone *not* marching and protesting *supported* his program. This lengthy and rather plodding speech has been the subject of perhaps more rhetorical analyses than any contemporary speech with the possible exception of Martin Luther King's "I Have a Dream". Indeed, it was initial televised commentaries about this speech that provoked Vice-President Spiro Agnew's attack on the network news organizations.

Although Theodore Roosevelt was largely responsible for building the Panama Canal and the Johnson, Nixon, and Ford Administrations were instrumental in negotiating treaties providing for Panamanian control of the canal while guaranteeing American access to it; it fell to Jimmy Carter to sell these bipartisan treaties to Congress and the public. This was not an easy task. The canal became for many a symbol of American dominance, while to others it represented an arrogant, bullying foreign policy. Sen. S. I. Hayakawa (R. CA.) is reputed to have explained his position as: "We ought to keep it. We stole it fair and square." The canal became a focal issue for the emergent New Right which employed mass mailings and the distribution of Illinois Congressman Phillip Crane's *Surrender in Panama*. Carter's speech was, literally, a fireside chat designed to allay fears. The speech is a stark contrast to the threatening tone of most of the other foreign policy speeches. Ironically, although the treaties were ultimately approved, the New Right emerged as a force to be reckoned with and President Carter's ability to lead the nation came under close scrutiny.

James Monroe
Seventh Annual Message
Washington, December 2, 1823

FELLOW CITIZENS OF THE SENATE AND HOUSE OF REPRESENTATIVES:

Many important subjects will claim your attention during the present session, of which I shall endeavor to give, in aid of your deliberations, a just idea in this communication. I undertake this duty with diffidence, from the vast extent of the interests on which I have to treat and of their great importance to every portion of our Union. I enter on it with zeal from a thorough conviction that there never was a period since the establishment of our Revolution when, regarding the condition of the civilized world and its bearing on us, there was greater necessity for devotion in the public servants to their respective duties, or for virtue, patriotism, and union in our constituents.

Meeting in you a new Congress, I deem it proper to present this view of public affairs in greater detail than might otherwise be necessary. I do it, however, with peculiar satisfaction, from a knowledge that in this respect I shall comply more fully with the sound principles of our Government. The people being with us exclusively the sovereign, it is indispensable that full information be laid before them on all important subjects, to enable them to exercise that high power with complete effect. If kept in the dark, they must be incompetent to it. We are all liable to error, and those who are engaged in the management of public affairs are more subject to excitement and to be led astray by their particular interests and passions than the great body of our constituents, who, living at home in the pursuit of their ordinary avocations, are calm but deeply interested spectators of events and of the conduct of those who are parties to them. To the people every department of the Government and every individual in each are responsible, and the more full their information the better they can judge of the wisdom of the policy pursued and of the conduct of each in regard to it. From their dispassionate judgment much aid may always be obtained, while their approbation will form the greatest incentive and most gratifying reward for virtuous actions, and the dread of their censure the best security against the abuse of their confidence. Their interests in all vital questions are the same, and the bond, by sentiment as well as by interest, will be proportionably strengthened as they are better informed of the real state of public affairs, especially in difficult conjunctures. It is by such knowledge that local prejudices and jealousies are surmounted, and that a national policy, extending its fostering care and protection to all the great interests of our Union, is formed and steadily adhered to.

A precise knowledge of our relations with foreign powers as respects our negotiations and transactions with each is thought to be particularly necessary. Equally necessary is it that we should form a just estimate of our resources, revenue, and progress in every kind of improvement connected with the national prosperity and public defense. It is by rendering justice to other nations that we may expect it from them. It is by our ability to resent injuries and redress wrongs that we may avoid them.

The commissioners under the fifth article of the treaty of Ghent, having disagreed in their opinions respecting that portion of the boundary between the Territories of the United States and of Great Britain the establishment of which had been submitted to them, have made their respective reports in compliance with that article, that the same might be referred to the decision of a friendly power. It being manifest, however, that it would be difficult, if not impossible, for any power to perform that office without great delay and much inconvenience to itself, a proposal has been made by this Government, and acceded to by that of Great Britain, to endeavor to establish that boundary by amicable negotiation. It appearing from long experience that no satisfactory arrangement could be formed of the commercial intercourse between the United States and the British colonies in this hemisphere by legislative acts while each party pursued its own course without agreement or concert with the other, a proposal has been made to the British

Government to regulate this commerce by treaty, as it has been to arrange in like manner the just claim of the citizens of the United States inhabiting the States and Territories bordering on the lakes and rivers which empty into the St. Lawrence to the navigation of that river to the ocean. For these and other objects of high importance to the interests of both parties a negotiation has been opened with the British Government which it is hoped will have a satisfactory result.

The commissioners under the sixth and seventh articles of the treaty of Ghent having successfully closed their labors in relation to the sixth, have proceeded to the discharge of those relating to the seventh. Their progress in the extensive survey required for the performance of their duties justifies the presumption that it will be completed in the ensuing year.

The negotiation which had been long depending with the French Government on several important subjects, and particularly for a just indemnity for losses sustained in the late wars by the citizens of the United States under unjustifiable seizures and confiscations of their property, has not as yet had the desired effect. As this claim rests on the same principle with others which have been admitted by the French Government, it is not perceived on what just ground it can be rejected. A minister will be immediately appointed to proceed to France and resume the negotiation on this and other subjects which may arise between the two nations.

At the proposal of the Russian Imperial Government, made through the minister of the Emperor residing here, a full power and instructions have been transmitted to the minister of the United States at St. Petersburg to arrange by amicable negotiation the respective rights and interests of the two nations on the northwest coast of this continent. A similar proposal had been made by His Imperial Majesty to the Government of Great Britain, which has likewise been acceded to. The Government of the United States has been desirous by this friendly proceeding of manifesting the great value which they have invariably attached to the friendship of the Emperor and their solicitude to cultivate the best understanding with his Government. In the discussions to which this interest has given rise and in the arrangement by which they may terminate the occasion has been judged proper for asserting, as a principle in which the rights and interests of the United States are involved, that the American continents, by the free and independent condition which they have assumed and maintain, are henceforth not to be considered as subjects for future colonization by any European powers.

Since the close of the last session of Congress the commissioners and arbitrators for ascertaining and determining the amount of indemnification which may be due to citizens of the United States under the decision of His Imperial Majesty the Emperor of Russia, in conformity to the convention concluded at St. Petersburg on the 12th of July 1822, have assembled in this city, and organized themselves as a board for the performance of the duties assigned to them by that treaty. The commission constituted under the eleventh article of the treaty of the 22d of February, 1819, between the United States and Spain is also in session here, and as the term of three years limited by the treaty for the execution of the trust will expire before the period of the next regular meeting of Congress, the attention of the Legislature will be drawn to the measures which may be necessary to accomplish the objects for which the commission was instituted.

In compliance with a resolution of the House of Representatives adopted at their last session, instructions have been given to all the ministers of the United States accredited to the powers of Europe and America to propose the proscription of the African slave trade by classing it under the denomination, and inflicting on its perpetrators the punishment, of piracy. Should this proposal be acceded to, it is not doubted that this odious and criminal practice will be promptly and entirely suppressed. It is earnestly hoped that it will be acceded to, from the firm belief that it is the most effectual expedient that can be adopted for the purpose.

At the commencement of the recent war between France and Spain it was declared by the French Government that it would grant no commissions to privateers, and that neither the commerce of Spain herself nor of neutral nations should be molested by the naval force of France, except in the breach of a lawful blockade. This declaration, which appears to have been faithfully carried into effect, concurring with principles proclaimed and cherished by the United States from the first establishment of their independence, suggested the hope that the time had arrived when the proposal for adopting it as a permanent and invariable rule in all future maritime wars might meet the favorable consideration of the great European powers. Instructions have accordingly been given to our ministers with France, Russia, and Great Britain to make those proposals to their respective Governments, and when the friends of humanity reflect on the essential amelioration to the condition of the human race which would result from the abolition of private war on the sea and on the great facility by which it might be accomplished, requiring only the consent of a few sovereigns, an earnest hope is indulged that these overtures will meet with an attention animated by the spirit in which they were made, and that they will ultimately be successful.

The ministers who were appointed to the Republics of Colombia and Buenos Ayres during the last session of Congress proceeded shortly afterwards to their destinations. Of their arrival there official intelligence has not yet been received. The minister appointed to the Republic of Chile will sail in a few days. An early appointment will also be made to Mexico. A minister has been received from Colombia, and the other governments have been informed that ministers, or diplomatic agents of inferior grade, would be received from each, accordingly as they might prefer the one or the other.

The minister appointed to Spain proceeded soon after his appointment for Cadiz, the residence of the Sovereign to whom he was accredited. In approaching that port the frigate which conveyed him was warned off by the commander of the French squadron by which it was blockaded and not permitted to enter, although apprised by the captain of the frigate of the public character of the person whom he had on board, the landing of whom was the sole object of his proposed entry. This act, being considered an infringement of the rights of ambassadors and of nations, will form a just cause of complaint to the Government of France against the officer by whom it was committed.

The actual condition of the public finances more than realizes the favorable anticipations that were entertained of it at the opening of the last session of Congress. On the 1st of January there was a balance in the Treasury of $4,237,427.55. From that time to the 30th September the receipts amounted to upward of $16,100,000, and the expenditures to $11,400,000. During the fourth quarter of the year it is estimated that the receipts will at least equal the expenditures, and that there will remain in the Treasury on the 1st day of January next a surplus of nearly $9,000,000.

On the 1st of January, 1825, a large amount of the war debt and a part of the Revolutionary debt become redeemable. Additional portions of the former will continue to become redeemable annually until the year 1835. It is believed, however, that if the United States remain at peace the whole of that debt may be redeemed by the ordinary revenue of those years during that period under the provision of the act of March 3, 1817, creating the sinking fund, and in that case the only part of the debt that will remain after the year 1835 will be the $7,000,000 of 5 per cent stock subscribed to the Bank of the United States, and the 3 per cent Revolutionary debt, amounting to $13,296,099.06, both of which are redeemable at the pleasure of the Government.

The state of the Army in its organization and discipline has been gradually improving for several years, and has now attained a high degree of perfection. The military disbursements have been regularly made and the accounts regularly and promptly rendered for settlement. The supplies of various descriptions have been of good quality, and regularly issued at all of the posts. A system of economy and accountability has been introduced into every branch of the service which admits of little additional improvement. This desirable state has been attained by the act reorganizing the staff of the Army, passed on the 14th of April, 1818.

The moneys appropriated for fortifications have been regularly and economically applied, and all the works advanced as rapidly as the amount appropriated would admit. Three important works will be completed in the course of this year—that is, Fort Washington, Fort Delaware, and the fort at the Rigolets, in Louisiana.

The Board of Engineers and the Topographical Corps have been in constant and active service in surveying the coast and projecting the works necessary for its defense.

The Military Academy has attained a degree of perfection in its discipline and instruction equal, as is believed, to any institution of its kind in any country.

The money appropriated for the use of the Ordnance Department has been regularly and economically applied. The fabrication of arms at the national armories and by contract with the Department has been gradually improving in quality and cheapness. It is believed that their quality is now such as to admit of but little improvement.

The completion of the fortifications renders it necessary that there should be a suitable appropriation for the purpose of fabricating the cannon and carriages necessary for those works.

Under the appropriation of $5,000 for exploring the Western waters for the location of a site for a Western armory, a commission was constituted, consisting of Colonel McRee, Colonel Lee, and Captain Talcott, who have been engaged in exploring the country. They have not yet reported the result of their labors, but it is believed that they will be prepared to do it at an early part of the session of Congress.

During the month of June last General Ashley and his party, who were trading under a license from the Government, were attacked by the Ricarees while peaceably trading with the Indians at their request. Several of the party were killed and wounded and their property taken or destroyed.

Colonel Leavenworth, who commanded Fort Atkinson, at the Council Bluffs, the most western post, apprehending that the hostile spirit of the Ricarees would extend to other tribes in that quarter, and that thereby the lives of the traders on the Missouri and the peace of the frontier would be endangered, took immediate measures to check the evil.

With a detachment of the regiment stationed at the Bluffs he successfully attacked the Ricaree village, and it is hoped that such an impression has been made on them as well as on the other tribes on the Missouri as will prevent a recurrence of future hostility.

The report of the Secretary of War, which is herewith transmitted, will exhibit in greater detail the condition of the Department in its various branches, and the progress which has been made in its administration during the three first quarters of the year.

I transmit a return of the militia of the several States according to the last reports which have been made by the proper officers in each to the Department of War. By reference to this return it will be seen that it is not complete, although great exertions have been made to make it so. As the defense and even the liberties of the country must depend in times of imminent danger on the militia, it is of the highest importance that it be well organized, armed, and disciplined throughout the Union. The report of the Secretary of War shews the progress made during the three first quarters of the present year by the application of the fund appropriated for arming the militia. Much difficulty is found in distributing the arms according to the act of Congress providing for it from the failure of the proper departments in many of the States to make regular returns. The act of May 12, 1820, provides that the system of tactics and regulations of the various corps of the Regular Army shall be extended to the militia. This act has been very imperfectly executed from the want of uniformity in the organization of the militia, proceeding from the defects of the system itself, and especially in its application to that main arm of the public defense. It is thought that this important subject in all its branches merits the attention of Congress.

The report of the Secretary of the Navy, which is now communicated, furnishes an account of the administration of that Department for the three first quarters of the present year, with the progress made in augmenting the Navy, and the manner in which the vessels in commission have been employed.

The usual force has been maintained in the Mediterranean Sea, the Pacific Ocean, and along the Atlantic coast, and has afforded the necessary protection to our commerce in those seas.

In the West Indies and the Gulf of Mexico our naval force has been augmented by the addition of several small vessels provided for by the " act authorizing an additional naval force for the suppression of piracy," passed by Congress at their last session. That armament has been eminently successful in the accomplishment of its object. The piracies by which our commerce in the neighborhood of the island of Cuba had been afflicted have been repressed and the confidence of our merchants in a great measure restored.

The patriotic zeal and enterprise of Commodore Porter, to whom the command of the expedition was confided, has been fully seconded by the officers and men under his command. And in reflecting with high satisfaction on the honorable manner in which they have sustained the reputation of their country and its Navy, the sentiment is alloyed only by a concern that in the fulfillment of that arduous service the diseases incident to the season and to the climate in which it was discharged have deprived the nation of many useful lives, and among them of several officers of great promise.

In the month of August a very malignant fever made its appearance at Thompsons Island, which threatened the destruction of our station there. Many perished, and the commanding officer was severely attacked. Uncertain as to his fate and knowing that most of the medical officers had been rendered incapable of discharging their duties, it was thought expedient to send to that post an officer of rank and experience, with several skillful surgeons, to ascertain the origin of the fever and the probability of its recurrence there in future seasons; to furnish every assistance to those who were suffering and, if practicable, to avoid the necessity of abandoning so important a station. Commodore Rodgers, with a promptitude which did him honor, cheerfully accepted that trust, and has discharged it in the manner anticipated from his skill and patriotism. Before his arrival Commodore Porter, with the greater part of the squadron, had removed from the island and returned to the United States in consequence of the prevailing sickness. Much useful information has, however, been obtained as to the state of the island and great relief afforded to those who had been necessarily left there.

Although our expedition, cooperating with an invigorated administration of the government of the island of Cuba, and with the corresponding active exertions of a British naval force in the same seas, have almost entirely destroyed the unlicensed piracies from that island, the success of our exertions has not been equally effectual to suppress the same crime, under other pretenses and colors, in the neighboring island of Porto Rico. They have been committed there under the abusive issue of Spanish commissions. At an early period of the present year remonstrances were made to the governor of that island, by an agent who was sent for the purpose, against those outrages on the peaceful commerce of the United States, of which many had occurred. That officer, professing his own want of authority to make satisfaction for our just complaints, answered only by a reference of them to the Government of Spain. The minister of the United States to that court was specially instructed to urge the necessity of the immediate and effectual interposition of that Government, directing restitution and indemnity for wrongs already committed and interdicting the repetition of them. The minister, as has been seen, was debarred access to the Spanish Government, and in the meantime several new cases of flagrant outrage have occurred, and citizens of the United States in the island of Porto Rico have suffered, and others been threatened with assassination for asserting their unquestionable rights even before the lawful tribunals of the country.

The usual orders have been given to all our public ships to seize American vessels engaged in the slave trade and bring them in for adjudication, and I have the gratification to state that not one so employed has been discovered, and there is good reason to believe that our flag is now seldom, if at all, disgraced by that traffic.

It is a source of great satisfaction that we are always enabled to recur to the conduct of our Navy with pride and commendation. As a means of national defense it enjoys the public confidence, and is steadily assuming additional importance. It is submitted whether a more efficient and equally economical organization of it might not in several respects be effected. It is supposed that higher grades than now exist by law would be useful. They would afford well-merited rewards to those who have long and faithfully served their country, present the best incentives to good conduct, and the best means of insuring a proper discipline; destroy the inequality in that respect between military and naval services, and relieve our officers from many inconveniences and mortifications which occur when our vessels meet those of other nations, ours being the only service in which such grades do not exist.

A report of the Postmaster General, which accompanies this communication, will shew the present state of the Post-Office Department and its general operations for some years past.

There is established by law 88,600 miles of post-roads, on which the mail is now transported 85,700 miles, and contracts have been made for its transportation on all the established routes, with one or two exceptions. There are 5,240 post-offices in the Union, and as many postmasters. The gross amount of postage which accrued from the 1st July, 1822, to the 1st July, 1823, was $1,114,345.12. During the same period the expenditures of the Post-Office Department amounted to $1,169,885.51, and consisted of the following items, viz: Compensation to postmasters, $353,995.98; incidental expenses, $30,866.37; transportation of the mail, $ 784,600.08; payments into the Treasury, $423.08. On the 1st of July last there was due to the Department from postmasters $135,245.28; from *late* postmasters and contractors, $256,749.31; making a total amount of balances due to the Department of $391,994.59. These balances embrace all delinquencies of postmasters and contractors which have taken place since the organization of the Department. There was due by the Department to contractors on the 1st of July last $26,548.64.

The transportation of the mail within five years past has been greatly extended, and the expenditures of the Department proportionably increased. Although the postage which has accrued within the last three years has fallen short of the expenditures $262,821.46, it appears that collections have been made from the outstanding balances to meet the principal part of the current demands.

It is estimated that not more than $250,000 of the above balances can be collected, and that a considerable part of this sum can only be realized by a resort to legal process. Some improvement in the receipts for postage is expected. A prompt attention to the collection of moneys received by postmasters, it is believed, will enable the Department to continue its operations without aid from the Treasury, unless the expenditures shall be increased by the establishment of new mail routes.

A revision of some parts of the post-office law may be necessary; and it is submitted whether it would not be proper to provide for the appointment of postmasters, where the compensation exceeds a certain amount, by nomination to the Senate, as other officers of the General Government are appointed.

Having communicated my views to Congress at the commencement of the last session respecting the encouragement which ought to be given to our manufactures and the principle on which it should be founded, I have only to add that those views remain unchanged, and that the present state of those countries with which we have the most immediate political relations and greatest commercial intercourse tends to confirm them. Under this impression I recommend a review of the tariff for the purpose of affording such additional protection to those articles which we are prepared to manufacture, or which are more immediately connected with the defense and independence of the country.

The actual state of the public accounts furnishes additional evidence of the efficiency of the present system of accountability in relation to the public expenditure. Of the moneys drawn from the Treasury since the 4th March, 1817, the sum remaining unaccounted for on the 30th of September last is more than a million and a half of dollars less than on the 30th of September preceding; and during the same period a reduction of nearly a million of dollars has been made in the amount of the unsettled accounts for moneys advanced previously to the 4th of March, 1817. It will be obvious that in proportion as the mass of accounts of the latter description is diminished by settlement the difficulty of settling the residue is increased from the consideration that in many instances it can be obtained only by legal process. For more precise details on this subject I refer to a report from the First Comptroller of the Treasury.

The sum which was appropriated at the last session for the repairs of the Cumberland road has been applied with good effect to that object. A final report has not yet been received from the agent who was appointed to superintend it. As soon as it is received it shall be communicated to Congress.

Many patriotic and enlightened citizens who have made the subject an object of particular investigation have suggested an improvement of still greater importance. They are of opinion that the waters of the Chesapeake and Ohio may be connected together by one continued canal, and at an expense far short of the value and importance of the object to be obtained. If this could be accomplished it is impossible to calculate the beneficial consequences which would result from it. A great portion of the produce of the very fertile country through which it would pass would find a market through that channel. Troops might be moved with great facility in war, with cannon and every kind of munition, and in either direction. Connecting the Atlantic with the Western country in a line passing through the seat of the National Government, it would contribute essentially to strengthen the bond of union itself. Believing as I do that Congress possess the right to appropriate money for such a national object (the jurisdiction remaining to the States through which the canal would pass), I submit it to your consideration whether it may not be advisable to authorize by an adequate appropriation the employment of a suitable number of the officers of the Corps of Engineers to examine the unexplored ground during the next season and to report their opinion thereon. It will likewise be proper to extend their examination to the several routes through which the waters of the Ohio may be connected by canals with those of Lake Erie.

As the Cumberland road will require annual repairs, and Congress have not thought it expedient to recommend to the States an amendment to the Constitution for the purpose of vesting in the United States a power to adopt and execute a system of internal improvement, it is also submitted to your consideration whether it may not be expedient to authorize the Executive to enter into an arrangement with the several States through which the road passes to establish tolls, each within its limits, for the purpose of defraying the expense of future repairs and of providing also by suitable penalties for its protection against future injuries.

The act of Congress of the 7th of May, 1822, appropriated the sum of $22,700 for the purpose of erecting two piers as a shelter for vessels from ice near Cape Henlopen, Delaware Bay. To effect the object of the act the officers of the Board of Engineers, with Commodore Bainbridge, were directed to prepare plans and estimates of piers sufficient to answer the purpose intended by the act. It appears by their report, which accompanies the documents from the War Department, that the appropriation is not adequate to the purpose intended; and as the piers would be of great service both to the navigation of the Delaware Bay and the protection of vessels on the adjacent parts of the coast, I submit for the consideration of Congress whether additional and sufficient appropriation should not be made.

The Board of Engineers were also directed to examine and survey the entrance of the harbor of the port of Presquille, in Pennsylvania, in order to make an estimate of the expense of removing the obstructions to the entrance, with a plan of the best mode of effecting the same, under the appropriation for that purpose by act of Congress passed 3d of March last. The report of the Board accompanies the papers from the War Department, and is submitted for the consideration of Congress.

A strong hope has been long entertained, founded on the heroic struggle of the Greeks, that they would succeed in their contest and resume their equal station among the nations of the earth. It is believed that the whole civilized world take a deep interest in their welfare. Although no power has declared in their favor, yet none, according to our information, has taken part against them. Their cause and their name have protected them from dangers which might ere this have overwhelmed any other people. The ordinary calculations of interest and of acquisition with a view to aggrandizement, which mingles so much in the transactions of nations, seem to have had no effect in regard to them. From the facts which have come to our knowledge there is good cause to believe that their enemy has lost forever all dominion over them; that Greece will become again an independent nation. That she may obtain that rank is the object of our most ardent wishes.

It was stated at the commencement of the last session that a great effort was then making in Spain and Portugal to improve the condition of the people of those countries, and that it appeared to be conducted with extraordinary moderation. It need scarcely be remarked that the result has been so far very different from what was then anticipated. Of events in that quarter of the globe, with which we have so much intercourse and from which we derive our origin, we have always been anxious and interested spectators. The citizens of the United States cherish sentiments the most friendly in favor of the liberty and happiness of their fellow-men on that side of the Atlantic. In the wars of the European powers in matters relating to themselves we have never taken any part, nor does it comport with our policy so to do. It is only when our rights are invaded or seriously menaced that we resent injuries or make preparation for our defense. With the movements in this hemisphere we are of necessity more immediately connected, and by causes which must be obvious to all enlightened and impartial observers. The political system of the allied powers is essentially different in this respect from that of America. This difference proceeds from that which exists in their respective Governments; and to the defense of our own, which has been achieved by the loss of so much blood and treasure, and matured by the wisdom of their most enlightened citizens, and under which we have enjoyed unexampled felicity, this whole nation is devoted. We owe it, therefore, to candor and to the amicable relations existing between the United States and those powers to declare that we should consider any attempt on their part to extend their system to any portion of this hemisphere as dangerous to our peace and safety. With the existing colonies or dependencies of any European power we have not interfered and shall not interfere. But with the Governments who have declared their independence and maintained it, and whose independence we have, on great consideration and on just principles, acknowledged, we could not view any interposition for the purpose of oppressing them, or controlling in any other manner their destiny, by any European power in any other light than as the manifestation of an unfriendly disposition toward the United States. In the war between those new Governments and Spain we declared our neutrality at the time of their recognition, and to this we have adhered, and shall continue to adhere, provided no change shall occur which, in the judgment of the competent authorities of this Government, shall make a corresponding change on the part of the United States indispensable to their security.

The late events in Spain and Portugal shew that Europe is still unsettled. Of this important fact no stronger proof can be adduced than that the allied powers should have thought it proper, on any principle satisfactory to themselves, to have interposed by force in the internal concerns of Spain. To what extent such interposition may be carried, on the same principle, is a question in which all independent powers whose governments differ from theirs are interested, even those most remote, and surely none more so than the United States. Our policy in regard to Europe, which was adopted at an early stage of the wars which have so long agitated that quarter of the globe, nevertheless remains the same, which is, not to interfere in the internal concerns of any of its powers; to consider the government *de facto* as the legitimate government for us; to cultivate friendly relations with it, and to preserve those relations by a frank, firm, and manly policy, meeting in all instances the just claims of every power, submitting to injuries from none. But in regard to those continents circumstances are eminently and conspicuously different. It is impossible that the allied powers should extend their political system to any portion of either continent without endangering our peace and happiness; nor can anyone believe that our southern brethren, if left to themselves, would adopt it of their own accord. It is equally impossible, therefore, that we should behold such interposition in any form with indifference. If we look to the comparative strength and resources of Spain and those new Governments, and their distance from each other, it must be obvious that she can never subdue them. It is still the true policy of the United States to leave the parties to themselves, in the hope that other powers will pursue the same course.

If we compare the present conditions of our Union with its actual state at the close of our Revolution, the history of the world furnishes no example of a progress in improvement in all the important circumstances which constitute the happiness of a nation which bears any resemblance to it. At the first epoch our population did not exceed 3,000,000. By the last census it amounted to about 10,000,000, and, what is more extraordinary, it is almost altogether native, for the immigration from other countries has been inconsiderable. At the first epoch half the territory within our acknowledged limits was uninhabited and a wilderness. Since then new territory has been acquired of vast extent, comprising within it many rivers, particularly the Mississippi, the navigation of which to the ocean was of the highest importance to the original States. Over this territory our population has expanded in every direction, and new States have been established almost equal in number to those which formed the first bond of our Union. This expansion of our population and accession of new States to our Union have had the happiest effect on all its highest interests. That it has eminently augmented our resources and added to our strength and respectability as a power is admitted by all. But it is not in these important circumstances only that this happy effect is felt. It is manifest that by enlarging the basis of our system and increasing the number of States the system itself has been greatly strengthened in both its branches. Consolidation and disunion have thereby been rendered equally impracticable. Each Government, confiding in its own strength, has less to apprehend from the other, and in consequence each, enjoying a greater freedom of action, is rendered more efficient for all the purposes for which it was instituted. It is unnecessary to treat here of the vast improvement made in the system itself by the adoption of this Constitution and of its happy effect in elevating the character and in protecting the rights of the nation as well as of individuals. To what, then, do we owe these blessings? It is known to all that we derive them from the excellence of our institutions. Ought we not, then, to adopt every measure which may be necessary to perpetuate them?

Woodrow Wilson
The League of Nations
September 15, 1919

MR. JACKSON, LADIES AND GENTLEMEN:

As I return to Portland I cannot help remembering that I learned a great deal in Oregon. When I was a teacher I used to prove to my own satisfaction—I do not know whether it was to the satisfaction of my classes or not—that the initiative and referendum would not work. I came to Oregon to find that they did work, and have since been apologizing for my earlier opinion. Because I have always taken this attitude toward facts, that I never let them get me if I see them coming first. There is nothing I respect so much as a fact. There is nothing that is so formidable as a fact, and the real difficulty in all political reform is to know whether you can translate your theories into facts or not, whether you can safely pick out the operative ideas and leave aside the inoperative ideas. For I think you will all agree with me that the whole progress of human affairs is the progress of ideas; not of ideas in the abstract form, but of ideas in the operative form, certain conceptions of justice and of freedom and of right that have got into men's natures and led those natures to insist upon the realization of those ideas in experience and in action.

The whole trouble about our civilization as it looks to me, is that it has grown complex faster than we have adjusted the simpler ideas to the existing conditions. There was a time when men would do in their business what they would not do as individuals. There was a time when they submerged their individual consciences in a corporation and persuaded themselves that it was legitimate for a corporation to do what they individually never would have dreamed of doing. That is what I mean by saying that the organization becomes complex faster than our adjustment of the simpler ideas of justice and right to the developing circumstances of our civilization. I say that because the errand that I am on concerns something that lies at the heart of all progress. I think we are all now convinced that we have not reached the right and final organization of our industrial society; that there are many features of our social life that ought to undergo correction; that while we call ourselves democrats—with a little "d"—while we believe in democratic government, we have not seen yet the successful way of making our life in fact democratic; that we have allowed classes to disclose themselves; that we have allowed lines of cleavage to be run through our community, so that there are antagonisms set up that breed heat, because they breed friction. The world must have leisure and order in which to see that these things are set right, and the world cannot have leisure and order unless it has a guaranteed peace.

For example, if the United States should conceivably—I think it inconceivable—stay out of the League of Nations, it would stay out at this cost: We would have to see, since we were not going to join our force with other nations, that our force was formidable enough to be respected by other nations. We would have to maintain a great Army and a great Navy. We would have to do something more than that: We would have to concentrate authority sufficiently to be able to use the physical force of the Nation quickly upon occasion. All of that is absolutely anti-democratic in its influence. All of that means that we should not be giving ourselves the leisure of thought or the release of material resources necessary to work out our own methods of civilization, our own methods of industrial organization and production and distribution; and our problems are exactly the problems of the rest of the world. I am more and more convinced, as I come in contact with the men who are trying to think for other countries as we are trying to think for this one, that our problems are identical, only there is this difference: Peoples of other countries have lost confidence in their Governments. Some of them have lost confidence in their form of government. That point, I hope and believe, has not been reached in the United States. We have not lost confidence in our Government. I am not now speaking of our administration; I am now thinking of our method of government.

We believe that we can manage our own affairs and that we have
the machinery through which we can manage our own affairs, and
that no clique or special interest is powerful enough to run away
with it. The other countries of the world also believe that about us.
They believe that we are successfully organized for justice, and
they therefore want us to take the lead and they want to follow the
lead. If we do not take the lead, then we throw them back upon
things in which they have no confidence and endanger a universal
disorder and discontent in the midst of which it will be impossible
to govern our own affairs with success and with constant
achievement. Whether you will or not, our fortunes are tied in with
the rest of the world, and the choice that we have to make now is
whether we will receive the influences of the rest of the world and
be affected by them or dominate the influences of the world and
lead them. That is a tremendous choice to make, but it is exactly
that tremendous choice that we have to make, and I deeply regret
the suggestions which are made on some sides that we should take
advantage of the present situation in the world but should not
shoulder any of the responsibility. Do you know of any business or
undertaking in which you can get the advantage without assuming
the responsibility? What are you going to be? Boys running
around the circus tent and peeping under the canvas? Men
declining to pay the admission and sitting on the roof and looking
on at the game. Or are you going to play your responsible part in
the game, knowing that you are trusted as leader and umpire
both?

Nothing has impressed me more, or impressed me more
painfully, if I may say so, than the degree in which the rest of the
world trusts us and looks to us. I say "painfully" because I am
conscious that they are expecting more than we can perform. They
are expecting miracles to be wrought by the influence of the
American spirit on the affairs of the world, and miracles cannot be
wrought. I have again and again recited to my fellow citizens on
this journey how deputations from peoples of every kind and every
color and every fortune, from all over the world, thronged to the
house in which I was living in Paris to ask the guidance and
assistance of the United States. They did not send similar
delegations to anybody else, and they did not send them to me
except because they thought they had heard in what I had been
saying the spirit of the American people uttered. Moreover, you

must not forget this, that almost all of them had kinsmen in America. You must not forget that America is made up out of all the world and that there is hardly a race of any influence in the world, at any rate hardly a Caucasian race, that has not scores and hundreds, and sometimes millions, of people living in America with whom they are in correspondence, from whom they receive the subtle suggestions of what is going on in American life, and of the ideals of American life. Therefore they feel that they know America from this contact they have had with us, and they want America to be the leading force in the world. Why, I received delegations there speaking tongues that I did not know anything about. I did not know what family of languages they belonged to, but fortunately for me they always brought an interpreter along who could speak English, and one of the significant facts was that the interpreter was almost always some young man who had lived in America. He did not talk English to me; he talked American to me. So there always seemed to be a little link of some sort tying them up with us, tying them up with us in fact, in relationship, in blood, as well as in life, and the world will be turned back to cynicism if America goes back on it.

We dare not go back on it. I ask you even as a business proposition whether it is more useful to trade with a cynic or with an optimist. I do not like to trade with a man with a grouch. I do not like to trade with a man who begins by not believing anything I am telling him. I like to trade with a man who is more or less susceptible to the eloquence which I address to him. A salesman has a much longer job if he approaches a grouch than if he approaches a friend. This trivial illustration illustrates, my fellow citizens, our relation to the rest of the world. If we do not do what the rest of the world expects of us, all the rest of the world will have a grouch toward America, and you will find it a hard job to reestablish your credit in the world. And back of financial credit lies mental credit. There is not a bit of credit that has not got an element of assessment of character. You do not limit your credit to men who can put up the collateral, who have the assets; you extend it also to the men in whose characters and abilities you believe; you think they are going to make good. Your credit is a sort of bet on their capacity, and that is the largest element in the kind of credit that expands enterprise. The credit that merely continues enterprise is based upon asset and past accomplishment, but the credit that expands enterprise is based upon your assessment of character. If you are going to put into the world this germ, I shall call it, of American enterprise and American faith and American vision, then you must be the principal partners in the new partnership which the world is forming.

I take leave to say, without intending the least disrespect to anybody, that, consciously or unconsciously, a man who opposes that proposition either has no imagination or no knowledge, or is a quitter. America has put her hand to this great enterprise already, in the men she sent overseas, and their part was the negative part merely. They were sent over there to see that a malign influence did not interfere with the just fortunes of the world. They stopped that influence, but they did not accomplish anything constructive, and what is the use clearing the table if you are going to put nothing on it? What is the use clearing the ground if you are not going to erect any building? What is the use of going to the pains that we went to, to draw up the specifications of the new building and then saying, "We will have nothing to do with its erection"? For the specifications of this treaty were American specifications, and we have got not only to be the architects, drawing up the specifications, but we have got to be the contractors, too. Isn't it a job worth while? Isn't it worth while, now that the chance has at last come, in the providence of God, that we should demonstrate to the world that America is what she claimed that she was? Every drop of blood that I have in me gets up and shouts when I think of the opportunity that America has.

I come of a race that, being bred on barren hills and unfertile plains in Scotland, being obliged to work where work was hard, somehow has the best zest in what it does when the job is hard, and I was repeating to my friend, Mr. Jackson, what I said the other day about my ancestry and about the implications of it. I come of a certain stock that raised Cain in the northern part of the larger of the British Isles, under the name of the Covenanters. They met in a churchyard—they were church people and they had a convention out of doors—and on the top of a flat tombstone they signed an immortal document called the "solemn league and covenant," which meant that they were going to stand by their religious principles in spite of the Crown of England and the force of England and every other influence, whether of man or the Devil, so long as any of them lived. Now, I have seen men of all nations sit around a table in Paris and sign a solemn league and covenant. They have become Covenanters, and I remain a Covenanter, and I am going to see this job through no matter what influence of evil I must withstand. [Loud applause.] Nothing has heartened me more on this journey than to feel that that really is the judgment of our fellow citizens. America is made up, as I have just said, out of all sorts of elements, but it is a singularly homogeneous people after all; homogeneous in its ideals, not in its blood; homogeneous in the infection which it has caught from a common light; homogeneous in its purpose. Every man has a sort of consciousness that America is put into the world for a purpose that is different in some respects from the purpose conceived by any other national organization.

Throughout America you have got a conducting medium. You do not put forth an American idea and find it halted by this man or that or the other, except he be particularly asleep or cantankerous, but it spreads, it spreads by the natural contact of similar ideas and similar ambitions and similar hopes. For, my fellow citizens, the only thing that lifts the world is hope. The only thing that can save the world is such arrangements as will convince the world that hope is not altogether without foundation. It is the spirit that is in it that is unconquerable. You can kill the bodies of insurgent men who are fighting for liberty, but the more of them you kill the more you seem to strengthen the spirit that springs up out of the bloody ground where they fell. The only thing in the world that is unconquerable is the thought of men. One looks back to that legendary story of the Middle Ages, in which certain men who were fighting under one of the semisavage chiefs of that obscure time refused to obey the order of their chief because they considered it inconsistent with the traditions of their tribe, and he said, "Don't you know that I have the power to kill you?" They said, "Yes; and don't you know that we have the power to die cursing you?" You cannot cut our spirits out. You cannot do anything but lay our bodies low and helpless. If you do, there will spring up, like dragon's teeth out of the earth, armed forces which will overcome you.

This is the field of the spirit here in America. This is the field of the single unconquerable force that there is in the world, and when the world learns, as it will learn, that America has put her whole force into the common harness of civilization, then it will know that the wheels are going to turn, the loads are going to be drawn, and men are going to begin to ascend those difficult heights of hope which have sometimes seemed so inaccessible. I am glad for one to have lived to see this day. I have lived to see a day in which, after saturating myself most of my life in the history and traditions of America, I seem suddenly to see the culmination of American hope and history—all the orators seeing their dreams realized, if their spirits are looking on; all the men who spoke the noblest sentiments of America heartened with the sight of a great Nation responding to and acting upon those dreams, and saying, "At last, the world knows America as the savior of the world!"

John F. Kennedy Commencement Address at American University in Washington June 10, 1963

PRESIDENT ANDERSON, MEMBERS OF THE FACULTY, BOARD OF TRUSTEES, DISTINGUISHED GUESTS, MY OLD COLLEAGUE, SENATOR BOB BYRD, WHO HAS EARNED HIS DEGREE THROUGH MANY YEARS OF ATTENDING NIGHT LAW SCHOOL, WHILE I AM EARNING MINE IN THE NEXT 30 MINUTES, LADIES AND GENTLEMEN:

It is with great pride that I participate in this ceremony of the American University, sponsored by the Methodist Church, founded by Bishop John Fletcher Hurst, and first opened by President Woodrow Wilson in 1914. This is a young and growing university, but it has already fulfilled Bishop Hurst's enlightened hope for the study of history and public affairs in a city devoted to the making of history and to the conduct of the public's business. By sponsoring this institution of higher learning for all who wish to learn, whatever their color or their creed, the Methodists of this area and the Nation deserve the Nation's thanks, and I commend all those who are today graduating.

Professor Woodrow Wilson once said that every man sent out from a university should be a man of his nation as well as a man of his time, and I am confident that the men and women who carry the honor of graduating from this institution will continue to give from their lives, from their talents, a high measure of public service and public support.

"There are few earthly things more beautiful than a university," wrote John Masefield, in his tribute to English universities—and his words are equally true today. He did not refer to spires and towers, to campus greens and ivied walls. He admired the splendid beauty of the university, he said, because it was "a place where those who hate ignorance may strive to know, where those who perceive truth may strive to make others see."

I have, therefore, chosen this time and this place to discuss a topic on which ignorance too often abounds and the truth is too rarely perceived—yet it is the most important topic on earth: world peace.

What kind of peace do I mean? What kind of peace do we seek? Not a Pax Americana enforced on the world by American weapons of war. Not the peace of the grave or the security of the slave. I am talking about genuine peace, the kind of peace that makes life on earth worth living, the kind that enables men and nations to grow and to hope and to build a better life for their children—not merely peace for Americans but peace for all men and women—not merely peace in our time but peace for all time.

I speak of peace because of the new face of war. Total war makes no sense in an age when great powers can maintain large and relatively invulnerable nuclear forces and refuse to surrender without resort to those forces. It makes no sense in an age when a single nuclear weapon contains almost ten times the explosive force delivered by all of the allied air forces in the Second World War. It makes no sense in an age when the deadly poisons produced by a nuclear exchange would be carried by wind and water and soil and seed to the far corners of the globe and to generations yet unborn.

Today the expenditure of billions of dollars every year on weapons acquired for the purpose of making sure we never need to use them is essential to keeping the peace. But surely the acquisition of such idle stockpiles—which can only destroy and never create—is not the only, much less the most efficient, means of assuring peace.

I speak of peace, therefore, as the necessary rational end of rational men. I realize that the pursuit of peace is not as dramatic as the pursuit of war—and frequently the words of the pursuer fall on deaf ears. But we have no more urgent task.

Some say that it is useless to speak of world peace or world law or world disarmament—and that it will be useless until the leaders of the Soviet Union adopt a more enlightened attitude. I hope they do. I believe we can help them do it. But I also believe that we must reexamine our own attitude—as individuals and as a Nation—for our attitude is as essential as theirs. And every graduate of this school, every thoughtful citizen who despairs of war and wishes to bring peace, should begin by looking inward—by examining his own attitude toward the possibilities of peace, toward the Soviet Union, toward the course of the cold war and toward freedom and peace here at home.

First: Let us examine our attitude toward peace itself. Too many of us think it is impossible. Too many think it unreal. But that is a dangerous, defeatist belief. It leads to the conclusion that war is inevitable—that mankind is doomed—that we are gripped by forces we cannot control.

We need not accept that view. Our problems are manmade—therefore, they can be solved by man. And man can be as big as he wants. No problem of human destiny is beyond human beings. Man's reason and spirit have often solved the seemingly unsolvable—and we believe that they can do it again.

I am not referring to the absolute, infinite concept of universal peace and good will of which some fantasies and fanatics dream. I do not deny the value of hopes and dreams but we merely invite discouragement and incredulity by making that our only and immediate goal.

Let us focus instead on a more practical, more attainable peace—based not on a sudden revolution in human nature but on a gradual evolution in human institutions—on a series of concrete actions and effective agreements which are in the interest of all concerned. There is no single, simple key to this peace—no grand or magic formula to be adopted by one or two powers. Genuine peace must be the product of many nations, the sum of many acts. It must be dynamic, not static, changing to meet the challenge of each new generation. For peace is a process—a way of solving problems.

With such a peace, there will still be quarrels and conflicting interests, as there are within families and nations. World peace, like community peace, does not require that each man love his neighbor—it requires only that they live together in mutual tolerance, submitting their disputes to a just and peaceful settlement. And history teaches us that enmities between nations, as between individuals, do not last forever. However fixed our likes and dislikes may seem, the tide of time and events will often bring surprising changes in the relations between nations and neighbors.

So let us persevere. Peace need not be impracticable, and war need not be inevitable. By defining our goal more clearly, by making it seem more manageable and less remote, we can help all peoples to see it, to draw hope from it, and to move irresistibly toward it.

Second: Let us reexamine our atittude toward the Soviet Union. It is discouraging to think that their leaders may actually believe what their propoagandists write. It is discouraging to read a recent authoritative Soviet text on *Military Strategy* and find, on page after page, wholly baseless and incredible claims—such as the allegation that "American imperialist circles are preparing to unleash different types of wars . . . that there is a very real threat of a preventive war being unleashed by American imperialists against the Soviet Union . . . [and that] the political aims of the American imperialists are to enslave economically and politically the European and other capitalist countries . . . [and] to achieve world domination . . . by means of aggressive wars."

Truly, as it was written long ago: "The wicked flee when no man pursueth." Yet it is sad to read these Soviet statements—to realize the extent of the gulf between us. But it is also a warning—a warning to the American people not to fall into the same trap as the Soviets, not to see only a distorted and desperate view of the other side, not to see conflict as inevitable, accommodation as impossible, and communication as nothing more than an exchange of threats.

No government or social system is so evil that its people must be considered as lacking in virtue. As Americans, we find communism profoundly repugnant as a negation of personal freedom and dignity. But we can still hail the Russian people for their many achievements—in science and space, in economic and industrial growth, in culture and in acts of courage.

Among the many traits the peoples of our two countries have in common, none is stronger than our mutual abhorrence of war. Almost unique, among the major world powers, we have never been at war with each other. And no nation in the history of battle ever suffered more than the Soviet Union suffered in the course of the Second World War. At least 20 million lost their lives. Countless millions of homes and farms were burned or sacked. A third of the nation's territory, including nearly two thirds of its industrial base, was turned into a wasteland—a loss equivalent to the devastation of this country east of Chicago.

Today, should total war ever break out again—no matter how—our two countries would become the primary targets. It is an ironic but accurate fact that the two strongest powers are the two in the most danger of devastation. All we have built, all we have worked for, would be destroyed in the first 24 hours. And even in the cold war, which brings burdens and dangers to so many countries, including this Nation's closest allies—our two countries bear the heaviest burdens. For we are both devoting massive sums of money to weapons that could be better devoted to combating ignorance, poverty, and disease. We are both caught up in a vicious and dangerous cycle in which suspicion on one side breeds suspicion on the other, and new weapons beget counterweapons.

In short, both the United States and its allies, and the Soviet Union and its allies, have a mutually deep interest in a just and genuine peace and in halting the arms race. Agreements to this end are in the interests of the Soviet Union as well as ours—and even the most hostile nations can be relied upon to accept and keep those treaty obligations, and only those treaty obligations, which are in their own interest.

So, let us not be blind to our differences—but let us also direct attention to our common interests and to the means by which those differences can be resolved. And if we cannot end now our differences, at least we can help make the world safe for diversity. For, in the final analysis, our most basic common link is that we all inhabit this small planet. We all breathe the same air. We all cherish our children's future. And we are all mortal.

Third: Let us reexamine our attitude toward the cold war, remembering that we are not engaged in a debate, seeking to pile up debating points. We are not here distributing blame or pointing the finger of judgment. We must deal with the world as it is, and not as it might have been had the history of the last 18 years been different.

We must, therefore, persevere in the search for peace in the hope that constructive changes within the Communist bloc might bring within reach solutions which now seem beyond us. We must conduct our affairs in such a way that it becomes in the Communists' interest to agree on a genuine peace. Above all, while defending our own vital interests, nuclear powers must avert those confrontations which bring an adversary to a choice of either a humiliating retreat or a nuclear war. To adopt that kind of course in the nuclear age would be evidence only of the bankruptcy of our policy—or of a collective death-wish for the world.

To secure these ends, America's weapons are nonprovocative, carefully controlled, designed to deter, and capable of selective use. Our military forces are committed to peace and disciplined in self-restraint. Our diplomats are instructed to avoid unnecessary irritants and purely rhetorical hostility.

For we can seek a relaxation of tensions without relaxing our guard. And, for our part, we do not need to use threats to prove that we are resolute. We do not need to jam foreign broadcasts out of fear our faith will be eroded. We are unwilling to impose our system on any unwilling people—but we are willing and able to engage in peaceful competition with any people on earth.

Meanwhile, we seek to strengthen the United Nations, to help solve its financial problems, to make it a more effective instrument for peace, to develop it into a genuine world security system—a system capable of resolving disputes on the basis of law, of insuring the security of the large and the small, and of creating conditions under which arms can finally be abolished.

At the same time we seek to keep peace inside the non-Communist world, where many nations, all of them our friends, are divided over issues which weaken Western unity, which invite Communist intervention or which threaten to erupt into war. Our efforts in West New Guinea, in the Congo, in the Middle East, and in the Indian subcontinent, have been persistent and patient despite criticism from both sides. We have also tried to set an example for others—by seeking to adjust small but significant differences with our own closest neighbors in Mexico and in Canada.

Speaking of other nations, I wish to make one point clear. We are bound to many nations by alliances. Those alliances exist because our concern and theirs substantially overlap. Our commitment to defend Western Europe and West Berlin, for example, stands undiminished because of the identity of our vital interests.

The United States will make no deal with the Soviet Union at the expense of other nations and other peoples, not merely because they are our partners, but also because their interests and ours converge.

Our interests converge, however, not only in defending the frontiers of freedom, but in pursuing the paths of peace. It is our hope—and the purpose of allied policies—to convince the Soviet Union that she, too, should let each nation choose its own future, so long as that choice does not interfere with the choices of others. The Communist drive to impose their political and economic system on others is the primary cause of world tension today. For there can be no doubt that, if all nations could refrain from interfering in the self-determination of others, the peace would be much more assured.

This will require a new effort to achieve world law—a new context for world discussions. It will require increased understanding between the Soviets and ourselves. And increased understanding will require increased contact and communication. One step in this direction is the proposed arrangement for a direct line between Moscow and Washington, to avoid on each side the dangerous delays, misunderstandings, and misreadings of the other's actions which might occur at a time of crisis.

We have also been talking in Geneva about other first-step measures of arms control, designed to limit the intensity of the arms race and to reduce the risks of accidental war. Our primary long-range interest in Geneva, however, is general and complete disarmament—designed to take place by stages, permitting parallel political developments to build the new institutions of peace which would take the place of arms. The pursuit of disarmament has been an effort of this Government since the 1920's. It has been urgently sought by the past three administrations. And however dim the prospects may be today, we intend to continue this effort—to continue it in order that all countries, including our own, can better grasp what the problems and possibilities of disarmament are.

The one major area of these negotiations where the end is in sight, yet where a fresh start is badly needed, is in a treaty to outlaw nuclear tests. The conclusion of such a treaty, so near and yet so far, would check the spiraling arms race in one of its most dangerous areas. It would place the nuclear powers in a position to deal more effectively with one of the greatest hazards which man faces in 1963, the further spread of nuclear arms. It would increase our security—it would decrease the prospects of war. Surely this goal is sufficiently important to require our steady pursuit, yielding neither to the temptation to give up the whole effort nor the temptation to give up our insistence on vital and responsible safeguards.

I am taking this opportunity, therefore, to announce two important decisions in this regard.

First: Chairman Khrushchev, Prime Minister Macmillan, and I have agreed that high-level discussions will shortly begin in Moscow looking toward early agreement on a comprehensive test ban treaty. Our hopes must be tempered with the caution of history—but with our hopes go the hopes of all mankind.

Second: To make clear our good faith and solemn convictions on the matter, I now declare that the United States does not propose to conduct nuclear tests in the atmosphere so long as other states do not do so. We will not be the first to resume. Such a declaration is no substitute for a formal binding treaty, but I hope it will help us achieve one. Nor would such a treaty be a substitute for disarmament, but I hope it will help us achieve it.

Finally, my fellow Americans, let us examine our attitude toward peace and freedom here at home. The quality and spirit of our own society must justify and support our efforts abroad. We must show it in the dedication of our own lives—as many of you who are graduating today will have a unique opportunity to do, by serving without pay in the Peace Corps abroad or in the proposed National Service Corps here at home.

But wherever we are, we must all, in our daily lives, live up to the age-old faith that peace and freedom walk together. In too many of our cities today, the peace is not secure because freedom is incomplete.

It is the responsibility of the executive branch at all levels of government—local, State, and National—to provide and protect that freedom for all of our citizens by all means within their authority. It is the responsibility of the legislative branch at all levels, wherever that authority is not now adequate, to make it adequate. And it is the responsibility of all citizens in all sections of this country to respect the rights of all others and to respect the law of the land.

All this is not unrelated to world peace. "When a man's ways please the Lord," the Scriptures tell us, "he maketh even his enemies to be at peace with him." And is not peace, in the last analysis, basically a matter of human rights—the right to live out our lives without fear of devastation—the right to breathe air as nature provided it—the right of future generations to a healthy existence?

While we proceed to safeguard our national interests, let us also safeguard human interests. And the elimination of war and arms is clearly in the interest of both. No treaty, however much it may be to the advantage of all, however tightly it may be worded, can provide absolute security against the risks of deception and evasion. But it can—if it is sufficiently effective in its enforcement and if it is sufficiently in the interests of its signers—offer far more security and far fewer risks than an unabated, uncontrolled, unpredictable arms race.

The United States, as the world knows, will never start a war. We do not want a war. We do not now expect a war. This generation of Americans has already had enough—more than enough—of war and hate and oppression. We shall be prepared if others wish it. We shall be alert to try to stop it. But we shall also do our part to build a world of peace where the weak are safe and the strong are just. We are not helpless before that task or hopeless of its success. Confident and unafraid, we labor on—not toward a strategy of annihilation but toward a strategy of peace.

NOTE

The President spoke at the John M. Reeves Athletic Field on the campus of American University after being awarded an honorary degree of doctor of laws. In his opening words he referred to Hurst R. Anderson, president of the university, and Robert C. Byrd, U.S. Senator from West Virginia.

John F. Kennedy
Remarks in the Rudolph Wilde Platz, Berlin
June 26, 1963

I am proud to come to this city as the guest of your distinguished Mayor, who has symbolized throughout the world the fighting spirit of West Berlin. And I am proud to visit the Federal Republic with your distinguished Chancellor who for so many years has committed Germany to democracy and freedom and progress, and to come here in the company of my fellow American, General Clay, who has been in this city during its great moments of crisis and will come again if ever needed.

Two thousand years ago the proudest boast was *"civis Romanus sum."* Today, in the world of freedom, the proudest boast is *"Ich bin ein Berliner."*

I appreciate my interpreter translating my German!

There are many people in the world who really don't understand, or say they don't, what is the great issue between the free world and the Communist world. Let them come to Berlin. There are some who say that communism is the wave of the future. Let them come to Berlin. And there are some who say in Europe and elsewhere we can work with the Communists. Let them come to Berlin. And there are even a few who say that it is true that communism is an evil system, but it permits us to make economic progress. *Lass' sie nach Berlin kommen.* Let them come to Berlin.

Freedom has many difficulties and democracy is not perfect, but we have never had to put a wall up to keep our people in, to prevent them from leaving us. I want to say, on behalf of my countrymen, who live many miles away on the other side of the Atlantic, who are far distant from you, that they take the greatest pride that they have been able to share with you, even from a distance, the story of the last 18 years. I know of no town, no city, that has been besieged for 18 years that still lives with the vitality and the force, and the hope and the determination of the city of West Berlin. While the wall is the most obvious and vivid demonstration of the failures of the Communist system, for all the world to see, we take no satisfaction in it, for it is, as your Mayor has said, an offense not only against history but an offense against humanity, separating families, dividing husbands and wives and brothers and sisters, and dividing a people who wish to be joined together.

What is true of this city is true of Germany—real, lasting peace in Europe can never be assured as long as one German out of four is denied the elementary rights of free men, and that is to make a free choice. In 18 years of peace and good faith, this generation of Germans has earned the right to be free, including the right to unite their families and their nation in lasting peace, with good will to all people. You live in a defended island of freedom, but your life is part of the main. So let me ask you, as I close, to lift your eyes beyond the dangers of today, to the hopes of tomorrow, beyond the freedom merely of this city of Berlin, or your country of Germany, to the advance of freedom everywhere, beyond the wall to the day of peace with justice, beyond yourselves and ourselves to all mankind.

Freedom is indivisible, and when one man is enslaved, all are not free. When all are free, then we can look forward to that day when this city will be joined as one and this country and this great Continent of Europe in a peaceful and hopeful globe. When that day finally comes, as it will, the people of West Berlin can take sober satisfaction in the fact that they were in the front lines for almost two decades.

All free men, wherever they may live, are citizens of Berlin, and, therefore, as a free man, I take pride in the words *"Ich bin ein Berliner."*

NOTE

The President spoke at 12:50 p.m. from a platform erected on the steps of the Schöneberger Rathaus, West Berlin's city hall, where he signed the Golden Book and remained for lunch. In his opening remarks he referred to Mayor Willy Brandt, Chancellor Adenauer, and Gen. Lucius D. Clay.

Richard M. Nixon
Address to the Nation on the War in Vietnam
November 3, 1969

GOOD EVENING, MY FELLOW AMERICANS:

Tonight I want to talk to you on a subject of deep concern to all Americans and to many people in all parts of the world—the war in Vietnam.

I believe that one of the reasons for the deep division about Vietnam is that many Americans have lost confidence in what their Government has told them about our policy. The American people cannot and should not be asked to support a policy which involves the overriding issues of war and peace unless they know the truth about that policy.

Tonight, therefore, I would like to answer some of the questions that I know are on the minds of many of you listening to me.

How and why did America get involved in Vietnam in the first place?

How has this administration changed the policy of the previous administration?

What has really happened in the negotiations in Paris and on the battlefront in Vietnam?

What choices do we have if we are to end the war?

What are the prospects for peace?

Now, let me begin by describing the situation I found when I was inaugurated on January 20.

—The war had been going on for 4 years.
—31,000 Americans had been killed in action.

—The training program for the South Vietnamese was behind schedule.

—540,000 Americans were in Vietnam with no plans to reduce the number.

—No progress had been made at the negotiations in Paris and the United States had not put forth a comprehensive peace proposal.

—The war was causing deep division at home and criticism from many of our friends as well as our enemies abroad.

In view of these circumstances there were some who urged that I end the war at once by ordering the immediate withdrawal of all American forces.

From a political standpoint this would have been a popular and easy course to follow. After all, we became involved in the war while my predecessor was in office. I could blame the defeat which would be the result of my action on him and come out as the peacemaker. Some put it to me quite bluntly: This was the only way to avoid allowing Johnson's war to become Nixon's war.

But I had a greater obligation than to think only of the years of my administration and of the next election. I had to think of the effect of my decision on the next generation and on the future of peace and freedom in America and in the world.

Let us all understand that the question before us is not whether some Americans are for peace and some Americans are against peace. The question at issue is not whether Johnson's war becomes Nixon's war.

The great question is: How can we win America's peace?

Well, let us turn now to the fundamental issue. Why and how did the United States become involved in Vietnam in the first place?

Fifteen years ago North Vietnam, with the logistical support of Communist China and the Soviet Union, launched a campaign to impose a Communist government on South Vietnam by instigating and supporting a revolution.

In response to the request of the Government of South Vietnam, President Eisenhower sent economic aid and military equipment to assist the people of South Vietnam in their efforts to prevent a Communist takeover. Seven years ago, President

Kennedy sent 16,000 military personnel to Vietnam as combat advisers. Four years ago, President Johnson sent American combat forces to South Vietnam.

Now, many believe that President Johnson's decision to send American combat forces to South Vietnam was wrong. And many others—I among them—have been strongly critical of the way the war has been conducted.

But the question facing us today is: Now that we are in the war, what is the best way to end it?

In January I could only conclude that the precipitate withdrawal of American forces from Vietnam would be a disaster not only for South Vietnam but for the United States and for the cause of peace.

For the South Vietnamese, our precipitate withdrawal would inevitably allow the Communists to repeat the massacres which followed their takeover in the North 15 years before.

—They then murdered more than 50,000 people and hundreds of thousands more died in slave labor camps.

—We saw a prelude of what would happen in South Vietnam when the Communists entered the city of Hue last year. During their brief rule there, there was a bloody reign of terror in which 3,000 civilians were clubbed, shot to death, and buried in mass graves.

—With the sudden collapse of our support, these atrocities of Hue would become the nightmare of the entire nation—and particularly for the million and a half Catholic refugees who fled to South Vietnam when the Communists took over in the North.

For the United States, this first defeat in our Nation's history would result in a collapse of confidence in American leadership, not only in Asia but throughout the world.

Three American Presidents have recognized the great stakes involved in Vietnam and understood what had to be done.

In 1963, President Kennedy, with his characteristic eloquence and clarity, said: "... we want to see a stable government there, carrying on a struggle to maintain its national independence.

"We believe strongly in that. We are not going to withdraw

from that effort. In my opinion, for us to withdraw from that effort would mean a collapse not only of South Viet-Nam, but Southeast Asia. So we are going to stay there."

President Eisenhower and President Johnson expressed the same conclusion during their terms of office.

For the future of peace, precipitate withdrawal would thus be a disaster of immense magnitude.

—A nation cannot remain great if it betrays its allies and lets down its friends.

—Our defeat and humiliation in South Vietnam without question would promote recklessness in the councils of those great powers who have not yet abandoned their goals of world conquest.

—This would spark violence wherever our commitments help maintain the peace—in the Middle East, in Berlin, eventually even in the Western Hemisphere.

Ultimately, this would cost more lives.

It would not bring peace; it would bring more war.

For these reasons, I rejected the recommendation that I should end the war by immediately withdrawing all of our forces. I chose instead to change American policy on both the negotiating front and battlefront.

In order to end a war fought on many fronts, I initiated a pursuit for peace on many fronts.

In a television speech on May 14, in a speech before the United Nations, and on a number of other occasions I set forth our peace proposals in great detail.

—We have offered the complete withdrawal of all outside forces within 1 year.

—We have proposed a cease-fire under international supervision.

—We have offered free elections under international supervision with the Communists participating in the organization and conduct of the elections as an organized political force. And the Saigon Government has pledged to accept the result of the elections.

We have not put forth our proposals on a take-it-or-leave-it basis. We have indicated that we are willing to discuss the proposals that have been put forth by the other side. We have declared that anything is negotiable except the right of the people of South Vietnam to determine their own future. At the Paris peace conference, Ambassador Lodge has demonstrated our flexibility and good faith in 40 public meetings.

Hanoi has refused even to discuss our proposals. They demand our unconditional acceptance of their terms, which are that we withdraw all American forces immediately and unconditionally and that we overthrow the Government of South Vietnam as we leave.

We have not limited our peace initiatives to public forums and public statements. I recognized, in January, that a long and bitter war like this usually cannot be settled in a public forum. That is why in addition to the public statements and negotiations I have explored every possible private avenue that might lead to a settlement.

Tonight I am taking the unprecedented step of disclosing to you some of our other initiatives for peace—initiatives we undertook privately and secretly because we thought we thereby might open a door which publicly would be closed.

I did not wait for my inauguration to begin my quest for peace.

—Soon after my election, through an individual who is directly in contact on a personal basis with the leaders of North Vietnam, I made two private offers for a rapid, comprehensive settlement. Hanoi's replies called in effect for our surrender before negotiations.

—Since the Soviet Union furnishes most of the military equipment for North Vietnam, Secretary of State Rogers, my Assistant for National Security Affairs, Dr. Kissinger, Ambassador Lodge, and I, personally, have met on a number of occasions with representatives of the Soviet Government to enlist their assistance in getting meaningful negotiations started. In addition, we have had extended discussions directed toward that same end with representatives of other governments which have diplomatic relations with North Vietnam. None of these initiatives have to date produced results.

—In mid-July, I became convinced that it was necessary to make a major move to break the deadlock in the Paris talks. I spoke directly in this office, where I am now sitting, with an individual who had known Ho Chi Minh [President, Democratic Republic of Vietnam] on a personal basis for 25 years. Through him I sent a letter to Ho Chi Minh.

I did this outside of the usual diplomatic channels with the hope that with the necessity of making statements for propaganda removed, there might be constructive progress toward bringing the war to an end. Let me read from that letter to you now.

"Dear Mr. President:
"I realize that it is difficult to communicate meaningfully across the gulf of four years of war. But precisely because of this gulf, I wanted to take this opportunity to reaffirm in all solemnity my desire to work for a just peace. I deeply believe that the war in Vietnam has gone on too long and delay in bringing it to an end can benefit no one—least of all the people of Vietnam. . . .
"The time time has come to move forward at the conference table toward an early resolution of this tragic war. You will find us forthcoming and open-minded in a common effort to bring the blessings of peace to the brave people of Vietnam. Let history record that at this critical juncture, both sides turned their face toward peace rather than toward conflict and war."

I received Ho Chi Minh's reply on August 30, 3 days before his death. It simply reiterated the public position North Vietnam had taken at Paris and flatly rejected my initiative.

The full text of both letters is being released to the press.

—In addition to the public meetings that I have referred to, Ambassador Lodge has met with Vietnam's chief negotiator in Paris in 11 private sessions.

—We have taken other significant initiatives which must remain secret to keep open some channels of communication which may still prove to be productive.

But the effect of all the public, private, and secret negotiations which have been undertaken since the bombing halt a year ago and since this administration came into office on January 20, can be summed up in one sentence. No progress whatever has been made except agreement on the shape of the bargaining table.

Well now, who is at fault?

It has become clear that the obstacle in negotiating an end to the war is not the President of the United States. It is not the South Vietnamese Government.

The obstacle is the other side's absolute refusal to show the least willingness to join us in seeking a just peace. And it will not do so while it is convinced that all it has to do is to wait for our next concession, and our next concession after that one, until it gets everything it wants.

There can now be no longer any question that progress in negotiation depends only on Hanoi's deciding to negotiate, to negotiate seriously.

I realize that this report on our efforts on the diplomatic front is discouraging to the American people, but the American people are entitled to know the truth—the bad news as well as the good news—where the lives of our young men are involved.

Now let me turn, however, to a more encouraging report on another front.

At the time we launched our search for peace I recognized we might not succeed in bringing an end to the war through negotiation. I, therefore, put into effect another plan to bring peace—a plan which will bring the war to an end regardless of what happens on the negotiating front.

It is in line with a major shift in U.S. foreign policy which I described in my press conference at Guam on July 25. Let me briefly explain what has been described as the Nixon Doctrine—a policy which not only will help end the war in Vietnam, but which is an essential element of our program to prevent future Vietnams.

We Americans are a do-it-yourself people. We are an impatient people. Instead of teaching someone else to do a job, we like to do it ourselves. And this trait has been carried over into our foreign policy.

In Korea and again in Vietnam, the United States furnished most of the money, most of the arms, and most of the men to help the people of those countries defend their freedom against Communist aggression.

Before any American troops were committed to Vietnam, a leader of another Asian country expressed this opinion to me when I was traveling in Asia as a private citizen. He said: "When you are trying to assist another nation defend its freedom, U.S. policy should be to help them fight the war but not to fight the war for them."

Well, in accordance with this wise counsel, I laid down in Guam three principles as guidelines for future American policy toward Asia:

—First, the United States will keep all of its treaty commitments.
—Second, we shall provide a shield if a nuclear power threatens the freedom of a nation allied with us or of a nation whose survival we consider vital to our security.
—Third, in cases involving other types of aggression, we shall furnish military and economic assistance when requested in accordance with our treaty commitments. But we shall look to the nation directly threatened to assume the primary responsibility of providing the manpower for its defense.

After I announced this policy, I found that the leaders of the Philippines, Thailand, Vietnam, South Korea, and other nations which might be threatened by Communist aggression, welcomed this new direction in American foreign policy.

The defense of freedom is everybody's business—not just America's business. And it is particularly the responsibility of the people whose freedom is threatened. In the previous administration, we Americanized the war in Vietnam. In this administration, we are Vietnamizing the search for peace.

The policy of the previous administration not only resulted in our assuming the primary responsibility for fighting the war, but even more significantly did not adequately stress the goal of strengthening the South Vietnamese so that they could defend themselves when we left.

The Vietnamization plan was launched following Secretary Laird's visit to Vietnam in March. Under the plan, I ordered first a substantial increase in the training and equipment of South Vietnamese forces.

In July, on my visit to Vietnam, I changed General Abrams' orders so that they were consistent with the objectives of our new policies. Under the new orders, the primary mission of our troops is to enable the South Vietnamese forces to assume the full responsibility for the security of South Vietnam.

Our air operations have been reduced by over 20 percent.

And now we have begun to see the results of this long overdue change in American policy in Vietnam.

—After 5 years of Americans going into Vietnam, we are finally bringing American men home. By December 15, over 60,000 men will have been withdrawn from South Vietnam—including 20 percent of all of our combat forces.

—The South Vietnamese have continued to gain in strength. As a result they have been able to take over combat responsibilities from our American troops.

Two other significant developments have occurred since this administration took office.

—Enemy infiltration, infiltration which is essential if they are to launch a major attack, over the last 3 months is less than 20 percent of what it was over the same period last year.

—Most important—United States casualties have declined during the last 2 months to the lowest point in 3 years.

Let me now turn to our program for the future.

We have adopted a plan which we have worked out in cooperation with the South Vietnamese for the complete withdrawal of all U.S. combat ground forces, and their replacement by South Vietnamese forces on an orderly scheduled timetable. This withdrawal will be made from strength and not from weakness. As

South Vietnamese forces become stronger, the rate of American withdrawal can become greater.

I have not and do not intend to announce the timetable for our program. And there are obvious reasons for this decision which I am sure you will understand. As I have indicated on several occasions, the rate of withdrawal will depend on developments on three fronts.

One of these is the progress which can be or might be made in the Paris talks. An announcement of a fixed timetable for our withdrawal would completely remove any incentive for the enemy to negotiate an agreement. They would simply wait until our forces had withdrawn and then move in.

The other two factors on which we will base our withdrawal decisions are the level of enemy activity and the progress of the training programs of the South Vietnamese forces. And I am glad to be able to report tonight progress on both of these fronts has been greater than we anticipated when we started the program in June for withdrawal. As a result, our timetable for withdrawal is more optimistic now than when we made our first estimates in June. Now, this clearly demonstrates why it is not wise to be frozen in on a fixed timetable.

We must retain the flexibility to base each withdrawal decision on the situation as it is at that time rather than on estimates that are no longer valid.

Along with this optimistic estimate, I must—in all candor—leave one note of caution.

If the level of enemy activity significantly increases we might have to adjust our timetable accordingly.

However, I want the record to be completely clear on one point.

At the time of the bombing halt just a year ago, there was some confusion as to whether there was an understanding on the part of the enemy that if we stopped the bombing of North Vietnam they would stop the shelling of cities in South Vietnam. I want to be sure that there is no misunderstanding on the part of the enemy with regard to our withdrawal program.

We have noted the reduced level of infiltration, the reduction of our casualties, and are basing our withdrawal decisions partially on those factors.

If the level of infiltration or our casualties increase while we are trying to scale down the fighting, it will be the result of a conscious decision by the enemy.

Hanoi could make no greater mistake than to assume that an increase in violence will be to its advantage. If I conclude that increased enemy action jeopardizes our remaining forces in Vietnam, I shall not hesitate to take strong and effective measures to deal with that situation.

This is not a threat. This is a statement of policy, which as Commander in Chief of our Armed Forces, I am making in meeting my responsibility for the protection of American fighting men wherever they may be.

My fellow Americans, I am sure you can recognize from what I have said that we really only have two choices open to us if we want to end this war.

—I can order an immediate, precipitate withdrawal of all Americans from Vietnam without regard to the effects of that action.

—Or we can persist in our search for a just peace through a negotiated settlement if possible, or through continued implementation of our plan for Vietnamization if necessary—a plan in which we will withdraw all of our forces from Vietnam on a schedule in accordance with our program, as the South Vietnamese become strong enough to defend their own freedom.

I have chosen this second course.

It is not the easy way.

It is the right way.

It is a plan which will end the war and serve the cause of peace—not just in Vietnam but in the Pacific and in the world.

In speaking of the consequences of a precipitate withdrawal, I mentioned that our allies would lose confidence in America.

Far more dangerous, we would lose confidence in ourselves. Oh, the immediate reaction would be a sense of relief that our men were coming home. But as we saw the consequences of what we had done, inevitable remorse and divisive recrimination would scar our spirit as a people.

We have faced other crises in our history and have become stronger by rejecting the easy way out and taking the right way in meeting our challenges. Our greatness as a nation has been our capacity to do what had to be done when we knew our course was right.

I recognize that some of my fellow citizens disagree with the plan for peace I have chosen. Honest and patriotic Americans have reached different conclusions as to how peace should be achieved.

In San Francisco a few weeks ago, I saw demonstrators carrying signs reading: "Lose in Vietnam, bring the boys home."

Well, one of the strengths of our free society is that any American has a right to reach that conclusion and to advocate that point of view. But as President of the United States, I would be untrue to my oath of office if I allowed the policy of this Nation to be dictated by the minority who hold that point of view and who try to impose it on the Nation by mounting demonstrations in the street.

For almost 200 years, the policy of this Nation has been made under our Constitution by those leaders in the Congress and the White House elected by all of the people. If a vocal minority, however fervent its cause, prevails over reason and the will of the majority, this Nation has no future as a free society.

And now I would like to address a word, if I may, to the young people of this Nation who are particularly concerned, and I understand why they are concerned, about this war.

I respect your idealism.

I share your concern for peace.

I want peace as much as you do.

There are powerful personal reasons I want to end this war. This week I will have to sign 83 letters to mothers, fathers, wives, and loved ones of men who have given their lives for America in Vietnam. It is very little satisfaction to me that this is only one-third as many letters as I signed the first week in office. There is nothing I want more than to see the day come when I do not have to write any of those letters.

—I want to end the war to save the lives of those brave young men in Vietnam.

—But I want to end it in a way which will increase the chance
that their younger brothers and their sons will not have to
fight in some future Vietnam someplace in the world.
—And I want to end the war for another reason. I want to end
it so that the energy and dedication of you, our young
people, now too often directed into bitter hatred against
those responsible for the war, can be turned to the great
challenges of peace, a better life for all Americans, a better
life for all people on this earth.

I have chosen a plan for peace. I believe it will succeed.

If it does succeed, what the critics say now won't matter. If it
does not succeed, anything I say then won't matter.

I know it may not be fashionable to speak of patriotism or
national destiny these days. But I feel it is appropriate to do so on
this occasion.

Two hundred years ago this Nation was weak and poor. But
even then, America was the hope of millions in the world. Today
we have become the strongest and richest nation in the world. And
the wheel of destiny has turned so that any hope the world has for
the survival of peace and freedom will be determined by whether
the American people have the moral stamina and the courage to
meet the challenge of free world leadership.

Let historians not record that when America was the most
powerful nation in the world we passed on the other side of the
road and allowed the last hopes for peace and freedom of millions
of people to be suffocated by the forces of totalitarianism.

And so tonight—to you, the great silent majority of my fellow
Americans—I ask for your support.

I pledged in my campaign for the Presidency to end the war in a
way that we could win the peace. I have initiated a plan of action
which will enable me to keep that pledge.

The more support I can have from the American people, the
sooner that pledge can be redeemed; for the more divided we are at
home, the less likely the enemy is to negotiate at Paris.

Let us be united for peace. Let us also be united against defeat.
Because let us understand: North Vietnam cannot defeat or
humiliate the United States. Only Americans can do that.

Fifty years ago, in this room and at this very desk,[1] President
Woodrow Wilson spoke words which caught the imagination of a

war-weary world. He said: "This is the war to end war." His dream for peace after World War I was shattered on the hard realities of great power politics and Woodrow Wilson died a broken man.

Tonight I do not tell you that the war in Vietnam is the war to end wars. But I do say this: I have initiated a plan which will end this war in a way that will bring us closer to that great goal to which Woodrow Wilson and every American President in our history has been dedicated—the goal of a just and lasting peace.

As President I hold the responsibility for choosing the best path to that goal and then leading the Nation along it.

I pledge to you tonight that I shall meet this responsibility with all of the strength and wisdom I can command in accordance with your hopes, mindful of your concerns, sustained by your prayers.

Thank you and goodnight.

NOTE

The President spoke at 9:32 p.m. in his office at the White House. The address was broadcast on radio and television.

On November 3, 1969, the White House Press Office released an advance text of the address.

1. Later research indicated that the desk had not been President Woodrow Wilson's as had long been assumed but was used by Vice President Henry Wilson during President Grant's administration.

Jimmy Carter
Panama Canal Treaties
February 1, 1978

GOOD EVENING

Seventy-five years ago, our Nation signed a treaty which gave us rights to build a canal across Panama, to take the historic step of joining the Atlantic and Pacific Oceans. The results of the agreement have been of great benefit to ourselves and to other nations throughout the world who navigate the high seas.

The building of the canal was one of the greatest engineering feats of history. Although massive in concept and construction, it's relatively simple in design and has been reliable and efficient in operation. We Americans are justly and deeply proud of this great achievement.

The canal has also been a source of pride and benefit to the people of Panama—but a cause of some continuing discontent. Because we have controlled a 10-mile-wide strip of land across the heart of their country and because they considered the original terms of the agreement to be unfair, the people of Panama have been dissatisfied with the treaty. It was drafted here in our country and was not signed by any Panamanian. Our own Secretary of State who did sign the original treaty said it was "vastly advantageous to the United States and . . . not so advantageous to Panama."

In 1964, after consulting with former Presidents Truman and Eisenhower, President Johnson committed our Nation to work towards a new treaty with the Republic of Panama. And last summer, after 14 years of negotiation under two Democratic Presidents and two Republican Presidents, we reached and signed an agreement that is fair and beneficial to both countries. The United States Senate will soon be debating whether these treaties should be ratified.

Throughout the negotiations, we were determined that our national security interests would be protected; that the canal would always be open and neutral and available to ships of all nations; that in time of need or emergency our warships would have the right to go to the head of the line for priority passage through the canal; and that our military forces would have the permanent right to defend the canal if it should ever be in danger. The new treaties meet all of these requirements.

Let me outline the terms of the agreement. There are two treaties—one covering the rest of this century, and the other guaranteeing the safety, openness, and neutrality of the canal after the year 1999, when Panama will be in charge of its operation.

For the rest of this century, we will operate the canal through a nine-person board of directors. Five members will be from the United States and four will be from Panama. Within the area of the present Canal Zone, we have the right to select whatever lands and waters our military and civilian forces need to maintain, to operate, and to defend the canal.

About 75 percent of those who now maintain and operate the canal are Panamanians; over the next 22 years, as we manage the canal together, this percentage will increase. The Americans who work on the canal will continue to have their rights of employment, promotion, and retirement carefully protected.

We will share with Panama some of the fees paid by shippers who use the canal. As in the past, the canal should continue to be self-supporting.

This is not a partisan issue. The treaties are strongly backed by President Gerald Ford and by Former Secretaries of State Dean Rusk and Henry Kissinger. They are endorsed by our business and professional leaders, especially those who recognize the benefits of good will and trade with other nations in this hemisphere. And they were endorsed overwhelmingly by the Senate Foreign Relations Committee which, this week, moved closer to ratification by approving the treaties, although with some recommended changes which we do not feel are needed.

And the treaties are supported enthusiastically by every member of the Joint Chiefs of Staff—General George Brown, the

Chairman, General Bernard Rogers, Chief of Staff of the Army, Admiral James Holloway, Chief of Naval Operations, General David Jones, Chief of Staff of the Air Force, and General Louis Wilson, Commandant of the Marine Corps—responsible men whose profession is the defense of this Nation and the preservation of our security.

The treaties also have been overwhelmingly supported throughout Latin America, but predictably, they are opposed abroad by some who are unfriendly to the United States and who would like to see disorder in Panama and a disruption of our political, economic, and military ties with our friends in Central and South America and in the Caribbean.

I know that the treaties also have been opposed by many Americans. Much of that opposition is based on misunderstanding and misinformation. I've found that when the full terms of the agreement are known, most people are convinced that the national interests of our country will be served best by ratifying the treaties.

Tonight, I want you to hear the facts. I want to answer the most serious questions and tell you why I feel the Panama Canal treaties should be approved.

The most important reason—the only reason—to ratify the treaties is that they are in the highest national interest of the United States and will strengthen our position in the world. Our security interests will be stronger. Our trade opportunities will be improved. We will demonstrate that as a large and powerful country, we are able to deal fairly and honorably with a proud but smaller sovereign nation. We will honor our commitment to those engaged in world commerce that the Panama Canal will be open and available for use by their ships—at a reasonable and competitive cost—both now and in the future.

Let me answer specifically the most common questions about the treaties.

Will our Nation have the right to protect and defend the canal against any armed attack or threat to the security of the canal or of ships going through it?

The answer is yes, and is contained in both treaties and also in the statement of understanding between the leaders of our two nations.

The first treaty says, and I quote: "The United States of

America and the Republic of Panama commit themselves to protect and defend the Panama Canal. Each Party shall act, in accordance with its constitutional processes, to meet the danger resulting from an armed attack or other actions which threaten the security of the Panama Canal or [of] ships transiting it."

The neutrality treaty says, and I quote again: "The United States of America and the Republic of Panama agree to maintain the regime of neutrality established in this Treaty, which shall be maintained in order that the Canal shall remain permanently neutral. . . . "

And to explain exactly what that means, the statement of understanding says, and I quote again: "Under (the Neutrality Treaty), Panama and the United States have the responsibility to assure that the Panama Canal will remain open and secure to ships of all nations. The correct interpretation of this principle is that each of the two countries shall, in accordance with their respective constitutional processes, defend the Canal against any threat to the regime of neutrality, and consequently [shall] have the right to act against the Canal or against the peaceful transit of vessels through the Canal."

It is obvious that we can take whatever military action is necessary to make sure that the canal always remains open and safe.

Of course, this does not give the United States any right to intervene in the internal affairs of Panama, nor would our military action ever be directed against the territorial integrity or the political independence of Panama.

Military experts agree that even with the Panamanian Armed Forces joined with us as brothers against a common enemy, it would take a large number of American troops to ward off a heavy attack. I, as President, would not hesitate to deploy whatever armed forces are necessary to defend the canal, and I have no doubt that even in a sustained combat, that we would be successful. But there is a much better way than sending our sons and grandsons to fight in the jungles of Panama.

We would serve our interests better by implementing the new treaties, an action that will help to avoid any attack on the Panama Canal.

What we want is the permanent right to use the canal—and we can defend this right through the treaties—through real cooperation with Panama. The citizens of Panama and their government have already shown their support of the new partnership, and a protocol to the neutrality treaty will be signed by many other nations, thereby showing their strong approval.

The new treaties will naturally change Panama from a passive and sometimes deeply resentful bystander into an active and interested partner, whose vital interests will be served by a well-operated canal. This agreement leads to cooperation and not confrontation between our country and Panama.

Another question is: Why should we give away the Panama Canal Zone? As many people say, "We bought it, we paid for it, it's ours."

I must repeat a very important point: We do not own the Panama Canal Zone. We have never had sovereignty over it. We have only had the right to use it.

The Canal Zone cannot be compared with United States territory. We bought Alaska from the Russians, and no one has ever doubted that we own it. We bought the Louisiana Purchases—Territories from France, and that's an integral part of the United States.

From the beginning, we have made an annual payment to Panama to use their land. You do not pay rent on your own land. The Panama Canal Zone has always been Panamanian territory. The U.S. Supreme Court and previous American Presidents have repeatedly acknowledged the sovereignty of Panama over the Canal Zone.

We've never needed to own the Panama Canal Zone, any more than we need to own a 10-mile-wide strip of land all the way through Canada from Alaska when we build an international gas pipeline.

The new treaties give us what we do need—not ownership of the canal, but the right to use it and to protect it. As the Chairman of the Joint Chiefs of Staff has said, "The strategic value of the canal lies in its use."

There's another question: Can our naval ships, our warships, in time of need or emergency, get through the canal immediately instead of waiting in line?

The treaties answer that clearly by guaranteeing that our ships will always have expeditious transit through the canal. To make sure that there could be no possible disagreement about what these words mean, the joint statement says that expeditious transit, and I quote, "is intended ... to assure the transit of such vessels through the Canal as quickly as possible, without any impediment, with expedited treatment, and in case of need of emergency, to go to the head of the line of vessels in order to transit the Canal rapidly."

Will the treaties affect our standing in Latin America? Will they create a so-called power vacuum, which our enemies might move in to fill? They will do just the opposite. The treaties will increase our Nation's influence in this hemisphere, will help to reduce any mistrust and disagreement, and they will remove a major source of anti-American feeling.

The new agreement has already provided vivid proof to the people of this hemisphere that a new era of friendship and cooperation is beginning and that what they regard as the last remnant of alleged American colonialism is being removed.

Last fall, I met individually with the leaders of 18 countries in this hemisphere. Between the United States and Latin America there is already a new sense of equality, a new sense of trust and mutual respect that exists because of the Panama Canal treaties. This opens up a fine opportunity for us in good will, trade, jobs, exports, and political cooperation.

If the treaties should be rejected, this would all be lost, and disappointment and despair among our good neighbors and traditional friends would be severe.

In the peaceful struggle against alien ideologies like communism, these treaties are a step in the right direction. Nothing could strengthen our competitors and adversaries in this hemisphere more than for us to reject this agreement.

What if a new sea-level canal should be needed in the future? This question has been studied over and over throughout this century, from before the time the canal was built up through the last few years. Every study has reached the same conclusion—that the best place to build a sea-level canal is in Panama.

The treaties say that if we want to build such a canal, we will build it in Panama, and if any canal is to be built in Panama, that we, the United States, will have the right to participate in the project.

This is a clear benefit to us, for it ensures that, say, 10 or 20 years from now, no unfriendly but wealthy power will be able to purchase the right to build a sea-level canal, to bypass the existing canal, perhaps leaving that other nation in control of the only usable waterway across the isthmus.

Are we paying Panama to take the canal? We are not. Under the new treaty, any payments to Panama will come from tolls paid by ships which use the canal.

What about the present and the future stability and the capability of the Panamanian Government? Do the people of Panama themselves support the agreement?

Well, as you know, Panama and her people have been our historical allies and friends. The present leader of Panama has been in office for more than 9 years, and he heads a stable government which has encouraged the development of free enterprise in Panama. Democratic elections will be held this August to choose the members of the Panamanian Assembly, who will in turn elect a President and a Vice President by majority vote. In the past, regimes have changed in Panama, but for 75 years, no Panamanian government has ever wanted to close the canal.

Panama wants the canal open and neutral—perhaps even more than we do. The canal's continued operation is very important to us, but it is much more than that to Panama. To Panama, it's crucial. Much of her economy flows directly or indirectly from the canal. Panama would be no more likely to neglect or to close the canal than we would be to close the Interstate Highway System here in the United States.

In an open and free referendum last October, which was monitored very carefully by the United Nations, the people of Panama gave the new treaties their support.

The major threat to the canal comes not from any government of Panama, but from misguided persons who may try to fan the flames of dissatisfaction with the terms of the old treaty.

There's a final question—about the deeper meaning of the treaties themselves, to us and to Panama.

Recently, I discussed the treaties with David McCullough, author of "The Path Between the Seas," the great history of the Panama Canal. He believes that the canal is something that we built and have looked after these many years; it is "ours" in that sense, which is very different from just ownership.

So, when we talk of the canal, whether we are old, young, for or against the treaties, we are talking about very deep and elemental feelings about our own strength.

Still, we Americans want a more humane and stable world. We believe in good will and fairness, as well as strength. This agreement with Panama is something we want because we know it is right. This is not merely the surest way to protect and save the canal, it's a strong, positive act of a people who are still confident, still creative, still great.

This new partnership can become a source of national pride and self-respect in much the same way that building the canal was 75 years ago. It's the spirit in which we act that is so very important.

Theodore Roosevelt, who was President when America built the canal, saw history itself as a force, and the history of our own time and the changes it has brought would not be lost on him. He knew that change was inevitable and necessary. Change is growth. The true conservative, he once remarked, keeps his face to the future.

But if Theodore Roosevelt were to endorse the treaties, as I'm quite sure he would, it would be mainly because he could see the decision as one by which we are demonstrating the kind of great power we wish to be.

"We cannot avoid meeting great issues," Roosevelt said. "All that we can determine for ourselves is whether we shall meet them well or ill."

The Panama Canal is a vast, heroic expression of that age-old desire to bridge the divide and to bring people closer together. This is what the treaties are all about.

We can sense what Roosevelt called "the lift toward nobler things which marks a great and generous people."

In this historic decision, he would join us in our pride for being a great and generous people, with the national strength and wisdom to do what is right for us and what is fair to others.

Thank you very much.

NOTE

The President spoke at 9 p.m. from the Library at the White House. His remarks were broadcast live on radio and television.

UNIT THREE

Selected Presidential Responsibilities

Chapter 5 Civil Rights

With a national, rather than state or local, constituency the president is in a unique position to act as an access point or advocate for minority interests. Had the presidents in this section followed their personal preferences or those of their home-town constituents they might have taken far less aggressive actions. But their presidential responsibility to the greater good of the nation and the necessities of the times directed their actions.

Although the effect of the Emancipation Proclamation is known to most Americans its rationale may surprise some readers. It is less a discussion of morality and justice than it is a set of terse military directives from the Commander-in-Chief. In fact, Lincoln drew his justification for taking this sweeping step from a wide interpretation of his war-making powers: there might not have been an emancipation had the Confederacy negotiated a settlement of the war.

President Eisenhower reluctantly ordered federal authorities to restore and maintain the peace while black children attended previously all-white Central High School in Little Rock, Arkansas. Eisenhower superceded the actions of Arkansas Governor Orville Faubus to assure the safe entrance of the students into the school, and then explained his action to the American people. The use of federal military force in domestic affairs has always been controversial and it was no less so in this case. Eisenhower emphasized his constitutional obligation to enforce the laws no matter what the content of those laws or court decisions might be.

President Kennedy inherited the civil rights controversy from Eisenhower. Integration of state universities in parts of the South produced organized opposition and ultimately presidential action.

When Governor George C. Wallace attempted to physically bar black students from admittance to the University of Alabama, Kennedy followed Eisenhower's example. He federalized the national guard and used federal marshalls to insure the black students' entrance into the university. But in his speech to the American people explaining his action Kennedy went a step beyond Eisenhower and called upon Congress to swiftly enact civil rights legislation. Additionally, he raised the ongoing argument from a legal to a moral plane, perhaps partly because Wallace's "Schoolhouse Door" speech had attempted to respond to the legal arguments for federal action.

President Johnson was more active than any other President in the area of civil rights, and he used many strategies to further his campaign. Using the potent symbolic nature of the presidency Johnson delivered the commencement address at prestigious all-black Howard University. By personally addressing a black audience he symbolically demonstrated their importance to both his presidency and the nation. This value-laden speech led to the controversial "affirmative action" initiatives.

Abraham Lincoln
Emancipation Proclamation
January 1, 1863

Whereas on the 22d day of September, A.D. 1862, a proclamation was issued by the President of the United States, containing, among other things, the following, to wit:

> That on the 1st day of January, A.D. 1863, all persons held as slaves within any State or designated part of a State the people whereof shall then be in rebellion against the United States shall be then, thenceforward, and forever free; and the executive government of the United States, including the military and naval authority thereof, will recognize and maintain the freedom of such persons and will do no act or acts to repress such persons, or any of them, in any efforts they may make for their actual freedom.

> That the Executive will on the 1st day of January aforesaid, by proclamation, designate the States and parts of States, if any, in which the people thereof, respectively, shall then be in rebellion against the United States; and the fact that any State or the people thereof shall on that day be in good faith represented in the Congress of the United States by members chosen thereto at elections wherein a majority of the qualified voters of such States shall have participated shall, in the absence of strong countervailing testimony, be deemed conclusive evidence that such State and the people thereof are not then in rebellion against the United States.

Now, therefore, I, Abraham Lincoln, President of the United States, by virtue of the power in me vested as Commander in Chief of the Army and Navy of the United States in time of actual armed rebellion against the authority and Government of the United States, and as a fit and necessary war measure for suppressing said rebellion, do, on this 1st day of January, A.D. 1863, and in accordance with my purpose so to do, publicly proclaimed for the full period of one hundred days from the day first above mentioned, order and designate as the States and parts of States wherein the people thereof, respectively, are this day in rebellion against the United States the following, to wit:

Arkansas, Texas, Louisiana (except the parishes of St. Bernard, Plaquemines, Jefferson, St. John, St. Charles, St. James, Ascension, Assumption, Terrebonne, Lafourche, St. Mary, St. Martin, and Orleans, including the city of New Orleans), Mississippi, Alabama, Florida, Georgia, South Carolina, North Carolina, and Virgina (except the forty-eight counties designated as West Virginia, and also the counties of Berkeley, Accomac, Northampton, Elizabeth City, York, Princess Anne, and Norfolk, including the cities of Norfolk and Portsmouth), and which excepted parts are for the present left precisely as if this proclamation were not issued.

And by virtue of the power and for the purpose aforesaid, I do order and declare that all persons held as slaves within said designated States and parts of States are and henceforward shall be free, and that the executive government of the United States, including the military and naval authorities thereof, will recognize and maintain the freedom of said persons.

And I hereby enjoin upon the people so declared to be free to abstain from all violence, unless in necessary self-defense; and I recommend to them that in all cases when allowed they labor faithfully for reasonable wages.

And I further declare and make known that such persons of suitable condition will be received into the armed service of the United States to garrison forts, positions, stations, and other places and to man vessels of all sorts in said service.

And upon this act, sincerely believed to be an act of justice, warranted by the Constitution upon military necessity, I invoke the considerate judgment of mankind and the gracious favor of Almighty God.

In witness whereof I have hereunto set my hand and caused the seal of the United States to be affixed.

[SEAL.]   Done at the city of Washington, this 1st day of January, A.D. 1863, and of the Independence of the United States of America the eighty-seventh.

ABRAHAM LINCOLN.

By the President:
WILLIAM H. SEWARD, *Secretary of State.*

Dwight D. Eisenhower
The Situation in Little Rock
September 24, 1957

GOOD EVENING, MY FELLOW CITIZENS:

For a few minutes this evening I want to speak to you about the serious situation that has arisen in Little Rock. To make this talk I have come to the President's office in the White House. I could have spoken from Rhode Island, where I have been staying recently, but I felt that, in speaking from the house of Lincoln, of Jackson and of Wilson, my words would better convey both the sadness I feel in the action I was compelled today to take and the firmness with which I intend to pursue this course until the orders of the Federal Court at Little Rock can be executed without unlawful interference.

In that city, under the leadership of demagogic extremists, disorderly mobs have deliberately prevented the carrying out of proper orders from a Federal Court. Local authorities have not eliminated that violent opposition and, under the law, I yesterday issued a Proclamation calling upon the mob to disperse.

This morning the mob again gathered in front of the Central High School of Little Rock, obviously for the purpose of again preventing the carrying out of the Court's order relating to the admission of Negro children to that school.

Whenever normal agencies prove inadequate to the task and it becomes necessary for the Executive Branch of the Federal Government to use its powers and authority to uphold Federal Courts, the President's responsibility is inescapable.

In accordance with that responsibility, I have today issued an Executive Order directing the use of troops under Federal authority to aid in the execution of Federal law at Little Rock, Arkansas. This became necessary when my Proclamation of yesterday was not observed, and the obstruction of justice still continues.

It is important that the reasons for my action be understood by all our citizens.

As you know, the Supreme Court of the United States has decided that separate public educational facilities for the races are inherently unequal and therefore compulsory school segregation laws are unconstitutional.

Our personal opinions about the decision have no bearing on the matter of enforcement; the responsibility and authority of the Supreme Court to interpret the Constitution are very clear. Local Federal Courts were instructed by the Supreme Court to issue such orders and decrees as might be necessary to achieve admission to public schools without regard to race—and with all deliberate speed.

During the past several years, many communities in our Southern States have instituted public school plans for gradual progress in the enrollment and attendance of school children of all races in order to bring themselves into compliance with the law of the land.

They thus demonstrated to the world that we are a nation in which laws, not men, are supreme.

I regret to say that this truth—the cornerstone of our liberties—was not observed in this instance.

It was my hope that this localized situation would be brought under control by city and State authorities. If the use of local police powers had been sufficient, our traditional method of leaving the problems in those hands would have been pursued. But when large gatherings of obstructionists made it impossible for the decrees of the Court to be carried out, both the law and the national interest demanded that the President take action.

Here is the sequence of events in the development of the Little Rock school case.

In May of 1955, the Little Rock School Board approved a moderate plan for the gradual desegregation of the public schools in that city. It provided that a start toward integration would be made at the present term in the high school, and that the plan would be in full operation by 1963. Here I might say that in a number of communities in Arkansas integration in the schools has already started and without violence of any kind. Now this Little Rock plan was challenged in the courts by some who believed that the period of time as proposed in the plan was too long.

The United States Court at Little Rock, which has supervisory responsibility under the law for the plan of desegregation in the public schools, dismissed the challenge, thus approving a gradual rather than an abrupt change from the existing system. The court found that the school board had acted in good faith in planning for a public school system free from racial discrimination.

Since that time, the court has on three separate occasions issued orders directing that the plan be carried out. All persons were instructed to refrain from interfering with the efforts of the school board to comply with the law.

Proper and sensible observance of the law then demanded the respectful obedience which the nation has a right to expect from all its people. This, unfortunately, has not been the case at Little Rock. Certain misguided persons, many of them imported into Little Rock by agitators, have insisted upon defying the law and have sought to bring it into disrepute. The orders of the court have thus been frustrated.

The very basis of our individual rights and freedoms rests upon the certainty that the President and the Executive Branch of Government will support and insure the carrying out of the decisions of the Federal Courts, even, when necessary with all the means at the President's command.

Unless the President did so, anarchy would result.

There would be no security for any except that which each one of us could provide for himself.

The interest of the nation in the proper fulfillment of the law's requirements cannot yield to opposition and demonstrations by some few persons.

Mob rule cannot be allowed to override the decisions of our courts.

Now, let me make it very clear that Federal troops are not being used to relieve local and state authorities of their primary duty to preserve the peace and order of the community. Nor are the troops there for the purpose of taking over the responsibility of the School Board and the other responsible local officials in running Central High School. The running of our school system and the maintenance of peace and order in each of our States are strictly local affairs and the Federal Government does not interfere except in a very few special cases and when requested by one of the several States. In the present case the troops are there, pursuant to law, solely for the purpose of preventing interference with the orders of the Court.

The proper use of the powers of the Executive Branch to enforce the orders of a Federal Court is limited to extraordinary and compelling circumstances. Manifestly, such an extreme situation has been created in Little Rock. This challenge must be met and with such measures as will preserve to the people as a whole their lawfully-protected rights in a climate permitting their free and fair exercise.

The overwhelming majority of our people in every section of the country are united in their respect for observance of the law— even in those cases where they may disagree with that law.

They deplore the call of extremists to violence.

The decision of the Supreme Court concerning school integration, of course, affects the South more seriously than it does other sections of the country. In that region I have many warm friends, some of them in the city of Little Rock. I have deemed it a great personal privilege to spend in our Southland tours of duty while in the military service and enjoyable recreational periods since that time.

So from intimate personal knowledge, I know that the overwhelming majority of the people in the South—including those of Arkansas and of Little Rock—are of good will, united in their efforts to preserve and respect the law even when they disagree with it.

They do not sympathize with mob rule. They, like the rest of our nation, have proved in two great wars their readiness to sacrifice for America.

A foundation of our American way of life is our national respect for law.

In the South, as elsewhere, citizens are keenly aware of the tremendous disservice that has been done to the people of Arkansas in the eyes of the nation, and that has been done to the nation in the eyes of the world.

At a time when we face grave situations abroad because of the hatred that Communism bears toward a system of government based on human rights; it would be difficult to exaggerate the harm that is being done to the prestige and influence, and indeed to the safety, of our nation and the world.

Our enemies are gloating over this incident and using it everywhere to misrepresent our whole nation. We are portrayed as a violator of those standards of conduct which the peoples of the world united to proclaim in the Charter of the United Nations. There they affirmed "faith in fundamental human rights" and "in the dignity and worth of the human person" and they did so "without distinction as to race, sex, language or religion."

And so, with deep confidence, I call upon the citizens of the State of Arkansas to assist in bringing to an immediate end all interference with the law and its processes. If resistance to the Federal Court orders cease at once, the further presence of Federal troops will be unnecessary and the City of Little Rock will return to its normal habits of peace and order and a blot upon the fair name and high honor of our nation in the world will be removed.

Thus will be restored the image of America and of all its parts as one nation, indivisible, with liberty and justice for all.

Good night, and thank you very much.

NOTE

The President referred to Proclamation 3204 "Obstruction of Justice in the State of Arkansas" and Executive Order 10730 "Providing Assistance for the Removal of an Obstruction of Justice Within the State of Arkansas," published in the Federal Register (22 F.R. 7628) and in Title 3 of the Code of Federal Regulations.

John F. Kennedy
Civil Rights
June 11, 1963

GOOD EVENING, MY FELLOW CITIZENS:

This afternoon, following a series of threats and defiant statements, the presence of Alabama National Guardsmen was required on the University of Alabama to carry out the final and unequivocal order of the United States District Court of the Northern District of Alabama. That order called for the admission of two clearly qualified young Alabama residents who happened to have been born Negro.

That they were admitted peacefully on the campus is due in good measure to the conduct of the students of the University of Alabama, who met their responsibilities in a constructive way.

I hope that every American, regardless of where he lives, will stop and examine his conscience about this and other related incidents. This Nation was founded by men of many nations and backgrounds. It was founded on the principle that all men are created equal, and that the rights of every man are diminished when the rights of one man are threatened.

Today we are committed to a worldwide struggle to promote and protect the rights of all who wish to be free. And when Americans are sent to Viet-Nam or West Berlin, we do not ask for whites only. It ought to be possible, therefore, for American students of any color to attend any public institution they select without having to be backed up by troops.

It ought to be possible for American consumers of any color to receive equal service in places of public accommodation, such as hotels and restaurants and theaters and retail stores, without being forced to resort to demonstrations in the street, and it ought to be possible for American citizens of any color to register and to vote in a free election without interference or fear of reprisal.

It ought to be possible, in short, for every American to enjoy the privileges of being American without regard to his race or his color. In short, every American ought to have the right to be treated as he would wish to be treated, as one would wish his children to be treated. But this is not the case.

The Negro baby born in America today, regardless of the section of the Nation in which he is born, has about one-half as much chance of completing a high school as a white baby born in the same place on the same day, one-third as much chance of completing college, one-third as much chance of becoming a professional man, twice as much chance of becoming unemployed, about one-seventh as much chance of earning $10,000 a year, a life expectancy which is 7 years shorter, and the prospects of earning only half as much.

This is not a sectional issue. Difficulties over segregation and discrimination exist in every city, in every State of the Union, producing in many cities a rising tide of discontent that threatens the public safety. Nor is this a partisan issue. In a time of domestic crisis men of good will and generosity should be able to unite regardless of party or politics. This is not even a legal or legislative issue alone. It is better to settle these matters in the courts than on the streets, and new laws are needed at every level, but law alone cannot make men see right.

We are confronted primarily with a moral issue. It is as old as the scriptures and is as clear as the American Constitution.

The heart of the question is whether all Americans are to be afforded equal rights and equal opportunities, whether we are going to treat our fellow Americans as we want to be treated. If an American, because his skin is dark, cannot eat lunch in a restaurant open to the public, if he cannot send his children to the best public school available, if he cannot vote for the public officials who represent him, if, in short, he cannot enjoy the full and free life which all of us want, then who among us would be content to have the color of his skin changed and stand in his place? Who among us would then be content with the counsels of patience and delay?

One hundred years of delay have passed since President Lincoln freed the slaves, yet their heirs, their grandsons, are not fully free. They are not yet freed from the bonds of injustice. They are not yet freed from social and economic oppression. And this Nation, for all its hopes and all its boasts, will not be fully free until all its citizens are free.

We preach freedom around the world, and we mean it, and we cherish our freedom here at home, but are we to say to the world, and much more importantly, to each other that this is a land of the free except for the Negroes; that we have no second-class citizens except Negroes; that we have no class or caste system, no ghettoes, no master race except with respect to Negroes?

Now the time has come for this Nation to fulfill its promise. The events in Birmingham and elsewhere have so increased the cries for equality that no city or State or legislative body can prudently choose to ignore them.

The fires of frustration and discord are burning in every city, North and South, where legal remedies are not at hand. Redress is sought in the streets, in demonstrations, parades, and protests which create tensions and threaten violence and threaten lives.

We face, therefore, a moral crisis as a country and as a people. It cannot be met by repressive police action. It cannot be left to increased demonstrations in the streets. It cannot be quieted by token moves or talk. It is a time to act in the Congress, in your State and local legislative body and, above all, in all of our daily lives.

It is not enough to pin the blame on others, to say this is a problem of one section of the country or another, or deplore the fact that we face. A great change is at hand, and our task, our obligation, is to make that revolution, that change, peaceful and constructive for all.

Those who do nothing are inviting shame as well as violence. Those who act boldly are recognizing right as well as reality.

Next week I shall ask the Congress of the United States to act, to make a commitment it has not fully made in this century to the proposition that race has no place in American life or law. The Federal judiciary has upheld that proposition in a series of forthright cases. The executive branch has adopted that proposition in the conduct of its affairs, including the employment of

Federal personnel, the use of Federal facilities, and the sale of federally financed housing.

But there are other necessary measures which only the Congress can provide, and they must be provided at this session. The old code of equity law under which we live commands for every wrong a remedy, but in too many communities, in too many parts of the country, wrongs are inflicted on Negro citizens and there are no remedies at law. Unless the Congress acts, their only remedy is in the street.

I am, therefore, asking the Congress to enact legislation giving all Americans the right to be served in facilities which are open to the public—hotels, restaurants, theaters, retail stores, and similar establishments.

This seems to me to be an elementary right. Its denial is an arbitrary indignity that no American in 1963 should have to endure, but many do.

I have recently met with scores of business leaders urging them to take voluntary action to end this discrimination and I have been encouraged by their response, and in the last 2 weeks over 75 cities have seen progress made in desegregating these kinds of facilities. But many are unwilling to act alone, and for this reason, nationwide legislation is needed if we are to move this problem from the streets to the courts

I am also asking Congress to authorize the Federal Government to participate more fully in lawsuits designed to end segregation in public education. We have succeeded in persuading many districts to desegregate voluntarily. Dozens have admitted Negroes without violence. Today a Negro is attending a State-supported institution in every one of our 50 States, but the pace is very slow.

Too many Negro children entering segregated grade schools at the time of the Supreme Court's decision 9 years ago will enter segregated high schools this fall, having suffered a loss which can never be restored. The lack of an adequate education denies the Negro a chance to get a decent job.

The orderly implementation of the Supreme Court decision, therefore, cannot be left solely to those who may not have the economic resources to carry the legal action or who may be subject to harassment.

Other features will be also requested, including greater protection for the right to vote. But legislation, I repeat, cannot solve this problem alone. It must be solved in the homes of every American in every community across our country.

In this respect, I want to pay tribute to those citizens North and South who have been working in their communities to make life better for all. They are acting not out of a sense of legal duty but out of a sense of human decency.

Like our soldiers and sailors in all parts of the world they are meeting freedom's challenge on the firing line, and I salute them for their honor and their courage.

My fellow Americans, this is a problem which faces us all—in every city of the North as well as the South. Today there are Negroes unemployed, two or three times as many compared to whites, inadequate in education, moving into the large cities, unable to find work, young people particularly out of work without hope, denied equal rights, denied the opportunity to eat at a restaurant or lunch counter or go to a movie theater, denied the right to a decent education, denied almost today the right to attend a State university even though qualified. It seems to me that these are matters which concern us all, not merely Presidents or Congressmen or Governors, but every citizen of the United States.

This is one country. It has become one country because all of us and all the people who came here had an equal chance to develop their talents.

We cannot say to 10 percent of the population that you can't have that right; that your children can't have the chance to develop whatever talents they have; that the only way that they are going to get their rights is to go into the streets and demonstrate. I think we owe them and we owe ourselves a better country than that.

Therefore, I am asking for your help in making it easier for us to move ahead and to provide the kind of equality of treatment which we would want ourselves; to give a chance for every child to be educated to the limit of his talents.

As I have said before, not every child has an equal talent or an equal ability or an equal motivation, but they should have the equal right to develop their talent and their ability and their motivation, to make something of themselves.

We have a right to expect that the Negro community will be

responsible, will uphold the law, but they have a right to expect that the law will be fair, that the Constitution will be color blind, as Justice Harlan said at the turn of the century.

This is what we are talking about and this is a matter which concerns this country and what it stands for, and in meeting it I ask the support of all our citizens.

Thank you very much.

Lyndon B. Johnson
Commencement Address at
Howard University
June 4, 1965

DR. NABRIT, MY FELLOW AMERICANS:

I am delighted at the chance to speak at this important and this historic institution. Howard has long been an outstanding center for the education of Negro Americans. Its students are of every race and color and they come from many countries of the world. It is truly a working example of democratic excellence.

Our earth is the home of revolution. In every corner of every continent men charged with hope contend with ancient ways in the pursuit of justice. They reach for the newest of weapons to realize the oldest of dreams, that each may walk in freedom and pride, stretching his talents, enjoying the fruits of the earth.

Our enemies may occasionally seize the day of change, but it is the banner of our revolution they take. And our own future is linked to this process of swift and turbulent change in many lands in the world. But nothing in any country touches us more profoundly, and nothing is more freighted with meaning for our own destiny than the revolution of the Negro American.

In far too many ways American Negroes have been another nation: deprived of freedom, crippled by hatred, the doors of opportunity closed to hope.

In our time change has come to this Nation, too. The American Negro, acting with impressive restraint, has peacefully protested and marched, entered the courtrooms and the seats of government, demanding a justice that has long been denied. The voice of the Negro was the call to action. But it is a tribute to America that, once aroused, the courts and the Congress, the President and most of the people, have been the allies of progress.

LEGAL PROTECTION FOR HUMAN RIGHTS

Thus we have seen the high court of the country declare that discrimination based on race was repugnant to the Constitution, and therefore void. We have seen in 1957, and 1960, and again in 1964, the first civil rights legislation in this Nation in almost an entire century.

As majority leader of the United States Senate, I helped to guide two of these bills through the Senate. And, as your President, I was proud to sign the third. And now very soon we will have the fourth—a new law guaranteeing every American the right to vote.

No act of my entire administration will give me greater satisfaction than the day when my signature makes this bill, too, the law of this land.

The voting rights bill will be the latest, and among the most important, in a long series of victories. But this victory—as Winston Churchill said of another triumph for freedom—"is not the end. It is not even the beginning of the end. But it is, perhaps, the end of the beginning."

That beginning is freedom; and the barriers to that freedom are tumbling down. Freedom is the right to share, share fully and equally, in American society—to vote, to hold a job, to enter a public place, to go to school. It is the right to be treated in every part of our national life as a person equal in dignity and promise to all others.

FREEDOM IS NOT ENOUGH

But freedom is not enough. You do not wipe away the scars of centuries by saying: Now you are free to go where you want, and do as you desire, and choose the leaders you please.

You do not take a person who, for years, has been hobbled by chains and liberate him, bring him up to the starting line of a race and then say, "you are free to compete with all the others," and still justly believe that you have been completely fair.

Thus it is not enough just to open the gates of opportunity. All our citizens must have the ability to walk through those gates. This is the next and the more profound stage of the battle for civil rights. We seek not just freedom but opportunity. We seek not just legal equity but human ability, not just equality as a right and a theory but equality as a fact and equality as a result.

For the task is to give 20 million Negroes the same chance as every other American to learn and grow, to work and share in society, to develop their abilities—physical, mental and spiritual, and to pursue their individual happiness.

To this end equal opportunity is essential, but not enough, not enough. Men and women of all races are born with the same range of abilities. But ability is not just the product of birth. Ability is stretched or stunted by the family that you live with, and the neighborhood you live in—by the school you go to and the poverty or the richness of your surroundings. It is the product of a hundred unseen forces playing upon the little infant, the child, and finally the man.

PROGRESS FOR SOME

This graduating class at Howard University is witness to the indomitable determination of the Negro American to win his way in American life.

The number of Negroes in schools of higher learning has almost doubled in 15 years. The number of nonwhite professional workers has more than doubled in 10 years. The median income of Negro college women tonight exceeds that of white college women. And there are also the enormous accomplishments of distinguished individual Negroes—many of them graduates of this institution, and one of them the first lady ambassador in the history of the United States.

These are proud and impressive achievements. But they tell only the story of a growing middle class minority, steadily narrowing the gap between them and their white counterparts.

A WIDENING GULF

But for the great majority of Negro Americans—the poor, the unemployed, the uprooted, and the dispossessed—there is a much grimmer story. They still, as we meet here tonight, are another nation. Despite the court orders and the laws, despite the legislative victories and the speeches, for them the walls are rising and the gulf is widening.

Here are some of the facts of this American failure.

Thirty-five years ago the rate of unemployment for Negroes and whites was about the same. Tonight the Negro rate is twice as high.

In 1948 the 8 percent unemployment rate for Negro teenage boys was actually less than that of whites. By last year that rate had grown to 23 percent, as against 13 percent for whites unemployed.

Between 1949 and 1959, the income of Negro men relative to white men declined in every section of this country. From 1952 to 1963 the median income of Negro families compared to white actually dropped from 57 percent to 53 percent.

In the years 1955 through 1957, 22 percent of experienced Negro workers were out of work at some time during the year. In 1961 through 1963 that proportion had soared to 29 percent.

Since 1947 the number of white families living in poverty has decreased 27 percent while the number of poorer nonwhite families decreased only 3 percent.

The infant mortality of nonwhites in 1940 was 70 percent greater than whites. Twenty-two years later it was 90 percent greater.

Moreover, the isolation of Negro from white communities is increasing, rather than decreasing as Negroes crowd into the central cities and become a city within a city.

Of course Negro Americans as well as white Americans have shared in our rising national abundance. But the harsh fact of the matter is that in the battle for true equality too many—far too many—are losing ground every day.

THE CAUSES OF INEQUALITY

We are not completely sure why this is. We know the causes are complex and subtle. But we do know the two broad basic reasons. And we do know that we have to act.

First, Negroes are trapped—as many whites are trapped—in inherited, gateless poverty. They lack training and skills. They are shut in, in slums, without decent medical care. Private and public poverty combine to cripple their capacities.

We are trying to attack these evils through our poverty program, through our education program, through our medical care and our other health programs, and a dozen more of the Great Society programs that are aimed at the root causes of this poverty.

We will increase, and we will accelerate, and we will broaden this attack in years to come until this most enduring of foes finally yields to our unyielding will.

But there is a second cause—much more difficult to explain, more deeply grounded, more desperate in its force. It is the devastating heritage of long years of slavery; and a century of oppression, hatred, and injustice.

SPECIAL NATURE OF NEGRO POVERTY

For Negro poverty is not white poverty. Many of its causes and many of its cures are the same. But there are differences—deep, corrosive, obstinate differences—radiating painful roots into the community, and into the family, and the nature of the individual.

These differences are not racial differences. They are solely and simply the consequence of ancient brutality, past injustice, and present prejudice. They are anguishing to observe. For the Negro they are a constant reminder of oppression. For the white they are a constant reminder of guilt. But they must be faced and they must be dealt with and they must be overcome, if we are ever to reach the time when the only difference between Negroes and whites is the color of their skin.

Nor can we find a complete answer in the experience of other American minorities. They made a valiant and a largely successful effort to emerge from poverty and prejudice.

The Negro, like these others, will have to rely mostly upon his own efforts. But he just can not do it alone. For they did not have the heritage of centuries to overcome, and they did not have a cultural tradition which had been twisted and battered by endless years of hatred and hopelessness, nor were they excluded—these others—because of race or color—a feeling whose dark intensity is matched by no other prejudice in our society.

Nor can these differences be understood as isolated infirmities.

They are a seamless web. They cause each other. They result from each other. They reinforce each other.

Much of the Negro community is buried under a blanket of history and circumstance. It is not a lasting solution to lift just one corner of that blanket. We must stand on all sides and we must raise the entire cover if we are to liberate our fellow citizens.

THE ROOTS OF INJUSTICE

One of the differences is the increased concentration of Negroes in our cities. More than 73 percent of all Negroes live in urban areas compared with less than 70 percent of the whites. Most of these Negroes live in slums. Most of these Negroes live together—a separated people.

Men are shaped by their world. When it is a world of decay, ringed by an invisible wall, when escape is arduous and uncertain, and the saving pressures of a more hopeful society are unknown, it can cripple the youth and it can desolate the men.

There is also the burden that a dark skin can add to the search for a productive place in our society. Unemployment strikes most swiftly and broadly at the Negro, and this burden erodes hope. Blighted hope breeds despair. Despair brings indifferences to the learning which offers a way out. And despair, coupled with indifferences, is often the source of destructive rebellion against the fabric of society.

There is also the lacerating hurt of early collision with white hatred or prejudice, distaste or condescension. Other groups have felt similar intolerance. But success and achievement could wipe it away. They do not change the color of a man's skin. I have seen this uncomprehending pain in the eyes of the little, young Mexican-American schoolchildren that I taught many years ago. But it can be overcome. But, for many, the wounds are always open.

FAMILY BREAKDOWN

Perhaps most important—its influence radiating to every part of life—is the breakdown of the Negro family structure. For this, most of all, white America must accept responsibility. It flows from centuries of oppression and persecution of the Negro man. It flows from the long years of degradation and discrimination, which have attacked his dignity and assaulted his ability to produce for his family.

This, too, is not pleasant to look upon. But it must be faced by those whose serious intent is to improve the life of all Americans.

Only a minority—less than half—of all Negro children reach the age of 18 having lived all their lives with both of their parents. At this moment, tonight, little less than two-thirds are at home with both of their parents. Probably a majority of all Negro children receive federally-aided public assistance sometime during their childhood.

The family is the cornerstone of our society. More than any other force it shapes the attitude, the hopes, the ambitions, and the values of the child. And when the family collapses it is the children that are usually damaged. When it happens on a massive scale the community itself is crippled.

So, unless we work to strengthen the family, to create conditions under which most parents will stay together—all the rest: schools and playgrounds, and public assistance, and private concern, will never be enough to cut completely the circle of despair and deprivation.

TO FULFILL THESE RIGHTS

There is no single easy answer to all of these problems.

Jobs are part of the answer. They bring the income which permits a man to provide for his family.

Decent homes in decent surroundings and a chance to learn— an equal chance to learn—are part of the answer.

Welfare and social programs better designed to hold families together are part of the answer.

Care for the sick is part of the answer.

An understanding heart by all Americans is another big part of the answer.

And to all of these fronts—and a dozen more—I will dedicate the expanding efforts of the Johnson administration.

But there are other answers that are still to be found. Nor do we fully understand even all of the problems. Therefore, I want to announce tonight that this fall I intend to call a White House conference of scholars, and experts, and outstanding Negro leaders—men of both races—and officials of Government at every level.

This White House conference's theme and title will be "To Fulfill These Rights."

Its object will be to help the American Negro fulfill the rights which, after the long time of injustice, he is finally about to secure.

To move beyond opportunity to achievement.

To shatter forever not only the barriers of law and public practice, but the walls which bound the condition of many by the color of his skin.

To dissolve, as best we can, the antique enmities of the heart which diminish the holder, divide the great democracy, and do wrong—great wrong—to the children of God.

And I pledge you tonight that this will be a chief goal of my administration, and of my program next year, and in the years to come. And I hope, and I pray, and I believe, it will be a part of the program of all America.

WHAT IS JUSTICE

For what is justice?

It is to fulfill the fair expectations of man.

Thus, American justice is a very special thing. For, from the first, this has been a land of towering expectations. It was to be a nation where each man could be ruled by the common consent of all—enshrined in law, given life by institutions, guided by men themselves subject to its rule. And all—all of every station and origin—would be touched equally in obligation and in liberty.

Beyond the law lay the land. It was a rich land, glowing with more abundant promise than man had ever seen. Here, unlike any place yet known, all were to share the harvest.

And beyond this was the dignity of man. Each could become whatever his qualities of mind and spirit would permit—to strive, to seek, and if he could, to find his happiness.

This is American justice. We have pursued it faithfully to the edge of our imperfections, and we have failed to find it for the American Negro.

So, it is the glorious opportunity of this generation to end the one huge wrong of the American Nation and, in so doing, to find America for ourselves, with the same immense thrill of discovery which gripped those who first began to realize that here, at last, was a home for freedom.

All it will take is for all of us to understand what this country is and what this country must become.

The Scripture promises: "I shall light a candle of understanding in thine heart, which shall not be put out."

Together, and with millions more, we can light that candle of understanding in the heart of all America.

And, once lit, it will never again go out.

NOTE

The President spoke at 6:35 p.m. on the Main Quadrangle in front of the library at Howard University in Washington, after being awarded an honorary degree of doctor of laws. His opening words referred to Dr. James M. Nabrit, Jr., President of the University. During his remarks he referred to Mrs. Patricia Harris, U.S. Ambassador to Luxembourg and former associate professor of law at Howard University.

The Voting Rights Act of 1965 was approved by the President on August 6, 1965

Chapter 6 The National Economy

The American electorate holds the President responsible for the economic well-being of the nation. Although, in fact, there is little that the Chief Executive can personally do to curb economic problems, we expect him to try. The Employment Act of 1946 codified the active role of the president in watching over our pluralistic economic system. The selections in this section deal with four very diverse Presidents' responses to their role as economic leaders.

President Herbert Hoover was not President at the most fortuitous time in our economic history. The stock market crashed in October of 1929 and the Great Depression began. The American people were frightened and confused. A few days after the crash President Hoover discussed the situation at a news conference. The former Secretary of Commerce and Labor's analysis of the crash today seems either paternalistically reassuring or terribly mistaken.

The second selection deals with a second president's handling of the same depression. President Roosevelt began his series of fireside chats with a discussion of banking. A president has an educative role to fulfill in many different policy areas, and this role takes on added importance in the often complex economic realm. Individual citizen cooperation with government initiatives will often spell success or failure for a president's program. This point was lost on neither Roosevelt nor President Truman.

President Johnson urged all-out "War on Poverty" that could only be waged by a cooperative Congress. The use of the State of the Union Address to initiate a major legislative program is not uncommon. Only rarely is the state of the union described to the

American people simply for description's sake. Instead, the current scene is viewed as a launching point for achieving prescribed goals. Although the goals will vary, the admonition to act quickly and firmly on economic matters is a common refrain in presidents' economic messages to the Congress.

Herbert Hoover
The National Economic Condition
November 5, 1929

THE PRESIDENT. I haven't anything of any news here to announce.

I thought perhaps you might like that I discuss the business situation with you just a little, but not from the point of view of publication at all—simply for your own information. I see no particular reasons for making any public statements about it, either directly or indirectly.

The question is one somewhat of analysis. We have had a period of overspeculation that has been extremely widespread, one of those waves of speculation that are more or less uncontrollable, as evidenced by the efforts of the Federal Reserve Board, and that ultimately results in a crash due to its own weight. That crash was perhaps a little expedited by the foreign situation, in that one result of this whole phenomenon has been the congestion of capital in the loan market in New York in the driving up of money rates all over the world.

The foreign central banks having determined that they would bring the crisis to an end, at least so far as their own countries were concerned, advanced money rates very rapidly in practically every European country in order to attract capital that had drifted from Europe into New York, back into their own industry and commerce. Incidentally, the effect of increasing discount rates in Europe is much greater on their business structure than it is with us. Our business structure is not so sensitive to interest rates as theirs is. So their sharp advancement of discount rates tended to affect this market, and probably expedited or even started this movement. But once the movement has taken place we have a number of phenomena that rapidly develop. The first is that the domestic banks in the interior of the United States, and corporations, withdraw their money from the call market.

There has been a very great movement out of New York into the interior of the United States, as well as some movement out of New York into foreign countries. The incidental result of that is to create a difficult situation in New York, but also to increase the available capital in the interior. In the interior there has been, in consequence, a tendency for interest rates to fall at once because of the unemployed capital brought back into interior points.

Perhaps the situation might be clearer on account of its parallel with the last very great crisis, 1907–1908. In that crash the same drain of money immediately took place into the interior. In that case there was no Federal Reserve System. There was no way to acquaint of capital movement over the country, and the interest rates ran up to 300 percent. The result was to bring about a monetary panic in the entire country.

Here with the Federal Reserve System and the activity of the Board, and the ability with which the situation has been handled, there has been a complete isolation of the stock market phenomenon from the rest of the business phenomena in the country. The Board, in cooperation with the banks in New York, has made ample capital available for the call market in substitution of the withdrawals. This has resulted in a general fall of interest rates, not only in the interior, but also in New York, as witness the reduction of the discount rate. So that instead of having a panic rise in interest rates with monetary rise following it, we have exactly the reverse phenomenon—we have a fallen interest rate. That is the normal thing to happen when capital is withdrawn from the call market through diminution in values.

The ultimate result of it is a complete isolation of the stock market phenomenon from the general business phenomenon. In other words, the financial world is functioning entirely normal and rather more easily today than it was 2 weeks ago, because interest rates are less and there is more capital available.

The effect on production is purely psychological. So far there might be said to be from such a shock some tendency on the part of people through alarm to decrease their activities, but there has been no cancellation of any orders whatsoever. There has been some lessening of buying in some of the luxury contracts, but that is not a phenomenon itself.

The ultimate result of the normal course of things would be that with a large release of capital from the speculative market there will be more capital available for the bond and mortgage market. That market has been practically starved for the last 4 or 5 months. There has been practically no—or very little at least—of mortgage or bond money available, practically no bond issues of any consequence. One result has been to create considerable reserves of business. A number of States have not been able to place their bonds for construction; a number of municipalities with bond issues have been held up because of the inability to put them out at what they considered fair rates. There are a great number of business concerns that would proceed with their activities in expansion through mortgage and bond money which have had to delay. All of which comprises a very substantial reserve in the country at the present time. The normal result will be for the mortgage and bond market to spring up again and those reserves to come in with increased activities.

The sum of it is, therefore, that we have gone through a crisis in the stock market, but for the first time in history the crisis has been isolated to the stock market itself. It has not extended into either the production activities of the country or the financial fabric of the country, and for that I think we may give the major credit to the constitution of the Federal Reserve System.

And that is about a summary of the whole situation as it stands at this moment.

NOTE

President Hoover's sixty-third news conference was held in the White House at 12 noon on Tuesday, November 5, 1929.

Franklin D. Roosevelt
"Fireside Chat" on Banking
March 12, 1933

I want to talk for a few minutes with the people of the United States about banking—with the comparatively few who understand the mechanics of banking but more particularly with the overwhelming majority who use banks for the making of deposits and the drawing of checks. I want to tell you what has been done in the last few days, why it was done, and what the next steps are going to be. I recognize that the many proclamations from State capitols and from Washington, the legislation, the Treasury regulations, etc., couched for the most part in banking and legal terms, should be explained for the benefit of the average citizen. I owe this in particular because of the fortitude and good temper with which everybody has accepted the inconvenience and hardships of the banking holiday. I know that when you understand what we in Washington have been about I shall continue to have your cooperation as fully as I have had your sympathy and help during the past week.

First of all, let me state the simple fact that when you deposit money in a bank the bank does not put the money into a safe deposit vault. It invests your money in many different forms of credit—bonds, commercial paper, mortgages and many other kinds of loans. In other words, the bank puts your money to work to keep the wheels of industry and of agriculture turning around. A comparatively small part of the money you put into the bank is kept in currency—an amount which in normal times is wholly sufficient to cover the cash needs of the average citizen. In other words, the total amount of all the currency in the country is only a small fraction of the total deposits in all of the banks.

What, then, happened during the last few days of February and the first few days of March? Because of undermined confidence on the part of the public, there was a general rush by a large portion of our population to turn bank deposits into currency or gold—a rush so great that the soundest banks could not get enough currency to meet the demand. The reason for this was that on the spur of the moment it was, of course, impossible to sell perfectly sound assets of a bank and convert them into cash except at panic prices far below their real value.

By the afternoon of March 3d scarcely a bank in the country was open to do business. Proclamations temporarily closing them in whole or in part had been issued by the Governors in almost all the States.

It was then that I issued the proclamation providing for the nationwide bank holiday, and this was the first step in the Government's reconstruction of our financial and economic fabric.

The second step was the legislation promptly and patriotically passed by the Congress confirming my proclamation and broadening my powers so that it became possible in view of the requirement of time to extend the holiday and lift the ban of that holiday gradually. This law also gave authority to develop a program of rehabilitation of our banking facilities. I want to tell our citizens in every part of the Nation that the national Congress—Republicans and Democrats alike—showed by this action a devotion to public welfare and a realization of the emergency and the necessity for speed that it is difficult to match in our history.

The third stage has been the series of regulations permitting the banks to continue their functions to take care of the distribution of food and household necessities and the payment of payrolls.

This bank holiday, while resulting in many cases in great inconvenience, is affording us the opportunity to supply the currency necessary to meet the situation. No sound bank is a dollar worse off than it was when it closed its doors last Monday. Neither is any bank which may turn out not to be in a position for immediate opening. The new law allows the twelve Federal Reserve Banks to issue additional currency on good assets and thus the banks which reopen will be able to meet every legitimate call. The new currency is being sent out by the Bureau of Engraving and Printing in large volume to every part of the country. It is sound currency because it is backed by actual, good assets.

A question you will ask is this: why are all the banks not to be reopened at the same time? The answer is simple. Your Government does not intend that the history of the past few years shall be repeated. We do not want and will not have another epidemic of bank failures.

As a result, we start tomorrow, Monday, with the opening of banks in the twelve Federal Reserve Bank cities—those banks which on first examination by the Treasury have already been found to be all right. This will be followed on Tuesday by the resumption of all their functions by banks already found to be sound in cities where there are recognized clearing houses. That means about 250 cities of the United States.

On Wednesday and succeeding days banks in smaller places all through the country will resume business, subject, of course, to the Government's physical ability to complete its survey. It is necessary that the reopening of banks be extended over a period in order to permit the banks to make applications for necessary loans, to obtain currency needed to meet their requirements and to enable the Government to make common sense checkups.

Let me make it clear to you that if your bank does not open the first day you are by no means justified in believing that it will not open. A bank that opens on one of the subsequent days is in exactly the same status as the bank that opens tomorrow.

I know that many people are worrying about the State banks not members of the Federal Reserve System. These banks can and will receive assistance from member banks and from the Reconstruction Finance Corporation. These State banks are following the same course as the National banks except that they get their licenses to resume business from the State authorities, and these authorities have been asked by the Secretary of the Treasury to permit their good banks to open up on the same schedule as the national banks. I am confident that the State Banking Departments will be as careful as the national Government in the policy relating to the opening of banks and will follow the same broad policy.

It is possible that when the banks resume a very few people who have not recovered from their fear may again begin withdrawals. Let me make it clear that the banks will take care of all needs—and it is my belief that hoarding during the past week has become an exceedingly unfashionable pastime. It needs no prophet to tell you that when the people find that they can get their money—that they can get it when they want it for all legitimate purposes—the phantom of fear will soon be laid. People will again be glad to have their money where it will be safely taken care of and where they can use it conveniently at any time. I can assure you that it is safer to keep your money in a reopened bank than under the mattress.

The success of our whole great national program depends, of course, upon the cooperation of the public—on its intelligent support and use of a reliable system.

Remember that the essential accomplishment of the new legislation is that it makes it possible for banks more readily to convert their assets into cash than was the case before. More liberal provision has been made for banks to borrow on these assets at the Reserve Banks and more liberal provision has also been made for issuing currency on the security of these good assets. This currency is not fiat currency. It is issued only on adequate security, and every good bank has an abundance of such security.

One more point before I close. There will be, of course, some banks unable to reopen without being reorganized. The new law allows the Government to assist in making these reorganizations quickly and effectively and even allows the Government to subscribe to at least a part of new capital which may be required.

I hope you can see from this elemental recital of what your Government is doing that there is nothing complex, or radical, in the process.

We had a bad banking situation. Some our our bankers had shown themselves either incompetent or dishonest in their handling of the people's funds. They had used the money entrusted to them in speculations and unwise loans. This was, of course, not true in the vast majority of our banks, but it was true in enough of them to shock the people for a time into a sense of insecurity and to put them into a frame of mind where they did not differentiate, but seemed to assume that the acts of a comparative few had tainted them all. It was the Government's job to straighten out this situation and do it as quickly as possible. And the job is being performed.

I do not promise you that every bank will be reopened or that individual losses will not be suffered, but there will be no losses that possibly could be avoided; and there would have been more and greater losses had we continued to drift. I can even promise you salvation for some at least of the sorely pressed banks. We shall be engaged not merely in reopening sound banks but in the creation of sound banks through reorganization.

It has been wonderful to me to catch the note of confidence from all over the country. I can never be sufficiently grateful to the people for the loyal support they have given me in their acceptance of the judgment that has dictated our course, even though all our processes may not have seemed clear to them.

After all, there is an element in the readjustment of our financial system more important than currency, more important than gold, and that is the confidence of the people. Confidence and courage are the essentials of success in carrying out our plan. You people must have faith; you must not be stampeded by rumors or guesses. Let us unite in banishing fear. We have provided the machinery to restore our financial system; it is up to you to support and make it work.

It is your problem no less than it is mine. Together we cannot fail.

Lyndon B. Johnson
The State of the Union
January 8, 1964

MR. SPEAKER, MR. PRESIDENT, MEMBERS OF THE HOUSE AND SENATE, MY FELLOW AMERICANS:

I will be brief, for our time is necessarily short and our agenda is already long.

Last year's congressional session was the longest in peacetime history. With that foundation, let us work together to make this year's session the best in the Nation's history.

Let this session of Congress be known as the session which did more for civil rights than the last hundred sessions combined; as the session which enacted the most far-reaching tax cut of our time; as the session which declared all-out war on human poverty and unemployment in these United States; as the session which finally recognized the health needs of all our older citizens; as the session which reformed our tangled transportation and transit policies; as the session which achieved the most effective, efficient foreign aid program ever; and as the session which helped to build more homes, more schools, more libraries, and more hospitals than any single session of Congress in the history of our Republic.

All this and more can and must be done. It can be done by this summer, and it can be done without any increase in spending. In fact, under the budget that I shall shortly submit, it can be done with an actual reduction in Federal expenditures and Federal employment.

We have in 1964 a unique opportunity and obligation—to prove the success of our system; to disprove those cynics and critics at home and abroad who question our purpose and our competence.

If we fail, if we fritter and fumble away our opportunity in needless, senseless quarrels between Democrats and Republicans, or between the House and the Senate, or between the South and North, or between the Congress and the administration, then history will rightfully judge us harshly. But if we succeed, if we can achieve these goals by forging in this country a greater sense of union, then, and only then, can we take full satisfaction in the State of the Union.

II.

Here in the Congress you can demonstrate effective legislative leadership by discharging the public business with clarity and dispatch, voting each important proposal up, or voting it down, but at least bringing it to a fair and a final vote.

Let us carry forward the plans and programs of John Fitzgerald Kennedy—not because of our sorrow or sympathy, but because they are right.

In his memory today, I especially ask all members of my own political faith, in this election year, to put your country ahead of your party, and to always debate principles; never debate personalities.

For my part, I pledge a progressive administration which is efficient, and honest and frugal. The budget to be submitted to the Congress shortly is in full accord with this pledge.

It will cut our deficit in half—from $10 billion to $4,900 million. It will be, in proportion to our national output, the smallest budget since 1951.

It will call for a substantial reduction in Federal employment, a feat accomplished only once before in the last 10 years. While maintaining the full strength of our combat defenses, it will call for the lowest number of civilian personnel in the Department of Defense since 1950.

It will call for total expenditures of $97,900 million—compared to $98,400 million for the current year, a reduction of more than $500 million. It will call for new obligational authority of $103,800 million—a reduction of more than $4 billion below last year's request of $107,900 million.

But it is not a standstill budget, for America cannot afford to stand still. Our population is growing. Our economy is more complex. Our people's needs are expanding.

But by closing down obsolete installations, by curtailing less urgent programs, by cutting back where cutting back seems to be wise, by insisting on a dollar's worth for a dollar spent, I am able to recommend in this reduced budget the most Federal support in history for education, for health, for retraining the unemployed, and for helping the economically and the physically handicapped.

This budget, and this year's legislative program, are designed to help each and every American citizen fulfill his basic hopes—his hopes for a fair chance to make good; his hopes for fair play from the law; his hopes for a full-time job on full-time pay; his hopes for a decent home for his family in a decent community; his hopes for a good school for his children with good teachers; and his hopes for security when faced with sickness or unemployment or old age.

III.

Unfortunately, many Americans live on the outskirts of hope—some because of their poverty, and some because of their color, and all too many because of both. Our task is to help replace their despair with opportunity.

This administration today, here and now, declares unconditional war on poverty in America. I urge this Congress and all Americans to join with me in that effort.

It will not be a short or easy struggle, no single weapon or strategy will suffice, but we shall not rest until that war is won. The richest Nation on earth can afford to win it. We cannot afford to lose it. One thousand dollars invested in salvaging an unemployable youth today can return $40,000 or more in his lifetime.

Poverty is a national problem, requiring improved national organization and support. But this attack, to be effective, must also be organized at the State and the local level and must be supported and directed by State and local efforts.

For the war against poverty will not be won here in Washington. It must be won in the field, in every private home, in every public office, from the courthouse to the White House.

The program I shall propose will emphasize this cooperative approach to help that one-fifth of all American families with incomes too small to even meet their basic needs.

Our chief weapon in a more pinpointed attack will be better schools, and better health, and better homes, and better training, and better job opportunities to help more Americans, especially young Americans, escape from squalor and misery and unemployment rolls where other citizens help to carry them.

Very often a lack of jobs and money is not the cause of poverty, but the symptom. The cause may lie deeper—in our failure to give our fellow citizens a fair chance to develop their own capacities, in a lack of education and training, in a lack of medical care and housing, in a lack of decent communities in which to live and bring up their children.

But whatever the cause, our joint Federal-local effort must pursue poverty, pursue it wherever it exists—in city slums and small towns, in sharecropper shacks or in migrant worker camps, on Indian Reservations, among whites as well as Negroes, among the young as well as the aged, in the boom towns and in the depressed areas.

Our aim is not only to relieve the symptom of poverty, but to cure it and, above all, to prevent it. No single piece of legislation, however, is going to suffice.

We will launch a special effort in the chronically distressed areas of Appalachia.

We must expand our small but our successful area redevelopment program.

We must enact youth employment legislation to put jobless, aimless, hopeless youngsters to work on useful projects.

We must distribute more food to the needy through a broader food stamp program.

We must create a National Service Corps to help the economically handicapped of our own country as the Peace Corps now helps those abroad.

We must modernize our unemployment insurance and establish a high-level commission on automation. If we have the brain power to invent these machines, we have the brain power to make certain that they are a boon and not a bane to humanity.

We must extend the coverage of our minimum wage laws to more than 2 million workers now lacking this basic protection of purchasing power.

We must, by including special school aid funds as part of our education program, improve the quality of teaching, training, and counseling in our hardest hit areas.

We must build more libraries in every area and more hospitals and nursing homes under the Hill-Burton Act, and train more nurses to staff them.

We must provide hospital insurance for our older citizens financed by every worker and his employer under Social Security, contributing no more than $1 a month during the employee's working career to protect him in his old age in a dignified manner without cost to the Treasury, against the devastating hardship of prolonged or repeated illness.

We must, as a part of a revised housing and urban renewal program, give more help to those displaced by slum clearance, provide more housing for our poor and our elderly, and seek as our ultimate goal in our free enterprise system a decent home for every American family.

We must help obtain more modern mass transit within our communities as well as low-cost transportation between them.

Above all, we must release $11 billion of tax reduction into the private spending stream to create new jobs and new markets in every area of this land.

IV.

These programs are obviously not for the poor or the underprivileged alone. Every American will benefit by the extension of social security to cover the hospital costs of their aged parents. Every American community will benefit from the construction or modernization of schools, libraries, hospitals, and nursing homes, from the training of more nurses and from the improvement of urban renewal in public transit. And every individual American taxpayer and every corporate taxpayer will benefit from the earliest possible passage of the pending tax bill from both the new investment it will bring and the new jobs that it will create.

That tax bill has been thoroughly discussed for a year. Now we need action. The new budget clearly allows it. Our taxpayers surely deserve it. Our economy strongly demands it. And every month of delay dilutes its benefits in 1964 for consumption, for investment, and for employment.

For until the bill is signed, its investment incentives cannot be deemed certain, and the withholding rate cannot be reduced—and the most damaging and devastating thing you can do to any businessman in America is to keep him in doubt and to keep him guessing on what our tax policy is. And I say that we should now reduce to 14 percent instead of 15 percent our withholding rate.

I therefore urge the Congress to take final action on this bill by the first of February, if at all possible. For however proud we may be of the unprecedented progress of our free enterprise economy over the last 3 years, we should not and we cannot permit it to pause.

In 1963, for the first time in history, we crossed the 70 million job mark, but we will soon need more than 75 million jobs. In 1963 our gross national product reached the $600 billion level—$100 billion higher than when we took office. But it easily could and it should be still $30 billion higher today than it is.

Wages and profits and family income are also at their highest levels in history—but I would remind you that 4 million workers and 13 percent of our industrial capacity are still idle today.

We need a tax cut now to keep this country moving.

V.

For our goal is not merely to spread the work. Our goal is to create more jobs. I believe the enactment of a 35-hour week would sharply increase costs, would invite inflation, would impair our ability to compete, and merely share instead of creating employment. But I am equally opposed to the 45- or 50-hour week in those industries where consistently excessive use of overtime causes increased unemployment.

So, therefore, I recommend legislation authorizing the creation of a tripartite industry committee to determine on an industry-by-industry basis as to where a higher penalty rate for overtime would increase job openings without unduly increasing costs, and authorizing the establishment of such higher rates.

VI.

Let me make one principle of this administration abundantly clear: All of these increased opportunities—in employment, in education, in housing, and in every field—must be open to Americans of every color. As far as the writ of Federal law will run, we must abolish not some, but all racial discrimination. For this is not merely an economic issue, or a social, political, or international issue. It is a moral issue, and it must be met by the passage this session of the bill now pending in the House.

All members of the public should have equal access to facilities open to the public. All members of the public should be equally eligible for Federal benefits that are financed by the public. All members of the public should have an equal chance to vote for public officials and to send their children to good public schools and to contribute their talents to the public good.

Today, Americans of all races stand side by side in Berlin and in Viet Nam. They died side by side in Korea. Surely they can work and eat and travel side by side in their own country.

VII.

We must also lift by legislation the bars of discrimination against those who seek entry into our country, particularly those who have much needed skills and those joining their families.

In establishing preferences, a nation that was built by the immigrants of all lands can ask those who now seek admission: "What can you do for our country?" But we should not be asking: "In what country were you born?"

VIII.

For our ultimate goal is a world without war, a world made safe for diversity, in which all men, goods, and ideas can freely move across every border and every boundary.

We must advance toward this goal in 1964 in at least 10 different ways, not as partisans, but as patriots.

First, we must maintain—and our reduced defense budget will

maintain—that margin of military safety and superiority obtained through 3 years of steadily increasing both the quality and the quantity of our strategic, our conventional, and our antiguerrilla forces. In 1964 we will be better prepared than ever before to defend the cause of freedom, whether it is threatened by outright aggression or by the infiltration practiced by those in Hanoi and Havana, who ship arms and men across international borders to foment insurrection. And we must continue to use that strength as John Kennedy used it in the Cuban crisis and for the test ban treaty—to demonstrate both the futility of nuclear war and the possibilities of lasting peace.

Second, we must take new steps—and we shall make new proposals at Geneva—toward the control and the eventual abolition of arms. Even in the absence of agreement, we must not stockpile arms beyond our needs or seek an excess of military power that could be provocative as well as wasteful.

It is in this spirit that in this fiscal year we are cutting back our production of enriched uranium by 25 percent. We are shutting down four plutonium piles. We are closing many nonessential military installations. And it is in this spirit that we today call on our adversaries to do the same.

Third, we must make increased use of our food as an instrument of peace—making it available by sale or trade or loan or donation—to hungry people in all nations which tell us of their needs and accept proper conditions of distribution.

Fourth, we must assure our pre-eminence in the peaceful exploration of outer space, focusing on an expedition to the moon in this decade—in cooperation with other powers if possible, alone if necessary.

Fifth, we must expand world trade. Having recognized in the Act of 1962 that we must *buy* as well as *sell*, we now expect our trading partners to recognize that we must *sell* as well as *buy*. We are willing to give them competitive access to our market, asking only that they do the same for us.

Sixth, we must continue, through such measures as the interest equalization tax, as well as the cooperation of other nations, our recent progress toward balancing our international accounts.

This administration must and will preserve the present gold value of the dollar.

Seventh, we must become better neighbors with the free states of the Americas, working with the councils of the OAS, with a stronger Alliance for Progress, and with all the men and women of this hemisphere who really believe in liberty and justice for all.

Eighth, we must strengthen the ability of free nations everywhere to develop their independence and raise their standard of living, and thereby frustrate those who prey on poverty and chaos. To do this, the rich must help the poor—and we must do our part. We must achieve a more rigorous administration of our development assistance, with larger roles for private investors, for other industrialized nations, and for international agencies and for the recipient nations themselves.

Ninth, we must strengthen our Atlantic and Pacific partnerships, maintain our alliances and make the United Nations a more effective instrument for national independence and international order.

Tenth, and finally, we must develop with our allies new means of bridging the gap between the East and the West, facing danger boldly wherever danger exists, but being equally bold in our search for new agreements which can enlarge the hopes of all, while violating the interests of none.

In short, I would say to the Congress that we must be constantly prepared for the worst, and constantly acting for the best. We must be strong enough to win any war, and we must be wise enough to prevent one.

We shall neither act as aggressors nor tolerate acts of aggression. We intend to bury no one, and we do not intend to be buried.

We can fight, if we must, as we have fought before, but we pray that we will never have to fight again.

IX.

My good friends and my fellow Americans: In these last 7 sorrowful weeks, we have learned anew that nothing is so enduring as faith, and nothing is so degrading as hate.

John Kennedy was a victim of hate, but he was also a great builder of faith—faith in our fellow Americans, whatever their creed or their color or their station in life; faith in the future of man, whatever his divisions and differences.

This faith was echoed in all parts of the world. On every continent and in every land to which Mrs. Johnson and I traveled, we found faith and hope and love toward this land of America and toward our people.

So I ask you now in the Congress and in the country to join with me in expressing and fulfilling that faith in working for a nation, a nation that is free from want and a world that is free from hate—a world of peace and justice, and freedom and abundance, for our time and for all time to come.

Chapter 7
Domestic Crisis Management

Presidential leadership is easy when the president's conscience and public opinion coincide. But when they disagree, the White House lights burn late into the night. A section of speeches about "domestic crises" could conceivably include speeches from almost every president on almost every sort of topic—choices must be made. We consider a "domestic crisis" to be a problem which meets the following criteria: (1) it emerges or peaks during the president's administration, (2) avoiding the problem poses potentially catastrophic consequences for the administration, and (3) any resolution of the problem deeply disturbs important presidential constituencies. In short, the president must act decisively, but every path including delay is fraught with danger.

The 1951–1952 negotiations between the steel companies and the steelworkers' union stalled. In the midst of the Korean War, inaction would have meant that war materials would not have been produced and the entire United Nations action in Korea could have been jeopardized. President Truman chose to pressure both labor and management by means of a nationally broadcast address. And lest this "moral suasion" prove insufficient, Truman ordered the Secretary of Commerce to seize the steel mills, rendering all parties to the dispute government employees. Although the seizure was declared unconstitutional shortly thereafter, it dramatized the president's determination to resolve the crisis.

The Watergate scandal began in June of 1972 when burglars were caught inside Democratic Party headquarters in Washington's Watergate hotel and office complex. Materials in the burglars' possession suggested a connection to the White House.

After personally avoiding the Watergate controversy for ten months, President Nixon addressed the nation on April 30, 1973. Denouncing the Watergate burglary, he accepted nominal responsibility and announced the resignation of his two top aides (John Ehrlichman and H. R. Haldeman), Attorney General Richard Kleindienst, and Presidential Counsel John Dean. Then Nixon absolved them of any wrongdoing and pledged to help investigators find and punish "all the guilty" parties. But Nixon's confused handling of the four strategies of *apologia* contributed to the escalation of the investigation.

First, one may deny that any misconduct occurred—either because the act in question never happened, or because it happened but was not improper. The question of propriety, in turn, can be argued either by differentiating the specific act from the class of similar improper acts, or by arguing that an ordinarily improper act was, in a specific case, necessary and proper because of extraordinary "transcendent" conditions.

A second strategy is to admit that an improper act did occur. But guilt requires punishment. "Mortification" involves taking full blame for the misconduct *and accepting punishment*. This is obviously unpleasant. But precisely because it *is* so unpleasant it often draws a sympathetic response. Ironically, admitting a lack of integrity seems to demonstrate strength of character (as in the familiar tale of George Washington's cherry tree). The alternative is "shifting blame" for the improper act to one or more others who may, or may not, have been connected with the improper act.

The third alternative is to argue that although the act was improper, it was not a unique transgression. One of the first lessons children learn is that "two wrongs don't make a right," and that lesson is rarely forgotten while listening to political speeches. Hence this strategy is both ethically and pragmatically dubious.

Nixon's first Watergate speech added to his problems by (1) continuing to argue that the break-in was both stupid and wrong, (2) implicating Haldeman, Ehrlichmann, and Kliendienst without *blaming* them for the misconduct, (3) exhorting further investigation of the matter, and (4) promising to cooperate with investigators. When Nixon finally resigned rather than face impeachment proceedings, his fate fell to Gerald Ford.

Gerald Ford was selected by Richard Nixon to fill the unexpired term of Vice-President Spiro Agnew, who had been implicated in a Maryland corruption investigation in 1973. Ford became the only president never to have been elected either president or vice-president when Nixon resigned. But the resignation left unsettled the question of Nixon's personal involvement. Had Ford not acted, Nixon would probably have been tried for his role in the cover-up. Would such a trial have been an unreasonable persecution or a necessary prosecution? President Ford decided that the prospective damage to Nixon's health and the country's recovery from the "long national nightmare" necessitated a pardon. Two years later the most frequent reason given by voters for not supporting Gerald Ford was his pardon of Nixon.

One of the most unusual domestic crises was brought to the nation's attention in 1979. Faced with a complex energy crisis and unable to secure congressional passage of his energy program, President Jimmy Carter talked to the nation about what he perceived as a deeper problem. The nation was experiencing, he said, a crisis of confidence in the form of a national "malaise." Most problems would be resolved if Americans would individually and collectively reform their character. But American audiences accustomed to hearing praise (whether justified or not) for our morality and effort applauded those who retorted that the reason for the crisis in confidence was Jimmy Carter himself. This speech illustrates the problems that arise when followers are not interested in moral leadership.

Harry S Truman
The Need for Government
Operation of the Steel Mills
April 8, 1952

MY FELLOW AMERICANS:

Tonight, our country faces a grave danger. We are faced by the possibility that at midnight tonight the steel industry will be shut down. This must not happen.

Steel is our key industry. It is vital to the defense effort. It is vital to peace.

We do not have a stockpile of the kinds of steel we need for defense. Steel is flowing directly from the plants that make it into defense production.

If steel production stops, we will have to stop making the shells and bombs that are going directly to our soldiers at the front in Korea. If steel production stops, we will have to cut down and delay the atomic energy program. If steel production stops, it won't be long before we have to stop making engines for the Air Force planes.

These would be the immediate effects if the steel mills close down. A prolonged shutdown would bring defense production to a halt and throw our domestic economy into chaos.

These are not normal times. These are times of crisis. We have been working and fighting to prevent the outbreak of world war. So far we have succeeded. The most important element in this successful struggle has been our defense program. If that is stopped, the situation can change overnight.

All around the world, we face the threat of military action by the forces of aggression. Our growing strength is holding these forces in check. If our strength fails, these forces may break out in renewed violence and bloodshed.

Our national security and our chances for peace depend on our defense production. Our defense production depends on steel.

As your President, I have to think about the effects that a steel shutdown here would have all over the world.

I have to think about our soldiers in Korea, facing the Chinese Communists, and about our soldiers and allies in Europe, confronted by the military power massed behind the Iron Curtain. I have to think of the danger to our security if we are forced, for lack of steel, to cut down on our atomic energy program.

I have no doubt that if our defense program fails, the danger of war, the possibility of hostile attack, grows that much greater.

I would not be faithful to my responsibilities as President if I did not use every effort to keep this from happening.

With American troops facing the enemy on the field of battle, I would not be living up to my oath of office if I failed to do whatever is required to provide them with the weapons and ammunitions they need for their survival.

Therefore, I am taking two actions tonight.

First, I am directing the Secretary of Commerce to take possession of the steel mills, and to keep them operating.

Second, I am directing the Acting Director of Defense Mobilization to get the representatives of the steel companies and the steelworkers down here to Washington at the earliest possible date in a renewed effort to get them to settle their dispute.

I am taking these measures because it is the only way to prevent a shutdown and to keep steel production rolling. It is also my hope that they will help bring about a quick settlement of the dispute.

I want you to understand clearly why these measures are necessary, and how this situation in the steel industry came about.

In normal times—if we were not in a national emergency—this dispute might not have arisen. In normal times, unions are entitled to whatever wages they can get by bargaining, and companies are entitled to whatever prices they can get in a competitive market.

But today, this is different. There are limitations on what wages employees can get, and there are limitations on what prices employers can charge.

We must have these limitations to prevent a wage-price spiral that would send prices through the roof, and wreck our economy and our defense program.

For more than a year we have prevented any such runaway inflation. We have done it by having rules that are fair to everyone—that require everyone to sacrifice some of his own interests to the national interest. These rules have been laid down under laws enacted by Congress, and they are applied by fair, impartial Government boards and agencies.

These rules have been applied in this steel case. They have been applied to the union, and they have been applied to the companies. The union has accepted these rules. The companies have not accepted them. The companies insist that they must have price increases that are out of line with the stabilization rules. The companies have said that unless they can get those increases they will not settle with the union. The companies have said, in short, that unless they can have what they want, the steel industry will shut down. That is the plain, unvarnished fact of the matter.

Let me tell you how this situation came about.

The steel companies and the steelworkers union had a contract that ran until December 31, 1951.

On November 1, 1951, the union gave notice that in view of the higher cost of living, and the wage increases already received by workers in other industries, the steelworkers wanted higher wages and better working conditions in their new contract for 1952.

The steel companies met with the union but the companies never really bargained. The companies all took the same position. They said there should be no changes in wages and working conditions—in spite of the fact that there had been substantial changes in many other industries, and in spite of the fact that the steel industry is making very high profits.

No progress was made, and a strike was threatened last December 31.

Before that happened, I sent the case to the Wage Stabilization Board. I asked them to investigate the facts and recommend a settlement that would be fair to both parties, and would also be in accordance with our rules for preventing inflation. Meanwhile, I asked both sides to keep the steel industry operating, and they did.

The Wage Board went into the facts very thoroughly. About 3 weeks ago, on March 20, the Wage Board recommended certain wage increases and certain changes in working conditions.

The Wage Board's recommendations were less than the union thought they ought to have. Nevertheless, the union accepted them as a basis for settlement.

There has been a lot of propaganda to the effect that the recommendations of the Wage Board were too high, that they would touch off a new round of wage increases, and that a new wage-price spiral would set in.

The facts are to the contrary. When you look into the matter, you find that the Wage Board's recommendations were fair and reasonable. They were entirely consistent with what has been allowed in other industries over the past 18 months. They are in accord with sound stabilization policies.

Under these recommendations, the steelworkers would simply be catching up with what workers in other major industries are already receiving.

The steelworkers have had no adjustment in their wages since December 1, 1950. Since that time the cost of living has risen, and workers in such industries as automobiles, rubber, electrical equipment, and meatpacking have received increases ranging from 13 to 17 cents an hour.

In the steel case the Wage Board recommended a general wage increase averaging 13¾ cents an hour in 1952. Obviously, this sets no new pattern and breaks no ceiling. It simply permits the steelworkers to catch up to what workers in other industries have already received.

The Board also recommended a 2½ cent wage increase to go into effect next January, if the union would agree to an 18-month contract. In addition, the Board recommended certain other provisions concerning such matters as paid holidays and extra pay for Sunday work. The steel industry has been lagging behind other industries in these matters, and the improvements suggested by the Board are moderate.

When you look at the facts, instead of the propaganda, it is perfectly plain that the Wage Board's recommendations in the steel case do provide a fair and reasonable basis for reaching a settlement on a new management-labor contract—a settlement that is consistent with our present stabilization program. Of course, neither party can ever get everything it thinks it deserves; and, certainly, the parties should bargain out the details. But in the present circumstances, both the companies and the union owe it to the American people to use these recommendations as a basis for reaching a settlement.

The fact of the matter is that the settlement proposed by the Board is fair to both parties and to the public interest. And what's more, I think the steel companies know it. They can read figures just as well as anybody else—just as well as I can or anybody in the business. I think they realize that the Board's recommendations on wages are reasonable, and they are raising all this hullabaloo in an attempt to force the Government to give them a big boost in prices.

Now, what about the price side? Is it true that the steel companies need a big increase in prices in order to be able to raise wages?

Here are the facts.

Steel industry profits are now running at the rate of about $2½ billion a year. The steel companies are now making a profit of about $19.50 on every ton of steel they produce. On top of that, they can get a price increase of close to $3 a ton under the Capehart amendment to the price control law. They don't need this, but we are going to have to give it to them, because the Capehart amendment requires it.

Now add this to the $19.50 a ton they are already making and you have profits of better than $22 a ton.

Now, what would the Wage Board's recommendations do to steel profits? To hear the steel companies talk, you would think the wage increase recommended by the Board would wipe out their profits altogether. Well, the fact of the matter is that if all the recommendations of the Wage Board were put into effect, they would cost the industry about $4 or $5 a ton.

In other words, if the steel companies absorbed every penny of the wage increase, they would still be making profits of $17 or $18 a ton on every ton of steel they made.

Now, a profit of $17 or $18 a ton for steel is extremely high. During 1947, 1948, and 1949, the 3 years before the Korean outbreak, steel profits averaged a little better than $11 a ton. The companies could absorb this wage increase entirely out of profits, and still be making higher profits than they made in the 3 prosperous years before Korea.

The plain fact is, though most people don't realize it, the steel industry has never been so profitable as it is today—at least not since the "profiteering" days of World War I.

And yet, in the face of these facts, the steel companies are now saying they ought to have a price increase of $12 a ton, giving them a profit of $26 or $27 a ton. That's about the most outrageous thing I ever heard of. They not only want to raise their prices to cover any wage increase; they want to double their money on the deal.

Suppose we were to yield to these demands. Suppose we broke out price control rules, and gave the steel companies a big price increase. That would be a terrible blow to the stability of the economy of the United States of America.

A big boost in steel prices would raise the prices of other things all up and down the line. Sooner or later, prices of all the products that use steel would go up—tanks and trucks and buildings, automobiles and vacuum cleaners and refrigerators, right on down to canned goods and egg beaters.

But even worse than this, if we broke our price control rules for steel, I don't see how we could keep them for any other industry.

There are plenty of other industries that would like to have big price increases. Our price control officials meet every day with industries that want to raise their prices. For months they have been turning down most of these requests, because most of the companies have had profits big enough to absorb cost increases and still leave a fair return.

The paper industry has been turned down. So has the brass industry, the truck industry, the auto parts industry, and many others.

All these industries have taken "no" for an answer, and they have gone home and kept right on producing. That's what any law abiding person does when he is told that what he'd like to do is against the rules.

But not the steel companies—not the steel companies. The steel industries doesn't want to come down and make its case, and abide by the decision like everybody else. The steel industry wants something special, something nobody else can get.

If we gave in to the steel companies on this issue, you could say goodby to stabilization. If we knuckled under to the steel industry, the lid would be off. Prices would start jumping up all around us— not just prices of things using steel, but prices of many other things we buy, including milk and groceries and meat.

You may think this steel dispute doesn't affect you. You may think it's just a matter between the Government and a few greedy companies. But it is not. If we granted the outrageous prices the steel industry wants, we would scuttle our whole price control program. And that comes pretty close to home for everybody in the country.

It is perfectly clear, from the facts I have cited, that the present danger to our stabilization program comes from the steel companies' insistence on a big jump in steel prices.

The plain fact of the matter is that the steel companies are recklessly forcing a shutdown of the steel mills. They are trying to get special, preferred treatment, not available to any other industry. And they are apparently willing to stop steel production to get it.

As President of the United States it is my plain duty to keep this from happening. And that is the reason for the measures I have taken tonight.

At midnight the Government will take over the steel plants. Both management and labor will then be working for the Government. And they will have a clear duty to heat up their furnaces again and go on making steel.

When management and labor meet down here in Washington they will have a chance to go back to bargaining and settle their dispute. As soon as they do that, we can turn the steel plants back to their private owners with the assurance that production will continue.

It is my earnest hope that the parties will settle without delay— tomorrow, if possible. I don't want to see the Government running the steel plants one minute longer than is absolutely necessary to prevent a shutdown.

A lot of people have been saying I ought to rely on the procedures of the Taft-Hartley Act to deal with this emergency.

This has not been done because the so-called emergency provisions of the Taft-Hartley Act would be of no help in meeting the situation that confronts us tonight.

That act provides that before anything else is done, the President must first set up a board of inquiry to find the facts on the dispute and report to him as to what they are. We would have to sit around a week or two for this board to report before we could take the next step. And meanwhile, the steel plants would be shut down.

Now there is another problem with the Taft-Hartley procedure. The law says that once a board of inquiry has reported, the Government can go to the courts for an injunction requiring the union to postpone a strike for 80 days. This is the only provision in the law to help us stop a strike. But the fact is that in the present case, the steelworkers' union has already postponed its strike since last December 31—99 days. In other words, the union has already done more, voluntarily, than it could be required to do under the Taft-Hartley Act. We do not need further delay and a prolonging of the crisis. We need a settlement and we need it fast.

Consequently, it is perfectly clear that the emergency provisions of the Taft-Hartley Act do not fit the needs of the present situation. We have already had the benefit of an investigation by one board. We have already had more delay than the Taft-Hartley Act provides.

But the overriding fact is that the Taft-Hartley procedure could not prevent a steel shutdown of at least a week or two.

We must have steel. We have taken the measures that are required to keep the steel mills in operation. But these are temporary measures and they ought to be ended as soon as possible.

The way we want to get steel production—the only way to get it in the long run—is for management and labor to sit down and settle their dispute. Sooner or later that's what will have to be done. So it might just as well be done now as any time.

There is no excuse for the present deadlock in negotiations. Everyone concerned knows what ought to be done. A settlement should be reached between the steel companies and the union. And the companies should then apply to the Office of Price Stabilization for whatever price increase they are entitled to under the law.

That is what is called for in the national interest.

On behalf of the whole country, I ask the steel companies and the steelworkers' union to compose their differences in the American spirit of fair play and obedience to the law of the land.

NOTE

Earlier that day the President had signed Executive Order 10340 "Directing the Secretary of Commerce to Take Possession of and Operate the Plants and Facilities of Certain Steel Companies." This order was ruled unconstitutional by the United States Supreme Court on June 2.

Richard M. Nixon
The Watergate Investigations
April 30, 1973

GOOD EVENING

I want to talk to you tonight from my heart on a subject of deep concern to every American.

In recent months, members of my Administration and officials of the Committee for the Re-Election of the President—including some of my closest friends and most trusted aides—have been charged with involvement in what has come to be known as the Watergate affair. These include charges of illegal activity during and preceding the 1972 Presidential election and charges that responsible officials participated in efforts to cover up that illegal activity.

The inevitable result of these charges has been to raise serious questions about the integrity of the White House itself. Tonight I wish to address those questions.

Last June 17, while I was in Florida trying to get a few days rest after my visit to Moscow, I first learned from news reports of the Watergate break-in. I was appalled at this senseless, illegal action, and I was shocked to learn that employees of the Re-Election Committee were apparently among those guilty. I immediately ordered an investigation by appropriate Government authorities. On September 15, as you will recall, indictments were brought against seven defendants in the case.

As the investigations went forward, I repeatedly asked those conducting the investigation whether there was any reason to believe that members of my Administration were in any way involved. I received repeated assurances that there were not.

Because of these continuing reassurances, because I believed the reports I was getting, because I had faith in the persons from whom I was getting them, I discounted the stories in the press that appeared to implicate members of my Administration or other officials of the campaign committee.

Until March of this year, I remained convinced that the denials were true and that the charges of involvement by members of the White House Staff were false. The comments I made during this period, and the comments made by my Press Secretary in my behalf, were based on the information provided to us at the time we made those comments. However, new information then came to me which persuaded me that there was a real possibility that some of these charges were true, and suggesting further that there had been an effort to conceal the facts both from the public, from you, and from me.

As a result, on March 21, I personally assumed the responsibility for coordinating intensive new inquiries into the matter, and I personally ordered those conducting the investigations to get all the facts and to report them directly to me, right here in this office.

I again ordered that all persons in the Government or at the Re-Election Committee should cooperate fully with the FBI, the prosecutors, and the grand jury. I also ordered that anyone who refused to cooperate in telling the truth would be asked to resign from Government service. And, with ground rules adopted that would preserve the basic constitutional separation of powers between the Congress and the Presidency, I directed that members of the White House Staff should appear and testify voluntarily under oath before the Senate committee which was investigating Watergate.

I was determined that we should get to the bottom of the matter, and that the truth should be fully brought out—no matter who was involved.

At the same time, I was determined not to take precipitate action and to avoid, if at all possible, any action that would appear to reflect on innocent people. I wanted to be fair. But I knew that in the final analysis, the integrity of this office—public faith in the integrity of this office—would have to take priority over all personal considerations.

Today, in one of the most difficult decisions of my Presidency, I accepted the resignations of two of my closest associates in the White House—Bob Haldeman, John Ehrlichman—two of the finest public servants it has been my privilege to know.

I want to stress that in accepting these resignations, I mean to leave no implication whatever of personal wrongdoing on their part, and I leave no implication tonight of implication on the part of others who have been charged in this matter. But in matters as sensitive as guarding the integrity of our democratic process, it is essential not only that rigorous legal and ethical standards be observed but also that the public, you, have total confidence that they are both being observed and enforced by those in authority and particularly by the President of the United States. They agreed with me that this move was necessary in order to restore that confidence.

Because Attorney General Kleindienst—though a distinguished public servant, my personal friend for 20 years, with no personal involvement whatever in this matter—has been a close personal and professional associate of some of those who are involved in this case, he and I both felt that it was also necessary to name a new Attorney General.

The Counsel to the President, John Dean, has also resigned.

As the new Attorney General, I have today named Elliot Richardson, a man of unimpeachable integrity and rigorously high principle. I have directed him to do everything necessary to ensure that the Department of Justice has the confidence and the trust of every law-abiding person in this country.

I have given him absolute authority to make all decisions bearing upon the prosecution of the Watergate case and related matters. I have instructed him that if he should consider it appropriate, he has the authority to name a special supervising prosecutor for matters arising out of the case.

Whatever may appear to have been the case before, whatever improper activities may yet be discovered in connection with this whole sordid affair, I want the American people, I want you to know beyond the shadow of a doubt that during my term as President, justice will be pursued fairly, fully, and impartially, no matter who is involved. This office is a sacred trust and I am determined to be worthy of that trust.

Looking back at the history of this case, two questions arise:
How could it have happened?

Who is to blame?

Political commentators have correctly observed that during my 27 years in politics I have always previously insisted on running my own campaigns for office.

But 1972 presented a very different situation. In both domestic and foreign policy, 1972 was a year of crucially important decisions, of intense negotiations, of vital new directions, particularly in working toward the goal which has been my overriding concern throughout my political career—the goal of bringing peace to America, peace to the world.

That is why I decided, as the 1972 campaign approached, that the Presidency should come first and politics second. To the maximum extent possible, therefore, I sought to delegate campaign operations, to remove the day-to-day campaign decisions from the President's office and from the White House. I also, as you recall, severely limited the number of my own campaign appearances.

Who, then, is to blame for what happened in this case?

For specific criminal actions by specific individuals, those who committed those actions must, of course, bear the liability and pay the penalty.

For the fact that alleged improper actions took place within the White House or within my campaign organization, the easiest course would be for me to blame those to whom I delegated the responsibility to run the campaign. But that would be a cowardly thing to do.

I will not place the blame on subordinates—on people whose zeal exceeded their judgment and who may have done wrong in a cause they deeply believed to be right.

In any organization, the man at the top must bear the responsibility. That responsibility, therefore, belongs here, in this office. I accept it. And I pledge to you tonight, from this office, that I will do everything in my power to ensure that the guilty are brought to justice and that such abuses are purged from our political processes in the years to come, long after I have left this office.

Some people, quite properly appalled at the abuses that occurred, will say that Watergate demonstrates the bankruptcy of the American political system. I believe precisely the opposite is true. Watergate represented a series of illegal acts and bad judgments by a number of individuals. It was the system that has brought the facts to light and that will bring those guilty to justice—a system that in this case has included a determined grand jury, honest prosecutors, a courageous judge, John Sirica, and a vigorous free press.

It is essential now that we place our faith in that system—and especially in the judicial system. It is essential that we let the judicial process go forward, respecting those safeguards that are established to protect the innocent as well as to convict the guilty. It is essential that in reacting to the excesses of others, we not fall into excesses ourselves.

It is also essential that we not be so distracted by events such as this that we neglect the vital work before us, before this nation, before America, at a time of critical importance to America and the world.

Since March, when I first learned that the Watergate affair might in fact be far more serious than I had been led to believe, it has claimed far too much of my time and my attention.

Whatever may now transpire in the case, whatever the actions of the grand jury, whatever the outcome of any eventual trials, I must now turn my full attention—and I shall do so—once again to the larger duties of this office. I owe it to this great office that I hold, and I owe it to you—to my country.

I know that as Attorney General, Elliot Richardson will be both fair and he will be fearless in pursuing this case wherever it leads. I am confident that with him in charge, justice will be done.

There is vital work to be done toward our goal of a lasting structure of peace in the world—work that cannot wait, work that I must do.

Tomorrow, for example, Chancellor Brandt of West Germany will visit the White House for talks that are a vital element of "The Year of Europe," as 1973 has been called. We are already preparing for the next Soviet-American summit meeting later this year.

This is also a year in which we are seeking to negotiate a mutual and balanced reduction of armed forces in Europe, which will reduce our defense budget and allow us to have funds for other purposes at home so desperately needed. It is the year when the United States and Soviet negotiators will seek to work out the second and even more important round of our talks on limiting nuclear arms and of reducing the danger of a nuclear war that would destroy civilization as we know it. It is a year in which we confront the difficult tasks of maintaining peace in Southeast Asia and in the potentially explosive Middle East.

There is also vital work to be done right here in America: to ensure prosperity, and that means a good job for everyone who wants to work; to control inflation, that I know worries every housewife, everyone who tries to balance a family budget in America; to set in motion new and better ways of ensuring progress toward a better life for all Americans.

When I think of this office—of what it means—I think of all the things that I want to accomplish for this Nation, of all the things I want to accomplish for you.

On Christmas Eve, during my terrible personal ordeal of the renewed bombing of North Vietnam, which after 12 years of war finally helped to bring America peace with honor, I sat down just before midnight. I wrote out some of my goals for my second term as President.

Let me read them to you.

"To make it possible for our children, and for our children's children, to live in a world of peace.

"To make this country be more than ever a land of opportunity—of equal opportunity, full opportunity for every American.

"To provide jobs for all who can work, and generous help for those who cannot work.

"To establish a climate of decency and civility, in which each person respects the feelings and the dignity and the God-given rights of his neighbor.

"To make this a land in which each person can dare to dream, can live his dreams—not in fear, but in hope—proud of his community, proud of his country, proud of what America has meant to himself and to the world."

These are great goals. I believe we can, we must work for them. We can achieve them. But we cannot achieve these goals unless we dedicate ourselves to another goal.

We must maintain the integrity of the White House, and that integrity must be real, not transparent. There can be no whitewash at the White House.

We must reform our political process—ridding it not only of the violations of the law but also of the ugly mob violence and other inexcusable campaign tactics that have been too often practiced and too readily accepted in the past, including those that may have been a response by one side to the excesses or expected excesses of the other side. Two wrongs do not make a right.

I have been in public life for more than a quarter of a century. Like any other calling, politics has good people and bad people. And let me tell you, the great majority in politics—in the Congress, in the Federal Government, in the State government—are good people. I know that it can be very easy, under the intensive pressures of a campaign, for even well-intentioned people to fall into shady tactics—to rationalize this on the grounds that what is at stake is of such importance to the Nation that the end justifies the means. And both of our great parties have been guilty of such tactics in the past.

In recent years, however, the campaign excesses that have occurred on all sides have provided a sobering demonstration of how far this false doctrine can take us. The lesson is clear: America, in its political campaigns, must not again fall into the trap of letting the end, however great that end is, justify the means.

I urge the leaders of both political parties, I urge citizens, all of you, everywhere, to join in working toward a new set of standards, new rules and procedures to ensure that future elections will be as nearly free of such abuses as they possibly can be made. This is my goal. I ask you to join in making it America's goal.

When I was inaugurated for a second time this past January 20, I gave each member of my Cabinet and each member of my senior White House Staff a special 4-year calendar, with each day marked to show the number of days remaining to the Administration. In the inscription on each calendar, I wrote these words: "The Presidential term which begins today consists of 1,461 days—no more, no less. Each can be a day of strengthening and renewal for America; each can add depth and dimension to the American experience. If we strive together, if we make the most of the challenge and the opportunity that these days offer us, they can stand out as great days for America, and great moments in the history of the world."

I looked at my own calendar this morning up at Camp David as I was working on this speech. It showed exactly 1,361 days remaining in my term. I want these to be the best days in America's history, because I love America. I deeply believe that America is the hope of the world. And I know that in the quality and wisdom of the leadership America gives lies the only hope for millions of people all over the world that they can live their lives in peace and freedom. We must be worthy of that hope, in every sense of the word. Tonight, I ask for your prayers to help me in everything that I do throughout the days of my Presidency to be worthy of their hopes and of yours.

God bless America and God bless each and every one of you.

NOTE

The President spoke at 9:01 p.m. from the Oval Office at the White House. His address was broadcast live on nationwide radio and television.

Gerald R. Ford
The Pardon to Richard Nixon
September 8, 1974

LADIES AND GENTLEMEN:

I have come to a decision which I felt I should tell you and all of my fellow American citizens, as soon as I was certain in my own mind and in my own conscience that it is the right thing to do.

I have learned already in this office that the difficult decisions always come to this desk. I must admit that many of them do not look at all the same as the hypothetical questions that I have answered freely and perhaps too fast on previous occasions.

My customary policy is to try and get all the facts and to consider the opinions of my countrymen and to take counsel with my most valued friends. But these seldom agree, and in the end, the decision is mine. To procrastinate, to agonize, and to wait for a more favorable turn of events that may never come or more compelling external pressures that may as well be wrong as right, is itself a decision of sorts and a weak and potentially dangerous course for a President to follow.

I have promised to uphold the Constitution, to do what is right as God gives me to see the right, and to do the very best that I can for America.

I have asked your help and your prayers, not only when I became President but many times since. The Constitution is the supreme law of our land and it governs our actions as citizens. Only the laws of God, which govern our consciences, are superior to it.

As we are a nation under God, so I am sworn to uphold our

laws with the help of God. And I have sought such guidance and searched my own conscience with special diligence to determine the right thing for me to do with respect to my predecessor in this place, Richard Nixon, and his loyal wife and family.

Theirs is an American tragedy in which we all have played a part. It could go on and on and on, or someone must write the end to it. I have concluded that only I can do that, and if I can, I must.

There are no historic or legal precedents to which I can turn in this matter, none that precisely fit the circumstances of a private citizen who has resigned the Presidency of the United States. But it is common knowledge that serious allegations and accusations hang like a sword over our former President's head, threatening his health as he tries to reshape his life, a great part of which was spent in the service of this country and by the mandate of its people.

After years of bitter controversy and divisive national debate, I have been advised, and I am compelled to conclude that many months and perhaps more years will have to pass before Richard Nixon could obtain a fair trial by jury in any jurisdiction of the United States under governing decisions of the Supreme Court.

I deeply believe in equal justice for all Americans, whatever their station or former station. The law, whether human or divine, is no respector of persons; but the law is a respecter of reality.

The facts, as I see them, are that a former President of the United States, instead of enjoying equal treatment with any other citizen accused of violating the law, would be cruelly and excessively penalized either in preserving the presumption of his innocence or in obtaining a speedy determination of his guilt in order to repay a legal debt to society.

During this long period of delay and potential litigation, ugly passions would again be aroused. And our people would again be polarized in their opinions. And the credibility of our free institutions of government would again be challenged at home and abroad.

In the end, the courts might well hold that Richard Nixon had been denied due process, and the verdict of history would even more be inconclusive with respect to those charges arising out of the period of his Presidency, of which I am presently aware.

But it is not the ultimate fate of Richard Nixon that most

concerns me, though surely it deeply troubles every decent and every compassionate person. My concern is the immediate future of this great country.

In this, I dare not depend upon my personal sympathy as a long-time friend of the former President, nor my professional judgment as a lawyer, and I do not.

As President, my primary concern must always be the greatest good of all the people of the United States whose servant I am. As a man, my first consideration is to be true to my own convictions and my own conscience.

My conscience tells me clearly and certainly that I cannot prolong the bad dreams that continue to reopen a chapter that is closed. My conscience tells me that only I, as President, have the constitutional power to firmly shut and seal this book. My conscience tells me it is my duty, not merely to proclaim domestic tranquility but to use every means that I have to insure it.

I do believe that the buck stops here, that I cannot rely upon public opinion polls to tell me what is right.

I do believe that right makes might and that if I am wrong, 10 angels swearing I was right would make no difference.

I do believe, with all my heart and mind and spirit, that I, not as President but as a humble servant of God, will receive justice without mercy if I fail to show mercy.

Finally, I feel that Richard Nixon and his loved ones have suffered enough and will continue to suffer, no matter what I do, no matter what we, as a great and good nation, can do together to make his goal of peace come true.

[At this point, the President began reading from the proclamation granting the pardon.]

"Now, therefore, I, Gerald R. Ford, President of the United States, pursuant to the pardon power conferred upon me by Article II, Section 2, of the Constitution, have granted and by these presents do grant a full, free, and absolute pardon unto Richard Nixon for all offenses against the United States which he, Richard Nixon, has committed or may have committed or taken part in during the period from July (January) 20, 1969 through August 9, 1974."

[The President signed the proclamation and then resumed reading.]

"In witness whereof, I have hereunto set my hand this eighth day of September, in the year of our Lord nineteen hundred and seventy-four, and of the Independence of the United States of America the one hundred and ninety-ninth."

NOTE

The President spoke at 11:05 a.m. in the Oval Office at the White House, where he signed Proclamation 4311 granting the pardon.

Jimmy Carter
Energy and National Goals
July 15, 1979

Good evening.

This is a special night for me. Exactly 3 years ago, on July 15, 1976, I accepted the nomination of my party to run for President of the United States. I promised you a President who is not isolated from the people, who feels your pain, and who shares your dreams and who draws his strength and his wisdom from you.

During the past 3 years I've spoken to you on many occasions about national concerns, the energy crisis, reorganizing the Government, our Nation's economy, and issues of war and especially peace. But over those years the subjects of the speeches, the talks, and the press conferences have become increasingly narrow, focused more and more on what the isolated world of Washington thinks is important. Gradually, you've heard more and more about what the Government thinks or what the Government should be doing and less and less about our Nation's hopes, our dreams, and our vision of the future.

Ten days ago I had planned to speak to you again about a very important subject—energy. For the fifth time I would have described the urgency of the problem and laid out a series of legislative recommendations to the Congress. But as I was preparing to speak, I began to ask myself the same question that I now know has been troubling many of you. Why have we not been able to get together as a nation to resolve our serious energy problem?

It's clear that the true problems of our Nation are much deeper—deeper than gasoline lines or energy shortages, deeper even than inflation or recession. And I realize more than ever that as President I need your help. So, I decided to reach out and listen to the voices of America.

I invited to Camp David people from almost every segment of our society—business and labor, teachers and preachers, Governors, mayors, and private citizens. And then I left Camp David to listen to other Americans, men and women like you. It has been an extraordinary 10 days, and I want to share with you what I've heard.

First of all, I got a lot of personal advice. Let me quote a few of the typical comments that I wrote down.

This from a southern Governor: "Mr. President, you are not leading this Nation—you're just managing the Government."

"You don't see the people enough any more."

"Some of your Cabinet members don't seem loyal. There is not enough discipline among your disciples."

"Don't talk to us about politics or the mechanics of government, but about an understanding of our common good."

"Mr. President, we're in trouble. Talk to us about blood and sweat and tears."

"If you lead, Mr. President, we will follow."

Many people talked about themselves and about the condition of our Nation. This from a young woman in Pennsylvania: "I feel so far from government. I feel like ordinary people are excluded from political power."

And this from a young Chicano: "Some of us have suffered from recession all our lives."

"Some people have wasted energy, but others haven't had anything to waste."

And this from a religious leader: "No material shortage can touch the important things like God's love for us or our love for one another."

And I like this one particularly from a black woman who happens to be the mayor of a small Mississippi town: "The bigshots are not the only ones who are important. Remember, you can't sell anything on Wall Street unless someone digs it up somewhere else first."

This kind of summarized a lot of other statements: "Mr. President, we are confronted with a moral and a spiritual crisis."

Several of our discussions were on energy, and I have a notebook full of comments and advice. I'll read just a few.

"We can't go on consuming 40 percent more energy than we produce. When we import oil we are also importing inflation plus unemployment."

"We've got to use what we have. The Middle East has only 5 percent of the world's energy, but the United States has 24 percent."

And this is one of the most vivid statements: "Our neck is stretched over the fence and OPEC has a knife."

"There will be other cartels and other shortages. American wisdom and courage right now can set a path to follow in the future."

This was a good one: "Be bold, Mr. President. We may make mistakes, but we are ready to experiment."

And this one from a labor leader got to the heart of it: "The real issue is freedom. We must deal with the energy problem on a war footing."

And the last that I'll read: "When we enter the moral equivalent of war, Mr. President, don't issue us BB guns."

These 10 days confirmed my belief in the decency and the strength and the wisdom of the American people, but it also bore out some of my longstanding concerns about our Nation's underlying problems.

I know, of course, being President, that government actions and legislation can be very important. That's why I've worked hard to put my campaign promises into law—and I have to admit, with just mixed success. But after listening to the American people I have been reminded again that all the legislation in the world can't fix what's wrong with America. So, I want to speak to you first tonight about a subject even more serious than energy or inflation. I want to talk to you right now about a fundamental threat to American democracy.

I do not mean our political and civil liberties. They will endure. And I do not refer to the outward strength of America, a nation that is at peace tonight everywhere in the world, with unmatched economic power and military might.

The threat is nearly invisible in ordinary ways. It is a crisis of confidence. It is a crisis that strikes at the very heart and soul and spirit of our national will. We can see this crisis in the growing doubt about the meaning of our own lives and in the loss of a unity of purpose for our Nation.

The erosion of our confidence in the future is threatening to destroy the social and the political fabric of America.

The confidence that we have always had as a people is not

simply some romantic dream or a proverb in a dusty book that we read just on the Fourth of July. It is the idea which founded our Nation and has guided our development as a people. Confidence in the future has supported everything else—public institutions and private enterprise, our own families, and the very Constitution of the United States. Confidence has defined our course and has served as a link between generations. We've always believed in something called progress. We've always had a faith that the days of our children would be better than our own.

Our people are losing that faith, not only in government itself but in the ability as citizens to serve as the ultimate rulers and shapers of our democracy. As a people we know our past and we are proud of it. Our progress has been part of the living history of America, even the world. We always believed that we were part of a great movement of humanity itself called democracy, involved in the search for freedom and that belief has always strengthened us in our purpose. But just as we are losing our confidence in the future, we are also beginning to close the door on our past.

In a nation that was proud of hard work, strong families, close-knit communities, and our faith in God, too many of us now tend to worship self-indulgence and consumption. Human identity is no longer defined by what one does, but by what one owns. But we've discovered that owning things and consuming things does not satisfy our longing for meaning. We've learned that piling up material goods cannot fill the emptiness of lives which have no confidence or purpose.

The symptoms of this crisis of the American spirit are all around us. For the first time in the history of our country a majority of our people believe that the next 5 years will be worse than the past 5 years. Two-thirds of our people do not even vote. The productivity of American workers is actually dropping, and the willingness of Americans to save for the future has fallen below that of all other people in the Western world.

As you know, there is a growing disrespect for government and for churches and for schools, the news media, and other institutions. This is not a message of happiness or reassurance, but it is the truth and it is a warning.

These changes did not happen overnight. They've come upon us gradually over the last generation, years that were filled with shocks and tragedy.

We were sure that ours was a nation of the ballot, not the bullet, until the murders of John Kennedy and Robert Kennedy and Martin Luther King, Jr. We were taught that our armies were always invincible and our causes were always just, only to suffer the agony of Vietnam. We respected the Presidency as a place of honor until the shock of Watergate.

We remember when the phrase "sound as a dollar" was an expression of absolute dependability, until 10 years of inflation began to shrink our dollar and our savings. We believed that our Nation's resources were limitless until 1973 when we had to face a growing dependence on foreign oil.

These wounds are still very deep. They have never been healed.

Looking for a way out of this crisis, our people have turned to the Federal Government and found it isolated from the mainstream of our Nation's life. Washington, D.C., has become an island. The gap between our citizens and our Government has never been so wide. The people are looking for honest answers, not easy answers; clear leadership, not false claims and evasiveness and politics as usual.

What you see too often in Washington and elsewhere around the country is a system of government that seems incapable of action. You see a Congress twisted and pulled in every direction by hundreds of well-financed and powerful special interests.

You see every extreme position defended to the last vote, almost to the last breath by one unyielding group or another. You often see a balanced and a fair approach that demands sacrifice, a little sacrifice from everyone, abandoned like an orphan without support and without friends.

Often you see paralysis and stagnation and drift. You don't like it, and neither do I. What can we do?

First of all, we must face the truth, and then we can change our course. We simply must have faith in each other, faith in our ability to govern ourselves, and faith in the future of this Nation. Restoring that faith and that confidence to America is now the most important task we face. It is a true challenge of this generation of Americans.

One of the visitors to Camp David last week put it this way: "We've got to stop crying and start sweating, stop talking and start walking, stop cursing and start praying. The strength we need will not come from the White House, but from every house in America."

We know the strength of America. We are strong. We can regain our unity. We can regain our confidence. We are the heirs of generations who survived threats much more powerful and awesome than those that challenge us now. Our fathers and mothers were strong men and women who shaped a new society during the Great Depression, who fought world wars, and who carved out a new charter of peace for the world.

We ourselves are the same Americans who just 10 years ago put a man on the Moon. We are the generation that dedicated our society to the pursuit of human rights and equality. And we are the generation that will win the war on the energy problem and in that process rebuild the unity and confidence of America.

We are at a turning point in our history. There are two paths to choose. One is a path I've warned about tonight, the path that leads to fragmentation and self-interest. Down that road lies a mistaken idea of freedom, the right to grasp for ourselves some advantage over others. That path would be one of constant conflict between narrow interests ending in chaos and immobility. It is a certain route to failure.

All the traditions of our past, all the lessons of our heritage, all the promises of our future point to another path, the path of common purpose and the restoration of American values. That path leads to true freedom for our Nation and ourselves. We can take the first steps down that path as we begin to solve our energy problem.

Energy will be the immediate test of our ability to unite this Nation, and it can also be the standard around which we rally. On the battlefield of energy we can win for our Nation a new confidence, and we can seize control again of our common destiny.

In little more than two decades we've gone from a position of energy independence to one in which almost half the oil we use comes from foreign countries, at prices that are going through the roof. Our excessive dependence on OPEC has already taken a tremendous toll on our economy and our people. This is the direct cause of the long lines which have made millions of you spend aggravating hours waiting for gasoline. It's a cause of the increased inflation and unemployment that we now face. This intolerable dependence on foreign oil threatens our economic independence and the very security of our Nation.

The energy crisis is real. It is worldwide. It is a clear and present danger to our Nation. These are facts and we simply must face them.

What I have to say to you now about energy is simple and vitally important.

Point one: I am tonight setting a clear goal for the energy policy of the United States. Beginning this moment, this Nation will never use more foreign oil than we did in 1977—never. From now on, every new addition to our demand for energy will be met from our own production and our own conservation. The generation-long growth in our dependence on foreign oil will be stopped dead in its tracks right now and then reversed as we move through the 1980's, for I am tonight setting the further goal of cutting our dependence on foreign oil by one-half by the end of the next decade—a saving of over 4½ million barrels of imported oil per day.

Point two: To ensure that we meet these targets, I will use my Presidential authority to set import quotas. I'm announcing tonight that for 1979 and 1980, I will forbid the entry into this country of one drop of foreign oil more than these goals allow. These quotas will ensure a reduction in imports even below the ambitious levels we set at the recent Tokyo summit.

Point three: To give us energy security, I am asking for the most massive peacetime commitment of funds and resources in our Nation's history to develop America's own alternative sources of fuel—from coal, from oil shale, from plant products for gasohol, from unconventional gas, from the Sun.

I propose the creation of an energy security corporation to lead this effort to replace 2½ million barrels of imported oil per day by 1990. The corporation will issue up to $5 billion in energy bonds, and I especially want them to be in small denominations so that average Americans can invest directly in America's energy security.

Just as a similar synthetic rubber corporation helped us win World War II, so will we mobilize American determination and ability to win the energy war. Moreover, I will soon submit legislation to Congress calling for the creation of this Nation's first solar bank which will help us achieve the crucial goal of 20 percent of our energy coming from solar power by the year 2000.

These efforts will cost money, a lot of money, and that is why Congress must enact the windfall profits tax without delay. It will be money well spent. Unlike the billions of dollars that we ship to foreign countries to pay for foreign oil, these funds will be paid by Americans to Americans. These funds will go to fight, not to increase, inflation and unemployment.

Point four: I'm asking Congress to mandate, to require as a matter of law, that our Nation's utility companies cut their massive use of oil by 50 percent within the next decade and switch to other fuels, especially coal, our most abundant energy source.

Point five: To make absolutely certain that nothing stands in the way of achieving these goals, I will urge Congress to create an energy mobilization board which, like the War Production Board in World War II, will have the responsibility and authority to cut through the redtape, the delays, and the endless roadblocks to completing key energy projects.

We will protect our environment. But when this Nation critically needs a refinery or a pipeline, we will build it.

Point six: I'm proposing a bold conservation program to involve every State, county, and city and every average American in our energy battle. This effort will permit you to build conservation into your homes and your lives at a cost you can afford.

I ask Congress to give me authority for mandatory conservation and for standby gasoline rationing. To further conserve energy, I'm proposing tonight an extra $10 billion over the next decade to strengthen our public transportation systems. And I'm asking you for your good and for your Nation's security to take no unnecessary trips, to use carpools or public transportation whenever you can, to park your car one extra day per week, to obey the speed limit, and to set your thermostats to save fuel. Every act of energy conservation like this is more than just common sense—I tell you it is an act of patriotism.

Our Nation must be fair to the poorest among us, so we will increase aid to needy Americans to cope with rising energy prices. We often think of conservation only in terms of sacrifice. In fact, it is the most painless and immediate way of rebuilding our Nation's strength. Every gallon of oil each one of us saves is a new form of production. It gives us more freedom, more confidence, that much more control over our own lives.

So, the solution of our energy crisis can also help us to conquer the crisis of the spirit in our country. It can rekindle our sense of unity, our confidence in the future, and give our Nation and all of us individually a new sense of purpose.

You know we can do it. We have the natural resources. We have more oil in our shale alone than several Saudi Arabias. We have more coal than any nation on Earth. We have the world's highest level of technology. We have the most skilled work force, with innovative genius, and I firmly believe that we have the national will to win this war.

I do not promise you that this struggle for freedom will be easy. I do not promise a quick way out of our Nation's problems, when the truth is that the only way out is an all-out effort. What I do promise you is that I will lead our fight, and I will enforce fairness in our struggle, and I will ensure honesty. And above all, I will act.

We can manage the short-term shortages more effectively and we will, but there are no short-term solutions to our long-range problems. There is simply no way to avoid sacrifice.

Twelve hours from now I will speak again in Kansas City, to expand and to explain further our energy program. Just as the search for solutions to our energy shortages has now led us to a new awareness of our Nation's deeper problems, so our willingness to work for those solutions in energy can strengthen us to attack those deeper problems.

I will continue to travel this country, to hear the people of America. You can help me to develop a national agenda for the 1980's. I will listen and I will act. We will act together. These were the promises I made 3 years ago, and I intend to keep them.

Little by little we can and we must rebuild our confidence. We can spend until we empty our treasuries, and we may summon all the wonders of science. But we can succeed only if we tap our greatest resources—America's people. America's values, and America's confidence.

I have seen the strength of America in the inexhaustible resources of our people. In the days to come, let us renew that strength in the struggle for an energy-secure nation.

In closing, let me say this: I will do my best, but I will not do it alone. Let your voice be heard. Whenever you have a chance, say something good about our country. With God's help and for the sake of our Nation, it is time for us to join hands in America. Let us commit ourselves together to a rebirth of the American spirit. Working together with our common faith we cannot fail.

Thank you and good night.

NOTE

The President spoke at 10 p.m. from the Oval Office at the White House. His remarks were broadcast live on radio and television.

Chapter 8 International Crisis Management

International crises demand delicate presidential action. In the nuclear age a mistake could prove catastrophic not only for the United States, but for the whole world. A wise president exercises his powers judiciously and, when extreme measures are necessary, he tries to mobilize public support for his action while reassuring his critics.

Two important points need to be made about presidential speeches on international crises. First, Americans rally around their president when they see him taking resolute action during any kind of international crisis—no matter how ill-advised that action might be. Second, a state of "crisis" is rhetorical, i.e. the sense of crisis is created and nurtured through the use of language. Therefore point three is that it is periodically useful for a president to label some situation a "crisis", to act boldly, and to thereby boost his popularity. Unfortunately, nationalistic jingoism does not encourage rational decisions by either leaders or followers. Finally, the paradox: the social judgment literature in psychology generally indicates that people are most likely to accurately judge new information when they experience low ego-involvement in the message topic. In other words, it seems generally advisable for Presidents (and their citizenry) to remain cool during a crisis. Put bluntly, a president must often (but certainly not always) choose between calmly resolving the crisis with little personal fanfare, and milking it for political advantage while probably exacerbating the crisis.

Isolationist sentiment in America was strong during the early years of World War II. But the attack on Pearl Harbor left little doubt that the United States would declare war on Japan.

Roosevelt's address to Congress served not only to insure passage of the war declaration, but to mobilize and inspire the frightened and angry nation. Additionally, his appeal for complete and absolute victory later constrained Truman's ability to conclude the war on terms acceptable to the American people.

American pilot Francis Gary Powers was shot down while flying his U-2 spy plane over the Soviet Union in May of 1960. The incident occurred during the presidential primary season and shortly before the planned Paris Summit Conference between President Dwight Eisenhower and Premier Nikita Khruschev. Eisenhower's terse statement later proved a serious embarassment, as the incident culminated in a disastrous summit conference.

Two years later American intelligence flights discovered that Russian missiles were being shipped into Cuba. Several Republicans had warned of the build-up during the late summer of 1962, but the Kennedy Administration denied that the missiles posed an offensive threat. But in mid-October new photographs convinced Kennedy that the missiles could not be allowed to remain. After prolonged discussion (now regarded as a classic example of crisis decision-making) Kennedy explained both the situation and his quarantine of Cuba on national television. This epitome of "brinksmanship" succeeded in persuading Khruschev to withdraw the missiles, and led both nations to review their foreign policy assumptions.

Direct involvement in the Vietnamese War began with the "Gulf of Tonkin Incident" in August of 1964. Although President Johnson comfortably led Senator Barry Goldwater in the polls, Goldwater's aggressive criticism of the Administration's passive advisory role in Vietnam raised bothersome issues for the President. When reports were received that two American ships had been fired upon in the Gulf of Tonkin, the president announced limited retaliation and asked Congress for a declaration of support. This "Gulf of Tonkin Resolution" became the justification for escalating American involvement in Vietnam. Subsequent questions have arisen as to the actual nature of the Tonkin attack, the Administration's planning for escalation as long as four months before the attack, and of course the constitutionality of this non-declaration of war.

On September 1, 1983 a commercial flight by Korean Air Lines wandered into Soviet airspace and was shot down by Russian fighter planes. Several Americans including Larry McDonald, the Democratic Congressman from Georgia and newly named head of the right-wing John Birch Society were among the hundreds of people killed. The Soviets denied the reports for several days as evidence to the contrary and world criticism mounted. When he finally addressed the nation, President Reagan summoned all the anger he could muster. Possibly exploiting the lack of Soviet leadership during the long terminal illness of Yuri Andropov, his language was highly inflammatory, and his speech allowed the Soviets no room to report an error and apologize. But unfortunately for Reagan, heinous crimes demand severe punishment. Thus his full-scale condemnation of the Soviet "massacre" rendered his various sanctions mild by comparison, which upset Mrs. McDonald, Senator Jesse Helms, and many other hardliners. The net effect for the Reagan Administration, however, was positive: the nation developed a greater distrust for the Soviets, patriotically rallied around their president, and Reagan heard welcome cries for harsher treatment of the Russians.

All five speeches rely on "narrative suasion" for their force. Each speech contains an early account of events and forces leading up to an impasse and fosters the impression that some other nation is (or has been) treating America unfairly. The sense of danger serves to enhance the audience's reliance upon the president for leadership (much as we rely on our doctor's advice when we are ill, and ignore his warnings when we feel fine).

Franklin D. Roosevelt
War Message
December 8, 1941

Yesterday, December 7, 1941—a date which will live in infamy—the United States of America was suddenly and deliberately attacked by naval and air forces of the Empire of Japan.

The United States was at peace with that nation and, at the solicitation of Japan, was still in conversation with its Government and its Emperor looking toward the maintenance of peace in the Pacific. Indeed, one hour after Japanese air squadrons had commenced bombing in the American Island of Oahu, the Japanese Ambassador to the United States and his colleague delivered to our Secretary of State a formal reply to a recent American message. And while this reply stated that it seemed useless to continue the existing diplomatic negotiations, it contained no threat or hint of war or of armed attack.

It will be recorded that the distance of Hawaii from Japan makes it obvious that the attack was deliberately planned many days or even weeks ago. During the intervening time the Japanese Government has deliberately sought to deceive the United States by false statements and expressions of hope for continued peace.

The attack yesterday on the Hawaiian Islands has caused severe damage to American naval and military forces. I regret to tell you that very many American lives have been lost. In addition American ships have been reported torpedoed on the high seas between San Francisco and Honolulu.

Yesterday the Japanese Government also launched an attack against Malaya.

Last night Japanese forces attacked Hong Kong.

Last night Japanese forces attacked Guam.

Last night Japanese forces attacked the Philippine Islands.

Last night the Japanese attacked Wake Island.

And this morning the Japanese attacked Midway Island.

Japan has, therefore, undertaken a surprise offensive extending throughout the Pacific area. The facts of yesterday and today speak for themselves. The people of the United States have already formed their opinions and well understand the implications to the very life and safety of our nation.

As Commander-in-Chief of the Army and Navy I have directed that all measures be taken for our defense.

But always will our whole nation remember the character of the onslaught against us.

No matter how long it may take us to overcome this premeditated invasion, the American people in their righteous might will win through to absolute victory.

I believe that I interpret the will of the Congress and of the people when I assert that we will not only defend ourselves to the uttermost but will make it very certain that this form of treachery shall never again endanger us.

Hostilities exist. There is no blinking at the fact that our people, our territory and our interests are in grave danger.

With confidence in our armed forces—with the unbounding determination of our people—we will gain the inevitable triumph—so help us God.

I ask that the Congress declare that since the unprovoked and dastardly attack by Japan on Sunday, December seventh, 1941, a state of war has existed between the United States and the Japanese Empire.

Dwight D. Eisenhower
The U-2 Affair
May 11, 1960

THE PRESIDENT [reading].

I have made some notes from which I want to talk to you about this U-2 incident.

A full statement about this matter has been made by the State Department, and there have been several statesmanlike remarks by leaders of both parties.

For my part, I supplement what the Secretary of State has had to say, with the following four main points. After that I shall have nothing further to say—for the simple reason I can think of nothing to add that might be useful at this time.

The first point is this: the need for intelligence-gathering activities.

No one wants another Pearl Harbor. This means that we must have knowledge of military forces and preparations around the world, especially those capable of massive surprise attacks.

Secrecy in the Soviet Union makes this essential. In most of the world no large-scale attack could be prepared in secret, but in the Soviet Union there is a fetish of secrecy and concealment. This is a major cause of international tension and uneasiness today. Our deterrent must never be placed in jeopardy. The safety of the whole free world demands this.

As the Secretary of State pointed out in his recent statement, ever since the beginning of my administration I have issued directives to gather, in every feasible way, the information required to protect the United States and the free world against surprise attack and to enable them to make effective preparations for defense.

My second point: the nature of intelligence-gathering activities.

These have a special and secret character. They are, so to speak, "below the surface" activities.

They are secret because they must circumvent measures designed by other countries to protect secrecy of military preparations.

They are divorced from the regular visible agencies of government which stay clear of operational involvement in specific detailed activities.

These elements operate under broad directives to seek and gather intelligence short of the use of force—with operations supervised by responsible officials within this area of secret activities.

We do not use our Army, Navy, or Air Force for this purpose, first, to avoid any possibility of the use of force in connection with these activities, and second, because our military forces, for obvious reasons, cannot be given latitude under broad directives but must be kept under strict control in every detail.

These activities have their own rules and methods of concealment which seek to mislead and obscure—just as in the Soviet allegation there are many discrepancies. For example, there is some reason to believe that the plane in question was not shot down at high altitude. The normal agencies of our Government are unaware of these specific activities or of the special efforts to conceal them.

Third point: how should we view all of this activity?

It is a distasteful but vital necessity.

We prefer and work for a different kind of world—and a different way of obtaining the information essential to confidence and effective deterrents. Open societies, in the day of present weapons, are the only answer.

This was the reason for my "open skies" proposal in 1955, which I was ready instantly to put into effect—to permit aerial observation over the United States and the Soviet Union which would assure that no surprise attack was being prepared against anyone. I shall bring up the "open skies" proposal again at Paris— since it is a means of ending concealment and suspicion.

My final point is that we must not be distracted from the real issues of the day by what is an incident or a symptom of the world situation today.

This incident has been given great propaganda exploitation. The emphasis given to a flight of an unarmed nonmilitary plane can only reflect a fetish of secrecy.

The real issues are the ones we will be working on at the summit—disarmament, search for solutions affecting Germany and Berlin, and the whole range of East-West relations, including the reduction of secrecy and suspicion.

Frankly, I am hopeful that we may make progress on these great issues. This is what we mean when we speak of "working for peace."

And as I remind you, I will have nothing further to say about this matter. [*Ends reading*]

John F. Kennedy
The Cuban Missile Crisis
October 22, 1962

GOOD EVENING, MY FELLOW CITIZENS:

This government, as promised, has maintained the closest surveillance of the Soviet military buildup on the island of Cuba. Within the past week, unmistakable evidence has established the fact that a series of offensive missile sites is now in preparation on that imprisoned island. The purpose of these bases can be none other than to provide a nuclear strike capability against the Western Hemisphere.

Upon receiving the first preliminary hard information of this nature last Tuesday morning at 9 a.m., I directed that our surveillance be stepped up. And having now confirmed and completed our evaluation of the evidence and our decision on a course of action, this Government feels obliged to report this new crisis to you in fullest detail.

The characteristics of these new missile sites indicate two distinct types of installations. Several of them include medium range ballistic missiles, capable of carrying a nuclear warhead for a distance of more than 1,000 nautical miles. Each of these missiles, in short, is capable of striking Washington, D.C., the Panama Canal, Cape Canaveral, Mexico City, or any other city in the southeastern part of the United States, in Central America, or in the Caribbean area.

Additional sites not yet completed appear to be designed for intermediate range ballistic missiles—capable of traveling more than twice as far—and thus capable of striking most of the major cities in the Western Hemisphere, ranging as far north as Hudson Bay, Canada, and as far south as Lima, Peru. In addition, jet bombers, capable of carrying nuclear weapons, are now being uncrated and assembled in Cuba, while the necessary air bases are being prepared.

This urgent transformation of Cuba into an important strategic base—by the presence of these large, long-range, and clearly offensive weapons of sudden mass destruction—constitutes an explicit threat to the peace and security of all the Americas, in flagrant and deliberate defiance of the Rio Pact of 1947, the traditions of this Nation and hemisphere, the joint resolution of the 87th Congress, the Charter of the United Nations, and my own public warnings to the Soviets on September 4 and 13. This action also contradicts the repeated assurances of Soviet spokesmen, both publicly and privately delivered, that the arms buildup in Cuba would retain its original defensive character, and that the Soviet Union had no need or desire to station strategic missiles on the territory of any other nation.

The size of this undertaking makes clear that it has been planned for some months. Yet only last month, after I had made clear the distinction between any introduction of ground-to-ground missiles and the existence of defensive antiaircraft missiles, the Soviet Government publicly stated on September 11 that, and I quote, "the armaments and military equipment sent to Cuba are designed exclusively for defensive purposes," that, and I quote the Soviet Government, "there is no need for the Soviet Government to shift its weapons . . . for a retaliatory blow to any other country, for instance Cuba," and that, and I quote their government, "the Soviet Union has so powerful rockets to carry these nuclear warheads that there is no need to search for sites for them beyond the boundaries of the Soviet Union." That statement was false.

Only last Thursday, as evidence of this rapid offensive buildup was already in my hand, Soviet Foreign Minister Gromyko told me in my office that he was instructed to make it clear once again, as he said his government had already done, that Soviet assistance to Cuba, and I quote, "pursued solely the purpose of contributing to the defense capabilities of Cuba," that, and I quote him, "training by Soviet specialists of Cuban nationals in handling defensive armaments was by no means offensive, and if it were otherwise,"

Mr. Gromyko went on, "the Soviet Government would never become involved in rendering such assistance." That statement also was false.

Neither the United States of America nor the world community of nations can tolerate deliberate deception and offensive threats on the part of any nation, large or small. We no longer live in a world where only the actual firing of weapons represents a sufficient challenge to a nation's security to constitute maximum peril. Nuclear weapons are so destructive and ballistic missiles are so swift, that any substantially increased possibility of their use or any sudden change in their deployment may well be regarded as a definite threat to peace.

For many years, both the Soviet Union and the United States, recognizing this fact, have deployed strategic nuclear weapons with great care, never upsetting the precarious status quo which insured that these weapons would not be used in the absence of some vital challenge. Our own strategic missiles have never been transferred to the territory of any other nation under a cloak of secrecy and deception; and our history—unlike that of the Soviets since the end of World War II—demonstrates that we have no desire to dominate or conquer any other nation or impose our system upon its people. Nevertheless, American citizens have become adjusted to living daily on the bull's-eye of Soviet missiles located inside the U.S.S.R. or in submarines.

In that sense, missiles in Cuba add to an already clear and present danger—although it should be noted the nations of Latin America have never previously been subjected to a potential nuclear threat.

But this secret, swift, and extraordinary buildup of Communist missiles—in an area well known to have a special and historical relationship to the United States and the nations of the Western Hemisphere, in violation of Soviet assurances, and in defiance of American and hemispheric policy—this sudden, clandestine decision to station strategic weapons for the first time outside of Soviet soil—is a deliberately provocative and unjustified change in the status quo which cannot be accepted by this country, if our courage and our commitments are ever to be trusted again by either friend or foe.

The 1930's taught us a clear lesson: aggressive conduct, if allowed to go unchecked and unchallenged, ultimately leads to war. This nation is opposed to war. We are also true to our word. Our unswerving objective, therefore, must be to prevent the use of these missiles against this or any other country, and to secure their withdrawal or elimination from the Western Hemisphere.

Our policy has been one of patience and restraint, as befits a peaceful and powerful nation, which leads a worldwide alliance. We have been determined not to be diverted from our central concerns by mere irritants and fanatics. But now further action is required—and it is under way; and these actions may only be the beginning. We will not prematurely or unnecessarily risk the costs of worldwide nuclear war in which even the fruits of victory would be ashes in our mouth—but neither will we shrink from that risk at any time it must be faced.

Acting, therefore, in the defense of our own security and of the entire Western Hemisphere, and under the authority entrusted to me by the Constitution as endorsed by the resolution of the Congress, I have directed that the following *initial* steps be taken immediately:

First: To halt this offensive buildup, a strict quarantine on all offensive military equipment under shipment to Cuba is being initiated. All ships of any kind bound for Cuba from whatever nation or port will, if found to contain cargoes of offensive weapons, be turned back. This quarantine will be extended, if needed, to other types of cargo and carriers. We are not at this time, however, denying the necessities of life as the Soviets attempted to do in their Berlin blockade of 1948.

Second: I have directed the continued and increased close surveillance of Cuba and its military buildup. The foreign ministers of the OAS, in their communique of October 6, rejected secrecy on such matters in this hemisphere. Should these offensive military preparations continue, thus increasing the threat to the hemisphere, further action will be justified. I have directed the Armed Forces to prepare for any eventualities; and I trust that in the interest of both the Cuban people and the Soviet technicians at the sites, the hazards to all concerned of continuing this threat will be recognized.

Third: It shall be the policy of this Nation to regard any nuclear missile launched from Cuba against any nation in the Western Hemisphere as an attack by the Soviet Union on the United States, requiring a full retaliatory response upon the Soviet Union.

Fourth: As a necessary military precaution, I have reinforced our base at Guantanamo, evacuated today the dependents of our personnel there, and ordered additional military units to be on a standby alert basis.

Fifth: We are calling tonight for an immediate meeting of the Organ of Consultation under the Organization of American States, to consider this threat to hemispheric security and to invoke articles 6 and 8 of the Rio Treaty in support of all necessary action. The United Nations Charter allows for regional security arrangements—and the nations of this hemisphere decided long ago against the military presence of outside powers. Our other allies around the world have also been alerted.

Sixth: Under the Charter of the United Nations, we are asking tonight that an emergency meeting of the Security Council be convoked without delay to take action against this latest Soviet threat to world peace. Our resolution will call for the prompt dismantling and withdrawal of all offensive weapons in Cuba, under the supervision of U.N. observers, before the quarantine can be lifted.

Seventh and finally: I call upon Chairman Khrushchev to halt and eliminate this clandestine, reckless, and provocative threat to world peace and to stable relations between our two nations. I call upon him further to abandon this course of world domination, and to join in an historic effort to end the perilous arms race and to transform the history of man. He has an opportunity now to move the world back from the abyss of destruction—by returning to his government's own words that it had no need to station missiles outside its own territory, and withdrawing these weapons from Cuba—by refraining from any action which will widen or deepen the present crisis—and then by participating in a search for peaceful and permanent solutions.

This Nation is prepared to present its case against the Soviet threat to peace, and our own proposals for a peaceful world, at any time and in any forum—in the OAS, in the United Nations, or in any other meeting that could be useful—without limiting our freedom of action. We have in the past made strenuous efforts to limit the spread of nuclear weapons. We have proposed the elimination of all arms and military bases in a fair and effective disarmament treaty. We are prepared to discuss new proposals for the removal of tensions on both sides—including the possibilities of a genuinely independent Cuba, free to determine its own destiny. We have no wish to war with the Soviet Union—for we are a peaceful people who desire to live in peace with all other peoples.

But it is difficult to settle or even discuss these problems in an atmosphere of intimidation. That is why this latest Soviet threat—or any other threat which is made either independently or in response to our actions this week—must and will be met with determination. Any hostile move anywhere in the world against the safety and freedom of peoples to whom we are committed—including in particular the brave people of West Berlin—will be met by whatever action is needed.

Finally, I want to say a few words to the captive people of Cuba, to whom this speech is being directly carried by special radio facilities. I speak to you as a friend, as one who knows of your deep attachment to your fatherland, as one who shares your aspirations for liberty and justice for all. And I have watched and the American people have watched with deep sorrow how your nationalist revolution was betrayed—and how your fatherland fell under foreign domination. Now your leaders are no longer Cuban leaders inspired by Cuban ideals. They are puppets and agents of an international conspiracy which has turned Cuba against your friends and neighbors in the Americas—and turned it into the first Latin American country to become a target for nuclear war—the first Latin American country to have these weapons on its soil.

These new weapons are not in your interest. They contribute nothing to your peace and well-being. They can only undermine it. But this country has no wish to cause you to suffer or to impose any system upon you. We know that your lives and land are being used as pawns by those who deny your freedom.

Many times in the past, the Cuban people have risen to throw out tyrants who destroyed their liberty. And I have no doubt that most Cubans today look forward to the time when they will be truly free—free from foreign domination, free to choose their own leaders, free to select their own system, free to own their own land, free to speak and write and worship without fear or degradation. And then shall Cuba be welcomed back to the society of free nations and to the associations of this hemisphere.

My fellow citizens: let no one doubt that this is a difficult and dangerous effort on which we have set out. No one can foresee precisely what course it will take or what costs or casualties will be incurred. Many months of sacrifice and self-discipline lie ahead—months in which both our patience and our will will be tested—months in which many threats and denunciations will keep us aware of our dangers. But the greatest danger of all would be to do nothing.

The path we have chosen for the present is full of hazards, as all paths are—but it is the one most consistent with our character and courage as a nation and our commitments around the world. The cost of freedom is always high—but Americans have always paid it. And one path we shall never choose, and that is the path of surrender or submission.

Our goal is not the victory of might, but the vindication of right—not peace at the expense of freedom, but both peace *and* freedom, here in this hemisphere, and, we hope, around the world. God willing, that goal will be achieved.

Thank you and good night.

Lyndon B. Johnson
The Gulf of Tonkin
August 4, 1964

MY FELLOW AMERICANS:

$\mathbf{A}$s President and Commander in Chief, it is my duty to the American people to report that renewed hostile actions against United States ships on the high seas in the Gulf of Tonkin have today required me to order the military forces of the United States to take action in reply.

The initial attack on the destroyer *Maddox*, on August 2, was repeated today by a number of hostile vessels attacking two U.S. destroyers with torpedoes. The destroyers and supporting aircraft acted at once on the orders I gave after the initial act of aggression. We believe at least two of the attacking boats were sunk. There were no U.S. losses.

The performance of commanders and crews in this engagement is in the highest tradition of the United States Navy. But repeated acts of violence against the Armed Forces of the United States must be met not only with alert defense, but with positive reply. That reply is being given as I speak to you tonight. Air action is now in execution against gunboats and certain supporting facilities in North Viet-Nam which have been used in these hostile operations.

In the larger sense this new act of aggression, aimed directly at our own forces, again brings home to all of us in the United States the importance of the struggle for peace and security in southeast Asia. Aggression by terror against the peaceful villagers of South Viet-Nam has now been joined by open aggression on the high seas against the United States of America.

The determination of all Americans to carry out our full commitment to the people and the government of South Viet-Nam will be redoubled by this outrage. Yet our response, for the present, will be limited and fitting. We Americans know, although others appear to forget, the risks of spreading conflict. We still seek no wider war.

I have instructed the Secretary of State to make this position totally clear to friends and to adversaries and, indeed, to all. I have instructed Ambassador Stevenson to raise this matter immediately and urgently before the Security Council of the United Nations. Finally, I have today met with the leaders of both parties in the Congress of the United States and I have informed them that I shall immediately request the Congress to pass a resolution making it clear that our Government is united in its determination to take all necessary measures in support of freedom and in defense of peace in southeast Asia.

I have been given encouraging assurance by these leaders of both parties that such a resolution will be promptly introduced, freely and expeditiously debated, and passed with overwhelming support. And just a few minutes ago I was able to reach Senator Goldwater and I am glad to say that he has expressed his support of the statement that I am making to you tonight.

It is a solemn responsibility to have to order even limited military action by forces whose overall strength is as vast and as awesome as those of the United States of America, but it is my considered conviction, shared throughout your Government, that firmness in the right is indispensable today for peace; that firmness will always be measured. Its mission is peace.

NOTE

The President began speaking at 11:36 p.m., Eastern daylight time.

For the President's special message to Congress, see Item 500. For his remarks upon signing the int resolution in support of freedom and in defense of peace in southeast Asia see Item 507.

Ronald Reagan
The Korean Airlines Massacre
September 5, 1983

MY FELLOW AMERICANS:

I'm coming before you tonight about the Korean airline massacre, the attack by the Soviet Union against 269 innocent men, women, and children aboard an unarmed Korean passenger plane. This crime against humanity must never be forgotten, here or throughout the world.

Our prayers tonight are with the victims and their families in their time of terrible grief. Our hearts go out to them—to brave people like Kathryn McDonald, the wife of a Congressman whose composure and eloquence on the day of her husband's death moved us all. He will be sorely missed by all of us here in government.

The parents of one slain couple wired me: "Our daughter . . . and her husband . . . died on Korean Airline Flight 007. Their deaths were the result of the Soviet Union violating every concept of human rights." The emotions of these parents—grief, shock, anger—are shared by civilized people everywhere. From around the world press accounts reflect an explosion of condemnation by people everywhere.

Let me state as plainly as I can: There was absolutely no justification, either legal or moral, for what the Soviets did. One newspaper in India said: "If every passenger plane . . . is fair game for home air forces . . . it will be the end of civil aviation as we know it."

This is not the first time the Soviet Union has shot at and hit a civilian airliner when it overflew its territory. In another tragic incident in 1978, the Soviets also shot down an unarmed civilian airliner after having positively identified it as such. In that instance, the Soviet interceptor pilot clearly identified the civilian markings on the side of the aircraft, repeatedly questioned the order to fire on a civilian airliner, and was ordered to shoot it down anyway. The aircraft was hit with a missile and made a crash landing. Several innocent people lost their lives in this attack, killed by shrapnel from the blast of a Soviet missile.

Is this a practice of other countries in the world? The answer is no. Commercial aircraft from the Soviet Union and Cuba on a number of occasions have overflown sensitive United States military facilities. They weren't shot down. We and other civilized countries believe in the tradition of offering help to mariners and pilots who are lost or in distress on the sea or in the air. We believe in following procedures to prevent a tragedy, not to provoke one.

But despite the savagery of their crime, the universal reaction against it, and the evidence of their complicity, the Soviets still refuse to tell the truth. They have persistently refused to admit that their pilot fired on the Korean aircraft. Indeed, they've not even told their own people that a plane was shot down.

They have spun a confused tale of tracking the plane by radar until it just mysteriously disappeared from their radar screens, but no one fired a shot of any kind. But then they coupled this with charges that it was a spy plane sent by us and that their planes fired tracer bullets past the plane as a warning that it was in Soviet airspace.

Let me recap for a moment and present the incontrovertible evidence that we have. The Korean airliner, a Boeing 747, left Anchorage, Alaska, bound for Seoul, Korea, on a course south and west which would take it across Japan. Out over the Pacific, in international waters, it was for a brief time in the vicinity of one of our reconnaissance planes, an RC-135, on a routine mission. At no time was the RC-135 in Soviet airspace. The Korean airliner flew on, and the two planes were soon widely separated.

The 747 is equipped with the most modern computerized navigation facilities, but a computer must resond to input provided by human hands. No one will ever know whether a mistake was made in giving the computer the course or whether there was a malfunction. Whichever, the 747 was flying a course further to the west than it was supposed to fly—a course which took it into Soviet airspace.

The Soviets tracked this plane for 2½ hours while it flew a straight-line course at 30 to 35,000 feet. Only civilian airliners fly in such a manner. At one point, the Korean pilot gave Japanese air control his position as east of Hokkaido, Japan, showing that he was unaware they were off course by as much or more than a hundred miles.

The Soviets scrambled jet interceptors from a base in Sakhalin Island. Japanese ground sites recorded the interceptor planes' radio transmissions—their conversations with their own ground control. We only have the voices from the pilots; the Soviet ground-to-air transmissions were not recorded. It's plain, however, from the pilot's words that he's responding to orders and queries from his own ground control.

Here is a brief segment of the tape which we're going to play in its entirety for the United Nations Security Council tomorrow.

[At this point, the tape was played.]

Those were the voices of the Soviet pilots. In this tape, the pilot who fired the missile describes his search for what he calls the target. He reports he has it in sight; indeed, he pulls up to within about a mile of the Korean plane, mentions its flashing strobe light and that its navigation lights are on. He then reports he's reducing speed to get behind the airliner, gives his distance from the plane at various points in this maneuver, and finally announces what can only be called the "Korean Airline Massacre." He says he has locked on the radar, which aims his missiles, has launched those missiles, the target has been destroyed, and he is breaking off the attack.

Let me point out something here having to do with his closeup view of the airliner on what we know was a clear night with a half moon. The 747 has a unique and distinctive silhouette, unlike any other plane in the world. There is no way a pilot could mistake this for anything other than a civilian airliner. And if that isn't enough, let me point out our RC-135 that I mentioned earlier had been back at its base in Alaska, on the ground for an hour, when the murderous attack took place over the Sea of Japan.

And make no mistake about it, this attack was not just against ourselves or the Republic of Korea. This was the Soviet Union against the world and the moral precepts which guide human relations among people everywhere. It was an act of barbarism, born of a society which wantonly disregards individual rights and the value of human life and seeks constantly to expand and dominate other nations.

They deny the deed, but in their conflicting and misleading protestations, the Soviets reveal that, yes, shooting down a plane—even one with hundreds of innocent men, women, children, and babies—is a part of their normal procedure if that plane is in what they claim as their airspace.

They owe the world an apology and an offer to join the rest of the world in working out a system to protect against this ever happening again. Among the rest of us there is one protective measure: an international radio wave length on which pilots can communicate with planes of other nations if they are in trouble or lost. Soviet military planes are not so equipped, because that would make it easier for pilots who might want to defect.

Our request to send vessels into Soviet waters to search for wreckage and bodies has received no satisfactory answer. Bereaved families of the Japanese victims were harassed by Soviet patrol boats when they tried to get near where the plane is believed to have gone down in order to hold a ceremony for their dead. But we shouldn't be surprised by such inhuman brutality. Memories come back of Czechoslovakia, Hungary, Poland, the gassing of villages in Afghanistan. If the massacre and their subsequent conduct is intended to intimidate, they have failed in their purpose. From every corner of the globe the word is defiance in the face of this unspeakable act and defiance of the system which excuses it and tries to cover it up. With our horror and our sorrow, there is a righteous and terrible anger. It would be easy to think in terms of vengeance, but that is not a proper answer. We want justice and action to see that this never happens again.

Our immediate challenge to this atrocity is to ensure that we make the skies safer and that we seek just compensation for the families of those who were killed.

Since my return to Washington, we've held long meetings, the most recent yesterday with the congressional leadership. There was a feeling of unity in the room, and I received a number of constructive suggestions. We will continue to work with the Congress regarding our response to this massacre.

As you know, we immediately made known to the world the shocking facts as honestly and completely as they came to us.

We have notified the Soviets that we will not renew our bilateral agreement for cooperation in the field of transportation so long as they threaten the security of civil aviation.

Since 1981 the Soviet airline Aeroflot has been denied the right to fly to the United States. We have reaffirmed that order and are examining additional steps we can take with regard to Aeroflot facilities in this country. We're cooperating with other countries to find better means to ensure the safety of civil aviation and to join us in not accepting Aeroflot as a normal member of the international civil air community unless and until the Soviets satisfy the cries of humanity for justice. I am pleased to report that Canada today suspended Aeroflot's landing and refueling privileges for 60 days.

We have joined with other countries to press the International Civil Aviation Organization to investigate this crime at an urgent special session of the Council. At the same time, we're listening most carefully to private groups, both American and international, airline pilots, passenger associations, and others, who have a special interest in civil air safety.

I am asking the Congress to pass a joint resolution of condemnation of this Soviet crime.

We have informed the Soviets that we're suspending negotiations on several bilateral arrangements we had under consideration.

Along with Korea and Japan, we called an emergency meeting of the U.N. Secretary Council which began on Friday. On that first day, Korea, Japan, Canada, Australia, the Netherlands, Pakistan, France, China, the United Kingdom, Zaire, New Zealand, and West Germany all joined us in denouncing the Soviet action and expressing our horror. We expect to hear from additional countries as debate resumes tomorrow.

We intend to work with the 13 countries who had citizens aboard the Korean airliner to seek reparations for the families of all those who were killed. The United States will be making a claim against the Soviet Union within the next week to obtain compensation for the benefit of the victims' survivors. Such compensation is an absolute moral duty which the Soviets must assume.

In the economic area in general, we're redoubling our efforts with our allies to end the flow of military and strategic items to the Soviet Union.

Secretary Shultz is going to Madrid to meet with representatives of 35 countries who, for 3 years, have been negotiating an agreement having to do with, among other things, human rights. Foreign Minister Gromyko of the Soviet Union is scheduled to attend that meeting. If he does come to the meeting, Secretary Schultz is going to present him with our demands for disclosure of the facts, corrective action, and concrete assurances that such a thing will not happen again and that restitution be made.

As we work with other countries to see that justice is done, the real test of our resolve is whether we have the will to remain strong, steady, and united. I believe more than ever—as evidenced by your thousands and thousands of wires and phone calls in these last few days—that we do.

I have outlined some of the steps we're taking in response to the tragic massacre. There is something I've always believed in, but which now seems more important than ever. The Congress will be facing key national security issues when it returns from recess. There has been legitimate difference of opinion on this subject, I know, but I urge the Members of that distinguished body to ponder long and hard the Soviets' aggression as they consider the security and safety of our people—indeed, all people who believe in freedom.

Senator Henry Jackson, a wise and revered statesman and one who probably understood the Soviets as well as any American in history, warned us, "the greatest threat the United States now faces is posed by the Soviet Union." But Senator Jackson said, "If America maintains a strong deterrent—and only if it does—this nation will continue to be a leader in the crucial quest for enduring pece among nations."

The late Senator made those statements in July on the Senate floor, speaking in behalf of the MX missile program he considered vital to restore America's strategic parity with the Soviets.

When John F. Kennedy was President, defense spending as a share of the Federal budget was 70 percent greater than it is today. Since then, the Soviet Union has carried on the most massive military buildup the world has ever seen. Until they are willing to join the rest of the world community, we must maintain the strength to deter their aggression.

But while we do so, we must not give up our effort to bring them into the world community of nations. Peace through strength as long as necessary, but never giving up our effort to bring peace closer through mutual, verifiable reduction in the weapons of war.

I've told you of negotiations we've suspended as a result of the Korean airline massacre, but we cannot, we must not give up our effort to reduce the arsenals of destructive weapons threatening the world. Ambassador Nitze has returned to Geneva to resume the negotiations on intermediate-range nuclear weapons in Europe. Equally, we will continue to press for arms reductions in the START talks that resume in October. We are more determined than ever to reduce and, if possible, eliminate the threat hanging over mankind.

We know it will be hard to make a nation that rules its own people through force to cease using force against the rest of the world. But we must try.

This is not a role we sought. We preach no manifest destiny. But like Americans who began this country and brought forth this last, best hope of mankind, history has asked much of the Americans of our own time. Much we have already given; much more we must be prepared to give.

Let us have faith, in Abraham Lincoln's words, "that right makes might, and in that faith let us, to the end dare to do our duty as we understand it." If we do, if we stand together and move forward with courage, then history will record that some good did come from this monstrous wrong that we will carry with us and remember for the rest of our lives.

Thank you. God bless you, and good night.

NOTE

The President spoke at 8 p.m. from the Oval Office of the White House. His address was broadcast live on nationwide radio and television.

UNIT FOUR

Looking Ahead

Chapter 11 Prophetic Farewells

$\mathbf{A}$ retiring President is in a unique position to speak frankly to the nation without direct regard for his personal political fortunes. If the president's administration has been perceived as successful, the president will have earned the respect of his listeners. Both selections in this section are messages from popular presidents to supportive audiences.

Alexander Hamilton helped President Washington prepare his lengthy but prescient farewell address. Beginning on a hopeful note, the address quickly turns to a discussion of the dangers confronting the new nation. Speaking from his experience after two terms, Washington warned of the "baneful effects" of political parties and the necessity (echoed later by Lincoln) of maintaining a national identity which supercedes regional attachments. But perhaps the most enduring theme of the address concerned foreign policy. Washington's advice to steer clear of foreign entanglements remained a lasting touchstone of American foreign policy.

Another military president speaking 164 years later also had some important parting words for his nation. President Eisenhower was both a successful general in World War II and a president who left office with the highest public opinion rating among contemporary presidents. As an acknowledged military leader, Eisenhower's warning against a military-industrial complex were particularly sobering. His pleas for moderation and balance reflect his concern that in Kennedy he had a successor of a far different political persuasion. Eisenhower's farewell address evidences the anxiety experienced by both the departing president and his countrymen as we constitutionally transfer the reigns of power.

George Washington
Farewell Address
September 19, 1796

Friends, and Fellow-Citizens: The period for a new election of a Citizen, to Administer the Executive government of the United States, being not far distant, and the time actually arrived, when your thoughts must be employed in designating the person, who is to be cloathed with that important trust, it appears to me proper, especially as it may conduce to a more distinct expression of the public voice, that I should now apprise you of the resolution I have formed, to decline being considered among the number of those, out of whom a choice is to be made.

I beg you, at the same time, to do me the justice to be assured, that this resolution has not been taken, without a strict regard to all the considerations appertaining to the relation, which binds a dutiful citizen to his country, and that, in with drawing the tender of service which silence in my situation might imply, I am influenced by no diminution of zeal for your future interest, no deficiency of grateful respect for your past kindness; but am supported by a full conviction that the step is compatible with both.

The acceptance of, and continuance hitherto in, the office to which your Suffrages have twice called me, have been a uniform sacrifice of inclination to the opinion of duty, and to a deference for what appeared to be your desire. I constantly hoped, that it would have been much earlier in my power, consistently with motives, which I was not at liberty to disregard, to return to that retirement, from which I had been reluctantly drawn. The strength of my inclination to do this, previous to the last Election, had even led to the preparation of an address to declare it to you; but mature reflection on the then perplexed and critical posture of our Affairs with foreign Nations, and the unanimous advice of persons entitled to my confidence, impelled me to abandon the idea.

I rejoice, that the state of your concerns, external as well as internal, no longer renders the pursuit of inclination incompatible with the sentiment of duty, or propriety; and am persuaded whatever partiality may be retained for my services, that in the present circumstances of our country, you will not disapprove my determination to retire.

The impressions, with which I first undertook the arduous trust, were explained on the proper occasion. In the discharge of this trust, I will only say, that I have, with good intentions, contributed towards the Organization and Administration of the government, the best exertions of which a very fallible judgment was capable. Not unconscious, in the outset, of the inferiority of my qualifications, experience in my own eyes, perhaps still more in the eyes of others, has strengthened the motives to diffidence of myself; and every day the encreasing weight of years admonishes me more and more, that the shade of retirement is as necessary to me as it will be welcome. Satisfied that if any circumstances have given peculiar value to my services, they were temporary, I have the consolation to believe, that while choice and prudence invite me to quit the political scene, patriotism does not forbid it.

In looking forward to the moment, which is intended to terminate the career of my public life, my feelings do not permit me to suspend the deep asknowledgment of that debt of gratitude which I owe to my beloved country, for the many honors it has conferred upon me; still more for the stedfast confidence with which it has supported me; and for the opportunities I have thence enjoyed of manifesting my inviolable attachment, by services faithful and persevering, though in usefulness unequal to my zeal. If benefits have resulted to our country from these services, let it always be remembered to your praise, and as an instructive example in our annals, that, under circumstances in which the Passions agitated in every direction were liable to mislead, amidst appearances sometimes dubious, viscissitudes of fortune often discouraging, in situations in which not unfrequently want of Success has countenanced the spirit of criticism, the constancy of your support was the essential prop of the efforts, and a guarantee of the plans by which they were effected. Profoundly penetrated with this idea, I shall carry it with me to my grave, as a strong incitement to unceasing vows that Heaven may continue to you the choicest tokens of its beneficence; that your Union and brotherly affection may be perpetual; that the free constitution, which is the work of your hands, may be sacredly maintained; that its Administration in every department may be stamped with wisdom and Virtue; that, in fine, the happiness of the people of these States, under the auspices of liberty, may be made complete, by so careful a preservation and so prudent a use of this blessing as will acquire to them the glory of recommending it to the applause, the affection, and adoption of every nation which is yet a stranger to it.

Here, perhaps, I ought to stop. But a solicitude for your welfare, which cannot end but with my life, and the apprehension of danger, natural to that solicitude, urge me on an occasion like the present, to offer to your solemn contemplation, and to recommend to your frequent review, some sentiments; which are the result of much reflection, of no inconsiderable observation, and which appear to me all important to the permanency of your felicity as a People. These will be offered to you with the more freedom, as you can only see in them the disinterested warnings of a parting friend, who can possibly have no personal motive to bias his counsel. Nor can I forget, as an encouragement to it, your endulgent reception of my sentiments on a former and not dissimilar occasion.

Interwoven as is the love of liberty with every ligament of your hearts, no recommendation of mine is necessary to fortify or confirm the attachment.

The Unity of Government which constitutes you one people is also now dear to you. It is justly so; for it is a main Pillar in the Edifice of your real independence, the support of your tranquility at home; your peace abroad; of your safety; of your prosperity; of that very Liberty which you so highly prize. But as it is easy to foresee, that from different causes and from different quarters, much pains will be taken, many artifices employed, to weaken in your minds the conviction of this truth; as this is the point in your political fortress against which the batteries of internal and external enemies will be most constantly and actively (though often covertly and insidiously) directed, it is of infinite moment, that you should properly estimate the immense value of your national Union to your collective and individual happiness; that you should cherish a cordial, habitual and immoveable attachment to it; accustoming yourselves to think and speak of it as of the Palladium of your political safety and prosperity; watching for its preservation with jealous anxiety; discountenancing whatever may suggest even a suspicion that it can in any event be abandoned, and indignantly frowning upon the first dawning of every attempt to alienate any portion of our Country from the rest, or to enfeeble the sacred ties which now link together the various parts.

For this you have every inducement of sympathy and interest. Citizens by birth or choice, of a common country, that country has a right to concentrate your affections. The name of AMERICAN, which belongs to you, in your national capacity, must always exalt the just pride of Patriotism, more than any appellation derived from local discriminations. With slight shades of difference, you have the same Religion, Manners, Habits and political Principles. you have in a common cause fought and triumphed together. The independence and liberty you possess are the work of joint councils, and joint efforts; of common dangers, sufferings and successes.

But these considerations, however powerfully they address themselves to your sensibility are greatly outweighed by those which apply more immediately to your Interest. Here every portion of our country finds the most commanding motives for carefully guarding and preserving the Union of the whole.

The *North*, in an unrestrained intercourse with the *South*, protected by the equal Laws of a common government, finds in the productions of the latter, great additional resources of maritime and commercial enterprise and precious materials of manufacturing industry. The *South* in the same Intercourse, benefitting by the Agency of the *North*, sees its agriculture grow and its commerce expand. Turning partly into its own channels the seamen of the *North*, it finds its particular navigation envigorated; and while it contributes, in different ways, to nourish and increase the general mass of the National navigation, it looks forward to the protection of a Maritime strength, to which itself is unequally adapted. The *East*, in a like intercourse with the *West*, already finds, and in the progressive improvement of interior communications, by land and water, will more and more find a valuable vent for the commodities which it brings from abroad, or manufactures at home. The *West* derives from the *East* supplies requisite to its growth and comfort, and what is perhaps of still greater consequence, it must of necessity owe the *secure* enjoyment of indispensable *outlets* for its own productions to the weight, influence, and the future Maritime strength of the Atlantic side of the Union, directed by an indissoluble community of Interest as *one Nation*. Any other tenure by which the *West* can hold this essential advantage, whether derived from it own seperate strength, or from an apostate and unnatural connection with any foreign Power, must be intrinsically precarious.

While then every part of our country thus feels an immediate and particular Interest in Union, all the parts combined cannot fail to find in the united mass of means and efforts greater strength, greater resource, proportionably greater security from external danger, a less frequent interruption of their Peace by foreign Nations; and, what is of inestimable value! they must derive from Union an exemption from those broils and Wars between themselves, which so frequently afflict neighbouring countries, not tied together by the same government; which their own rivalships alone would be sufficient to produce, but which opposite foreign alliances, attachments and intrigues would stimulate and imbitter. Hence likewise they will avoid the necessity of those overgrown Military establishments, which under any form of Government are inauspicious to liberty, and which are to be regarded as particularly hostile to Republican Liberty: In this sense it is, that your Union ought to be considered as a main prop of your liberty, and that the love of the one ought to endear to you the preservation of the other.

These considerations speak a persuasive language to every reflecting and virtuous mind, and exhibit the continuance of the UNION as a primary object of Patriotic desire. Is there a doubt, whether a common government can embrace so large a sphere? Let experience solve it. To listen to mere speculation in such a case were criminal. We are authorized to hope that a proper organization of the whole, with the auxiliary agency of governments for the respective Sub divisions, will afford a happy issue to the experiment. 'Tis well worth a fair and full experiment. With such powerful and obvious motives to Union, affecting all parts of our country, while experience shall not have demonstrated its impracticability, there will always be reason, to distrust the patriotism of those, who in any quarter may endeavor to weaken its bands.

In contemplating the causes which may disturb our Union, it occurs as matter of serious concern, that any ground should have been furnished for characterizing parties by *Geographical* discriminations: *Northern* and *Southern; Atlantic* and *Western;* whence designing men may endeavour to excite a belief that there is a real difference of local interests and views. One of the expedients of Party to acquire influence, within particular districts, is to misrepresent the opinions and aims of other Districts. You cannot shield yourselves too much against the jealousies and heart burnings which spring from these misrepresentations. They tend to render Alien to each other those who ought to be bound together by fraternal affection. The Inhabitants of our Western country have lately had a useful lesson on this head. They have seen, in the Negotiation by the Executive, and in the unanimous ratification by the Senate, of the Treaty with Spain, and in the universal satisfaction at that event, throughout the United States, a decisive proof how unfounded were the suspicions propagated among them of a policy in the General Government and in the Atlantic States unfriendly to their Interests in regard to the MISSISSIPPI. They have been witnesses to the formation of two Treaties, that with G: Britain and that with Spain, which secure to them every thing they could desire, in respect to our Foreign relations, towards confirming their prosperity. Will it not be their wisdom to rely for the preservation of [*sic*] these advantages on the UNION by which they were procured? Will they not henceforth be deaf to those advisers, if such there are, who would sever them from their Brethren and connect them with Aliens?

To the efficacy and permanency of Your Union, a Government for the whole is indispensable. No Alliances however strict between the parts can be an adequate substitute. They must inevitably experience the infractions and interruptions which all Alliances in all times have experienced. Sensible of this momentous truth, you have improved upon your first essay, by the adoption of a Constitution of Government, better calculated than your former for an intimate Union, and for the efficacious management of your common concerns. This government, the offspring of your own choice uninfluenced and unawed, adopted upon full investigation and mature deliberation, completely free in its principles, in the distribution of its powers, uniting security with energy, and containing within itself a provision for its own amendment, has a just claim to your confidence and your support. Respect for its authority, compliance with its Laws, acquiescence in its measures, are duties enjoined by the fundamental maxims of true Liberty. The basis of our political systems is the right of the people to make and to alter their Constitutions of Government. But the Constitution which at any time exists, 'till changed by an explicit and authentic act of the whole People, is sacredly obligatory upon all. The very idea of the power and the right of the People to establish Government presupposes the duty of every Individual to obey the established Government.

All obstructions to the execution of the Laws, all combinations and Associations, under whatever plausible character with the real design to direct, control counteract, or awe the regular deliberation and action of the Constituted authorities are distructive of this fundamental principle and of fatal tendency. They serve to organize faction, to give it an artificial and extraordinary force; to put in the place of the delegated will of the Nation, the will of a party; often a small but artful and enterprizing minority of the Community; and, according to the alternate triumph of different parties, to make the public administration the Mirror of the ill concerted and incongruous projects of faction, rather than the organ of consistent and wholesome plans digested by common councils and modefied by mutual interests. However combinations or Associations of the above description may now and then answer popular ends, they are likely, in the course of time and things, to become potent engines, by which cunning, ambitious and unprincipled men will be enabled to subvert the Power of the People, and to usurp for themselves the reins of Government; destroying afterwards the very engines which have lifted them to unjust dominion.

Towards the preservation of your Government and the permanency of your present happy state, it is requisite, not only that you steadily discountenance irregular oppositions to its acknowledged authority, but also that you resist with care the spirit of innovation upon its principles however specious the pretexts. One method of assault may be to effect, in the forms of the Constitution, alterations which will impair the energy of the system, and thus to undermine what cannot be directly overthrown. In all the changes to which you may be invited, remember that time and habit are at least as necessary to fix the true character of Governments, as of other human institutions; that experience is the surest standard, by which to test the real tendency of the existing Constitution of a country; that facility in changes upon the credit of mere hypotheses and opinion exposes to perpetual change, from the endless variety of hypotheses and opinion; and remember, especially, that for the efficient management of your common interests, in a country so extensive as ours, a Government of as much vigour as is consistent with the perfect security of Liberty is indispensable. Liberty itself will find in such Government, with powers properly distributed and adjusted, its surest Guardian. It is indeed little else than a name, where the Government is too feeble to withstand the enterprises of faction, to confine each member of the Society within the limits prescribed by the laws and to maintain all in the secure and tranquil enjoyment of the rights of person and property.

I have already intimated to you the danger of Parties in the State, with particular reference to the founding of them on Geographical discriminations. Let me now take a more comprehensive view, and warn you in the most solemn manner against the baneful effects of the Spirit of Party, generally.

This spirit, unfortunately, is inseperable from our nature, having its root in the strongest passions of the human Mind. It exists under different shapes in the all Governments, more or less stifled, controlled, or repressed; but, in those of the popular form it is seen in its greatest rankness and is truly their worst enemy.

The alternate domination of one faction over another, sharpened by the spirit of revenge natural to party dissention, which in different ages and countries has perpetrated the most horrid enormities, is itself a frightful despotism. But this leads at length to a more formal and permanent despotism. The disorders and miseries, which result, gradually incline the minds of men to seek security and repose in the absolute power of an Individual: and sooner or later the chief of some prevailing faction more able or more fortunate than his competitors, turns this disposition to the purposes of his own elevation, on the ruins of Public Liberty.

Without looking forward to an extremity of this kind (which nevertheless ought not to be entirely out of sight) the common and continual mischiefs of the spirit of Party are sufficient to make it the interest and the duty of a wise People to discourage and restrain it.

It serves always to distract the Public Councils and enfeeble the Public administration. It agitates the Community with ill founded jealousies and false alarms, kindles the animosity of one part against another, foments occasionally riot and insurrection. It opens the door to foreign influence and corruption, which find a facilitated access to the government itself through the channels of party passions. Thus the policy and and [sic] the will of one country, are subjected to the policy and will of another.

There is an opinion that parties in free countries are useful checks upon the Administration of the Government and serve to keep alive the spirit of Liberty. This within certain limits is probably true, and in Governments of a Monarchical cast Patriotism may look with endulgence, if not with favour, upon the spirit of party. But in those of the popular character, in Governments purely elective, it is a spirit not to be encouraged. From their natural tendency, it is certain there will always be enough of that spirit for every salutary purpose. And there being constant danger of excess, the effort ought to be, by force of public opinion, to mitigate and assuage it. A fire not to be quenched; it demands a uniform vigilance to prevent its bursting into a flame, lest instead of warming it should consume.

It is important, likewise, that the habits of thinking in a free Country should inspire caution in those entrusted with its administration, to confine themselves within their respective Constitutional spheres; avoiding in the exercise of the Powers of one department to encroach upon another. The spirit of encroachment tends to consolidate the powers of all the departments in one, and thus to create whatever the form of government, a real despotism. A just estimate of that love of power, and proneness to abuse it, which predominates in the human heart is sufficient to satisfy us of the truth of this position. The necessity of reciprocal checks in the exercise of political power; by dividing and distributing it into different depositories, and constituting each the Guardian of the Public Weal against invasions by the others, has been evinced by experiments ancient and modern; some of them in our country and under our own eyes. To preserve them must be as necessary as to institute them. If in the opinion of the People, the distribution or modification of the Constitutional powers be in any particular wrong, let it be corrected by an amendment in the way which the Constitution designates. But let there be no change by usurpation; for though this, in one instance, may be the instrument of good, it is the customary weapon by which free governments are destroyed. The precedent must always greatly overbalance in permanent evil any partial or transient benefit which the use can at any time yield.

Of all the dispositions and habits which lead to political prosperity, Religion and morality are indispensable supports. In vain would that man claim the tribute of Patriotism, who should labour to subvert these great Pillars of human happiness, these firmest props of the duties of Men and citizens. The mere Politician, equally with the pious man ought to respect and to cherish them. A volume could not trace all their connections with private and public felicity. Let it simply be asked where is the security for property, for reputation, for life, if the sense of religious obligation *desert* the oaths, which are the instruments of investigation in Courts of Justice? And let us with caution indulge the supposition, that morality can be maintained without religion. Whatever may be conceded to the influence of refined education on minds of peculiar structure, reason and experience both forbid us to expect that National morality can prevail in exclusion of religious principle.

'Tis substantially true, that virtue or morality is a necessary spring of popular government. The rule indeed extends with more or less force to every species of free Government. Who that is a sincere friend to it, can look with indifference upon attempts to shake the foundation of the fabric

Promote then as an object of primary importance, Institutions for the general diffusion of knowledge. In proportion as the structure of a government gives force to public opinion, it is essential that public opinion should be enlightened.

As a very important source of strength and security, cherish public credit. One method of preserving it is to use it as sparingly as possible: avoiding occasions of expence by cultivating peace, but remembering also that timely disbursements to prepare for danger frequently prevent much greater disbursements to repel it; avoiding likewise the accumulation of debt, not only by shunning occasions of expence, but by vigorous exertions in time of Peace to discharge the Debts which unavoidable wars may have occasioned, not ungenerously throwing upon posterity the burthen which we ourselves ought to bear. The execution of these maxims belongs to your Representatives, but it is necessary that public opinion should cooperate. To facilitate to them the performance of their duty, it is essential that you should practically bear in mind, that towards the payment of debts there must be Revenue; that to have Revenue there must be taxes; that no taxes can be devised which are not more or less inconvenient and unpleasant; that the intrinsic embarrassment inseperable from the selection of the proper objects (which is always a choice of difficulties) ought to be a decisive motive for a candid construction of the Conduct of the Government in making it, and for a spirit of acquiescence in the measures for obtaining Revenue which the public exigencies may at any time dictate.

Observe good faith and justice towards all Nations. Cultivate peace and harmony with all. Religion and morality enjoin this conduct; and can it be that good policy does not equally enjoin it? It will be worthy of a free, elightened, and, at no distant period, a great Nation, to give to mankind the magnanimous and too novel example of a People always guided by an exalted justice and benevolence. Who can doubt that in the course of time and things the fruits of such a plan would richly repay any temporary advantages which might be lost by a steady adherence to it? Can it be, that Providence has not connected the permanent felicity of a Nation with its virtue? The experiment, at least, is recommended by every sentiment which ennobles human Nature. Alas! is it rendered impossible by its vices?

In the execution of such a plan nothing is more essential that that permanent, inveterate antipathies against particular Nations and passionate attachments for others should be excluded; and that in place of them just and amicable feelings towards all should be cultivated. The Nation, which indulges towards another an habitual hatred, or an habitual fondness, is in some degree a slave. It is a slave to its animosity or to its affection, either of which is sufficient to lead it astray from its duty and its interest. Antipathy in one Nation against another, disposes each more readily to offer insult and injury, to lay hold of slight causes of umbrage, and to be haughty and intractable, when accidental or trifling occasions of dispute occur. Hence frequent collisions, obstinate envenomed and bloody contests. The Nation, prompted by illwill and resentment sometimes impels to War the Government, contrary to the best calculations of policy. The Government sometimes participates in the national propensity, and adopts through passion what reason would reject; at other times, it makes the animosity of the Nation subservient to projects of hostility instigated by pride, ambition and other sinister and pernicious motives. The peace often, sometimes perhaps the Liberty, of Nations has been the victim.

So likewise, a passionate attachment of one Nation for another produces a variety of evils. Sympathy for the favourite nation, facilitating the illusion of an imaginary common interest, in cases where no real common interest exists, and infusing into one the enmities of the other, betrays the former into a participation in the quarrels and Wars of the latter, without adequate inducement or justification: It leads also to concessions to the favourite Nation of priviledges denied to others, which is apt doubly to injure the Nation making the concessions; by unnecessarily parting with what ought to have been retained; and by exciting jealousy, ill will, and a disposition to retaliate, in the parties from whom equal priviledges are withheld: And it gives to ambitious, corrupted, or deluded citizens (who devote themselves to the favourite Nation) facility to betray, or sacrifice the interests of their own country, without odium, sometimes even with popularity; gilding with the appearances of a virtuous sense of obligation a commendable deference for public opinion, or a laudable zeal for public good, the base or foolish compliances of ambition corruption or infatuation.

As avenues to foreign influence in unnumerable ways, such attachments are particularly alarming to the truly enlightened and independent Patriot. How many opportunities do they afford to tamper with domestic factions, to practice the arts of seduction, to mislead public opinion, to influence or awe the public Councils! Such an attachment of a small or weak, towards a great and powerful Nation, dooms the former to be the satellite of the latter.

Against the insidious wiles of foreign influence (I conjure you to believe me fellow citizens) the jealousy of a free people ought to be *constantly* awake; since history and experience prove that foreign influence is one of the most baneful foes of Republican Government. But that jealousy to be useful must be impartial; else it becomes the instrument of the very influence to be avoided, instead of a defence against it. Excessive partiality for one foreign nation and excessive dislike of another, cause those whom they actuate to see danger only on one side, and serve to veil and even second the arts of influence on the other. Real Patriots, who may resist the intrigues of the favourite, are liable to become suspected and

odious; while its tools and dupes usurp the applause and confidence of the people, to surrender their interests.

The Great rule of conduct for us, in regard to foreign Nations is
in extending our commercial relations to have with them as little
political connection as possible. So far as we have already formed
engagements let them be fulfilled, with perfect good faith. Here let
us stop.

Europe has a set of primary interests, which to us have none, or
a very remote relation. Hence she must be engaged in frequent
controversies, the causes of which are essentially foreign to our
concerns. Hence, therefore, it must be unwise in us to implicate
ourselves, by artificial ties, in the ordinary vicissitudes of her
politics, or the ordinary combinations and collisions of her
friendships, or enmities:

Our detached and distant situation invites and enables us to
pursue a different course. If we remain one People, under an
efficient government, the period is not far off, when we may defy
material injury from external annoyance; when we may take such
an attitude as will cause the neutrality we may at any time resolve
upon to be scrupulously respected; when belligerent nations, under
the impossibility of making acquisitions upon us, will not lightly
hazard the giving us provocation; when we may choose peace or
war, as our interest guided by our justice shall Counsel.

Why forego the advantages of so peculiar a situation? Why quit
our own to stand upon foreign ground? Why, by interweaving our
destiny with that of any part of Europe, entangle our peace and
prosperity in the toils of European Ambition, Rivalship, Interest,
Humour or Caprice?

'Tis our true policy to steer clear of permanent Alliances, with
any portion of the foreign world. So far, I mean, as we are now at
liberty to do it, for let me not be understood as capable of
patronising infidility to existing engagements (I hold the maxim no
less applicable to public than to private affairs, that honesty is
always the best policy). I repeat it therefore, let those engagements
be observed in the genuine sense. But in my opinion, it is
unnecessary and would be unwise to extend them.

Taking care always to keep ourselves, by suitable establishments, on a respectably defensive posture, we may safely trust to
temporary alliances for extraordinary emergencies.

Harmony, liberal intercourse with all Nations, are recommended by policy, humanity and interest. But even our Commercial policy should hold an equal and impartial hand: neither seeking nor granting exclusive favours or preferences; consulting the natural course of things; diffusing and diversifying by gentle means the streams of Commerce, but forcing nothing; establishing with Powers so disposed; in order to give to trade a stable course, to define the rights of our Merchants, and to enable the Government to support them; conventional rules of intercourse, the best that present circumstances and mutual opinion will permit, but temporary, and liable to be from time to time abandoned or varied, as experience and circumstances shall dictate; constantly keeping in view, that 'tis folly in one Nation to look for disinterested favors from another; that it must pay with a portion of its Independence for whatever it may accept under that character; that by such acceptance, it may place itself in the condition of having given equivalents for nominal favours and yet of being reproached with ingratitude for not giving more. There can be no greater error than to expect, or calculate upon real favours from Nation to Nation. 'Tis an illusion which experience must cure, which a just pride ought to discard.

In offering to you, my Countrymen these counsels of an old and affectionate friend, I dare not hope they will make the strong and lasting impression, I could wish; that they will controul the usual current of the passions, or prevent our Nation from running the course which has hitherto marked the Destiny of Nations: But if I may even flatter myself, that they may be productive of some partial benefit, some occasional good; that they may now and then recur to moderate the fury of party spirit, to warn against the mischiefs of foreign Intrigue, to guard against the Impostures of pretended patriotism; this hope will be a full recompence for the solicitude for your welfare, by which they have been dictated.

How far in the discharge of my Official duties, I have been guided by the principles which have been delineated, the public Records and other evidences of my conduct must Witness to You and to the world. To myself, the assurance of my own conscience is, that I have at least believed myself to be guided by them.

In relation to the still subsisting War in Europe, my Proclamation of the 22d. of April 1793 is the index to my Plan. Sanctioned by your approving voice and by that of Your Representatives in both Houses of Congress, the spirit of that measure has continually governed me; uninfluenced by any attempts to deter or divert me from it.

After deliberate examination with the aid of the best lights I could obtain I was well satisfied that our Country, under all the circumstances of the case, had a right to take, and was bound in duty and interest, to take a Neutral position. Having taken it, I determined, as far as should depend upon me, to maintain it, with moderation, perseverence and firmness.

The consideration, which respect the right to hold this conduct, it is not necessary on this occasion to detail. I will only observe, that according to my understanding of the matter, that right, so far from being denied by any of the Belligerent Powers has been virtually admitted by all.

The duty of holding a Neutral conduct may be inferred, without any thing more, from the obligation which justice and humanity impose on every Nation, in cases in which it is free to act, to maintain inviolate the relations of Peace and amity towards other Nations.

The inducements of interest for observing that conduct will best be referred to your own reflections and experience. With me, a predominant motive has been to endeavour to gain time to our country to settle and mature its yet recent institutions, and to progress without interruption, to that degree of strength and consistency, which is necessary to give it, humanly speaking, the command of its own fortunes.

Though in reviewing the incidents of my Administration, I am unconscious of intentional error, I am nevertheless too sensible of my defects not to think it probable that I may have committed many errors. Whatever they may be I fervently beseech the Almighty to avert or mitigate the evils to which they may tend. I shall also carry with me the hope that my country will never cease to view them with indulgence; and that after forty five years of my life dedicated to its Service, with an upright zeal, the faults of incompetent abilities will be consigned to oblivion, as myself must soon be to the Mansions of rest.

Relying on its kindness in this as in other things, and actuated by that fervent love towards it, which is so natural to a Man, who views in it the native soil of himself and his progenitors for several Generations; I anticipate with pleasing expectation that retreat, in which I promise myself to realize, without alloy, the sweet enjoyment of partaking, in the midst of my fellow Citizens, the benign influence of good Laws under a free Government, the ever favourite object of my heart, and the happy reward, as I trust, of our mutual cares, labours and dangers.

Dwight D. Eisenhower
Farewell to the American People
January 17, 1961

MY FELLOW AMERICANS:

Three days from now, after half a century in the service of our country, I shall lay down the responsibilities of office as, in traditional and solemn ceremony, the authority of the Presidency is vested in my successor.

This evening I come to you with a message of leave-taking and farewell, and to share a few final thoughts with you, my countrymen.

Like every other citizen, I wish the new President, and all who will labor with him, Godspeed. I pray that the coming years will be blessed with peace and prosperity for all.

Our people expect their President and the Congress to find essential agreement on issues of great moment, the wise resolution of which will better shape the future of the Nation.

My own relations with the Congress, which began on a remote and tenuous basis when, long ago, a member of the Senate appointed me to West Point, have since ranged to the intimate during the war and immediate post-war period, and, finally, to the mutually interdependent during these past eight years.

In this final relationship, the Congress and the Administration have, on most vital issues, cooperated well, to serve the national good rather than mere partisanship, and so have assured that the business of the Nation should go forward. So, my official relationship with the Congress ends in a feeling, on my part, of gratitude that we have been able to do so much together.

II.

We now stand ten years past the midpoint of a century that has witnessed four major wars among great nations. Three of these involved our own country. Despite these holocausts America is today the strongest, the most influential and most productive nation in the world. Understandably proud of this pre-eminence, we yet realize that America's leadership and prestige depend, not merely upon our unmatched material progress, riches and military strength, but on how we use our power in the interests of world peace and human betterment.

III.

Throughout America's adventure in free government, our basic purposes have been to keep the peace; to foster progress in human achievement, and to enhance liberty, dignity and integrity among people and among nations. To strive for less would be unworthy of a free and religious people. Any failure traceable to arrogance, or our lack of comprehension or readiness to sacrifice would inflict upon us grievous hurt both at home and abroad.

Progress toward these noble goals is persistently threatened by the conflict now engulfing the world. It commands our whole attention, absorbs our very beings. We face a hostile ideology—global in scope, atheistic in character, ruthless in purpose, and insidious in method. Unhappily the danger it poses promises to be of indefinite duration. To meet it successfully, there is called for, not so much the emotional and transitory sacrifices of crisis, but rather those which enable us to carry forward steadily, surely, and without complaint the burdens of a prolonged and complex struggle—with liberty the stake. Only thus shall we remain, despite every provocation, on our charted course toward permanent peace and human betterment.

Crises there will continue to be. In meeting them, whether foreign or domestic, great or small, there is a recurring temptation to feel that some spectacular and costly action could become the miraculous solution to all current difficulties. A huge increase in newer elements of our defense; development of unrealistic programs to cure every ill in agriculture; a dramatic expansion in basic and applied research—these and many other possibilities, each possibly promising in itself, may be suggested as the only way to the road we wish to travel.

But each proposal must be weighed in the light of a broader consideration: the need to maintain balance in and among national programs—balance between the private and the public economy, balance between cost and hoped for advantage—balance between the clearly necessary and the comfortably desirable; balance between our essential requirements as a nation and the duties imposed by the nation upon the individual; balance between actions of the moment and the national welfare of the future. Good judgment seeks balance and progress; lack of it eventually finds imbalance and frustration.

The record of many decades stands as proof that our people and their government have, in the main, understood these truths and have responded to them well, in the face of stress and threat. But threats, new in kind or degree, constantly arise. I mention two only.

IV.

A vital element in keeping the peace is our military establishment. Our arms must be mighty, ready for instant action, so that no potential aggressor may be tempted to risk his own destruction.

Our military organization today bears little relation to that known by any of my predecessors in peacetime, or indeed by the fighting men of World War II or Korea.

Until the latest of our world conflicts, the United States had no armaments industry. American makers of plowshares could, with time and as required, make swords as well. But now we can no longer risk emergency improvisation of national defense; we have been compelled to create a permanent armaments industry of vast proportions. Added to this, three and a half million men and women are directly engaged in the defense establishment. We annually spend on military security more than the net income of all United States corporations.

This conjunction of an immense military establishment and a large arms industry is new in the American experience. The total influence—economic, political, even spiritual—is felt in every city, every State house, every office of the Federal government. We recognize the imperative need for this development. Yet we must not fail to comprehend its grave implications. Our toil, resources and livelihood are all involved; so is the very structure of our society.

In the councils of government, we must guard against the acquisition of unwarranted influence, whether sought or unsought, by the military-industrial complex. The potential for the disastrous rise of misplaced power exists and will persist.

We must never let the weight of this combination endanger our liberties or democratic processes. We should take nothing for granted. Only an alert and knowledgeable citizenry can compel the proper meshing of the huge industrial and military machinery of defense with our peaceful methods and goals, so that security and liberty may prosper together.

Akin to, and largely responsible for the sweeping changes in our industrial-military posture, has been the technological revolution during recent decades.

In this revolution, research has become central; it also becomes more formalized, complex, and costly. A steadily increasing share is conducted for, by, or at the direction of, the Federal government.

Today, the solitary inventor, tinkering in his shop, has been overshadowed by task forces of scientists in laboratories and testing fields. In the same fashion, the free university, historically the fountainhead of free ideas and scientific discovery, has experienced a revolution in the conduct of research. Partly because of the huge costs involved, a government contract becomes virtually a substitute for intellectual curiosity. For every old blackboard there are now hundreds of new electronic computers.

The prospect of domination of the nation's scholars by Federal employment, project allocations, and the power of money is ever present—and is gravely to be regarded.

Yet, in holding scientific research and discovery in respect, as we should, we must also be alert to the equal and opposite danger that public policy could itself become the captive of a scientific-technological elite.

It is the task of statesmanship to mold, to balance, and to integrate these and other forces, new and old, within the principles of our democratic system—ever aiming toward the supreme goals of our free society.

V.

Another factor in maintaining balance involves the element of time. As we peer into society's future, we—you and I, and our government—must avoid the impulse to live only for today, plundering, for our own ease and convenience, the precious resources of tomorrow. We cannot mortgage the material assets of our grandchildren without risking the loss also of their political and spiritual heritage. We want democracy to survive for all generations to come, not to become the insolvent phantom of tomorrow.

VI.

Down the long lane of the history yet to be written America knows that this world of ours, ever growing smaller, must avoid becoming a community of dreadful fear and hate, and be, instead, a proud confederation of mutual trust and respect.

Such a confederation must be one of equals. The weakest must come to the conference table with the same confidence as do we, protected as we are by our moral, economic, and military strength. That table, though scarred by many past frustrations, cannot be abandoned for the certain agony of the battlefield.

Disarmament, with mutual honor and confidence, is a continuing imperative. Together we must learn how to compose differences, not with arms, but with intellect and decent purpose. Because this need is so sharp and apparent I confess that I lay down my official responsibilities in this field with a definite sense of disappointment. As one who has witnessed the horror and the lingering sadness of war—as one who knows that another war could utterly destroy this civilization which has been so slowly and painfully built over thousands of years—I wish I could say tonight that a lasting peace is in sight.

Happily, I can say that war has been avoided. Steady progress toward our ultimate goal has been made. But, so much remains to be done. As a private citizen, I shall never cease to do what little I can to help the world advance along that road.

VII.

So—in this my last good night to you as your President—I thank you for the many opportunities you have given me for public service in war and peace. I trust that in that service you find some things worthy; as for the rest of it, I know you will find ways to improve performance in the future.

You and I—my fellow citizens—need to be strong in our faith that all nations, under God, will reach the goal of peace with justice. May we be ever unswerving in devotion to principle, confident but humble with power, diligent in pursuit of the Nation's great goals.

To all the peoples of the world, I once more give expression to America's prayerful and continuing aspiration:

We pray that peoples of all faiths, all races, all nations, may have their great human needs satisfied; that those now denied opportunity shall come to enjoy it to the full; that all who yearn for freedom may experience its spiritual blessings; that those who have freedom will understand, also, its heavy responsibilities, that all who are insensitive to the needs of others will learn charity; that the scourges of poverty, disease and ignorance will be made to disappear from the earth, and that, in the goodness of time, all peoples will come to live together in a peace guaranteed by the binding force of mutual respect and love.

Sources

Baker, Ray Stannard and William W. Dodd, (ed.) *Public Papers of Woodrow Wilson* (New York: Harper Brothers, 1923).

Basler, Roy P. (ed.), *The Collected Works of Abraham Lincoln* (New Brunswick, N.J.: Rutgers University Press, 1953).

Fitzpatrick, John C. (ed.), *The Writings of George Washington* (Washington, D.C.: U.S. Government Printing Office, 1940).

Rauch, Basil (ed.), *Franklin D. Roosevelt: Selected Speeches, Messages, Press Conferences and Letters* (New York: Rinehart and Company, 1957).

Richardson, James D. (ed.), *Messages and Papers of the Presidents* (New York: 1897).

Rosenman, Samuel (ed.), *Public Papers of the President: Franklin D. Roosevelt* (New York: Harper Brothers, 1950).

Public Papers of the Presidents (Washington, D.C.: U.S. Government Printing Office).

WESTMAR COLLEGE LIBRARY